Secret rites and secret writing
Royalist literature, 1641–1660

This book is a study of the various kinds of royalist writing during the period of the English Civil War and the Interregnum, when printing and publishing were largely controlled by Parliament.

Lois Potter examines the effectiveness of this control and the means by which writers evaded it: illicit publication; the use of various kinds of code, such as ciphers, emblems, secret languages, symbolism and allegory; the exploitation of genres such as romance and tragicomedy; the submerging of personal identity through literary quotation and allusion.

A final chapter considers the place of Charles I in royalist literature, with particular emphasis on the effect of the *Eikon Basilike*, once believed in, and revered, as his work.

By looking at a very wide sample of texts, ranging from anonymous pamphlets to the works of well-known 'Cavalier poets', the book brings greater precision to the controversial subject of the relation of literature to politics and of the relation of both to the psychology of secrecy.

Secret rites and secret writing
Royalist literature, 1641–1660

LOIS POTTER

Senior Lecturer in English,
University of Leicester

The right of the
University of Cambridge
to print and sell
all manner of books
was granted by
Henry VIII in 1534.
The University has printed
and published continuously
since 1584.

CAMBRIDGE UNIVERSITY PRESS

Cambridge
New York   Port Chester
Melbourne   Sydney

CAMBRIDGE UNIVERSITY PRESS
Cambridge, New York, Melbourne, Madrid, Cape Town, Singapore, São Paulo, Delhi

Cambridge University Press
The Edinburgh Building, Cambridge CB2 8RU, UK

Published in the United States of America by Cambridge University Press, New York

www.cambridge.org
Information on this title: www.cambridge.org/9780521107969

First published 1989
This digitally printed version 2009

A catalogue record for this publication is available from the British Library

Library of Congress Cataloguing in Publication data
Potter, Lois.
Secret rites and secret writing: royalist literature, 1641–1660 /
Lois Potter.
p.   cm.
Bibliography.
Includes index.
ISBN 0–521–25512–0
1. English literature – Early modern, 1500–1700 – History and
criticism.   2. Great Britain – History – Civil War, 1642–1649 –
Literature and the war.   3. Charles I, King of England, 1600–1649,
in fiction, drama, poetry, etc.   4. Politics and literature – Great
Britain – History – 17th century.   5. Royalists – Great Britain –
History – 17th century.   6. Monarchy in literature.   7. Ciphers in
literature.   8. Figures of speech.   9. Literary form.   I. Title.
PR435.P68   1990
820.9′004 – dc20   89–31660 CIP

ISBN 978-0-521-25512-7 hardback
ISBN 978-0-521-10796-9 paperback

IN MEMORIAM

J. C. HILSON

Sensus. Amicum perdidi.
Ratio. Iam eum te habuisse certum est.

Seneca, *De Remediis Fortuitorum*

CONTENTS

PLATES

PREFACE

Until recently, it was the habit of literary historians to leap rapidly from 1642 to 1660, on the grounds that the intervening period belonged to the history of politics and religion, not literature. One of the chief factors encouraging the creation of this Great Divide was the way in which writers themselves tended to refer to it. Milton's autobiographical asides (e.g. in *Reason of Church Government*) frequently remind the reader that his political activities are an interruption of his true vocation, writing an epic poem. Dryden's splendid phrase for the pre-war dramatists, 'the giant race before the flood' ('To My Dear Friend Mr. Congreve'), not only encapsulates his *fin de siècle* view of their successors, it also makes the closure of the public theatres between 1642 and 1660 part of a general catastrophe from which only a few survivors were left to begin a new world. The Age of Dryden, on this account, begins only in 1660.

All three of these statements need qualification. Milton's poetic career did not come to a complete stop during the 1640s and 1650s. Dryden's was already beginning in 1649. Theatrical activity continued in various forms. Writers had reasons for creating their particular images of the period. In Milton's case, to emphasise the effects of civil war on a pastoral poet was to stress the resemblance between his life and Virgil's, which was one of his personal myths. Dryden, like other writers who had gone into print in praise of Cromwell, had every reason to represent the period before 1660 as an aberration best forgotten. And the concept of the 'reformed' or refined stage, already in use in the 1650s, meant that the new theatre managers who received their patents from Charles II found it in their interest to play down those elements of the pre-war drama which had managed to continue during the previous eighteen years.

In fact, one of the main reasons why literary historians have avoided the period is not that there is too little material, but too much. A great deal of this material, however, poses problems of definition. It is often meaningless – and even, so to speak, genre-less – without an understanding of its context. Few scholars any longer argue for a bellettrist definition of literature; it is obvious that we read everything in a context of some sort. There is no real reason why a work which assumes a knowledge of how metaphors work, how one is supposed to talk about love and women, and how an English garden looks in the spring, should be superior to one which assumes, say, the ability to recognise an ironic tone and some knowledge of the proceedings of the Westminster Assembly. But the territory where literature and history meet is frightening enough as it is without the added hazards created by the existence of more material of both kinds than any one person can assimilate.

This book began with the intention of surveying the relation between literature and public events throughout the period. This seemed not only an important but a feasible study, since writers themselves frequently represent the civil war as a conflict about language. The dispute over the Prayer Book and the liturgy of the Church of England, for instance, is to some extent a dispute as to whether words create devotion or devotion creates words. Writers also comment on each other's vocabulary. Clarendon notes 'the new phrase' which the Scots had brought to England with the Covenant (Hyde 1888, vol. III, p. 456); a Parliamentary newsbook describes the word 'sanguine', used in one of the king's captured letters, as 'a new coyned expression at Court': the fact that it means both 'merry' and 'bloody' proves to him that the royalists 'are never merry or jocund but when they are sanguine, bloody, glutted with the blood of faithfull subjects' (*Mercurius Britanicus*, 28 July–4 Aug., 1645).

It seemed possible, then, to follow these signposts towards a study of the extent to which ideology influences literary style. Was there such a thing as a specifically royalist or parliamentarian aesthetic? Some scholars have tried to find one. The historian S. R. Gardiner linked Edmund Waller's political views to his 'subordination of independent thought and fancy to the severest artificial laws of style' (Gardiner 1897, vol. 1, p. 8). Joan Webber (1968) distinguishes (with respect only to writers of non-fictional prose) what she calls 'conservative Anglican' – meditative, anti-historical, obscure and ambiguous, symbolic' (p. 7) – from 'radical Puritan' – 'active, timebound, as simple and visible as possible' (p. 8). The problem with this kind of analysis, however, is that the terms keep shifting. Anti-Episcopal sentiment, in the sense of a dislike of the political role played by some bishops, and suspicion of the pro-Catholic direction which the court was thought to be taking united much of England in the period 1637–42. By the outbreak of the war, some of those who had been 'Puritans' in this wide sense had already joined the royalist camp. The war in its early years, and especially at the time of the Scots' entrance and the taking of the Covenant

in 1643, could have been described as Anglican versus Presbyterian. Taking
the Covenant had vastly different meanings for different people: by 1647,
there were 'Presbyterians' who would have accepted not only monarchy
but modified episcopacy (McCormack 1973, pp. 146–9), or who used the
term, as one of them put it much later, 'not in the sense of anti-Episcopal
but anti-Independent' (Wallis MS, Letter of 29 Jan. 1696–7). Many who
supported Parliament in the war were royalists after it ended; many who
loathed the Long Parliament were willing to accept Cromwell's rule.
Waller, court poet and member of the Long Parliament, exiled for his
part in a royalist conspiracy, later wrote a panegyric on Cromwell;
he was attacked for this by a Presbyterian clergyman, Robert Wild, who
was also a 'cavalier poet'. Both men wrote poems welcoming the restoration of Charles II. Are they turncoats, and, if so, at what point did they
turn them? Given these shifting alignments, it is only with reference to a
specific date that one can safely describe a writer as belonging to one party
or the other. Moreover, the background of controversy, though it may
make writers hyper-conscious of their opponents' style, also makes them
totally unscrupulous as literary critics. Few of them stick to their theories
about style and vocabulary when by abandoning them they can score a point.

In view of the problem created by the overabundance of material and the
complexity of the situation I was trying to analyse, I finally made two
decisions. One was to concentrate on royalist literature. It has the advantage of being easier to identify than any other of the period. Cromwell
may have said that he knew what he did not want, but not what he did; the
royalists, however, knew exactly what they wanted: Charles I, and, after
his death, Charles II. My second decision followed from the first. It was to
look particularly at the concept of secrecy and encoded meaning, which is
essential to any party whose opponents control access to the media.
Finally, I hoped to find out what purpose this literature, and its elliptical
presentation, was serving. It was easy enough to see the connection between secrecy and political absolutism: the concept of *arcana imperii*, the
idea that, as Solomon said, 'it is the glory of God to conceal a thing: but the
honour of kings is to search out a matter' (Proverbs 25:2). But how did the
royalist writers reconcile these abstractions with the events of the 1640s?
Was their own secrecy really protecting them from danger, and, if so, of
what kind?

It will be evident that my approach implies a sense of the hermeneutics of
literature similar to that of Annabel Patterson's brilliant *Censorship and
Interpretation* (1984), which has as its central thesis the idea 'that it is to
censorship that we in part owe our very concept of "literature," as a kind of

discourse with rules of its own' (p. 4). My book differs from hers in being confined to a smaller time span and exploring it in more detail, with perhaps more emphasis on the factual than the theoretical. Whereas Patterson sees censorship as *creating* a psychology of secrecy, my concentration on the royalists has led me to see the threat of censorship as only part of a psychological *need* for secrecy whose motivation I shall be trying to clarify in the chapters that follow.

In order to understand the process by which experience is encoded as literature, one obviously has to know what events have been in the public consciousness at any given period. This is one reason why I have made so much use of pamphlets and newsbooks, which, being brief, were usually published quickly and can be dated relatively precisely. In my first chapter I describe the means of production and distribution of this literature, with special emphasis on the publishers and newsbooks whose names will recur throughout this book. Readers who prefer a less factual and more critical approach might prefer to start with the second chapter. Here and in chapters 3 and 4 the subject of secret writing moves from the literal to the metaphorical. I look at the various kinds of code available to writers, from ciphers to pictorial and verbal tricks, to the more subtle effects of genre, allusion and quotation. In a study of royalism it seems important above all to take account of the effect of the personality and writings (real or supposed) of Charles I himself. This is why my final chapter deals with the way in which the image of the king, in the arts, on the scaffold, and in the *Eikon Basilike*, comes to embody, but also to exhaust, the complex of royalist images and beliefs.

The writers discussed here in some detail include Cleveland, Davenant, Fanshawe, Lovelace, Marvell, Waller, Vaughan, and several other canonical figures; Milton is very much present as a voice of opposition, and an important aspect of the book is its study of the practice of quotation from earlier authors, particularly Jonson, Webster, Shakespeare, and Burton. It is also true, however, that many of the works referred to are anonymous or pseudonymous, and that others are by writers who are scarcely household names, if indeed they can be called writers at all: John Crouch, George Digby, Samuel Sheppard, Robert Wild. This book is marginal in the strictest sense of the word, since it is concerned not only with the margins of literary history but, fleetingly at least, with the margins of books: the acknowledgement of sources, the marginalia of readers. I also discuss some odd non-literary episodes: the case of the Sussex Picture, the Abingdon double-cross, the curious affair of the substitute frontispiece. If these sound like the titles of unwritten Sherlock Holmes stories, it is not surprising. 'The Musgrave Ritual' does in fact deal with a secret code dating from the civil war, and T. S. Eliot incorporated some lines from it in *Murder in the Cathedral*, a 'mystery play' which is also a play of martyrdom. There is probably some meaning in this conjunction of events, but I shall not pursue it here.

Because this book quotes from a large number of brief and obscure works, many of which are mentioned only once, I have tried to streamline its documentation as far as was consistent with clarity. Where possible, I have adopted the author–date method of citation after quotations; in the case of anonymous works, I have used a short title instead. For manuscripts, I have used whatever abbreviation seemed easiest to recognise. A single alphabetical list gives the full references; it is confined to works cited in the text. This method of documentation means that it is difficult to explain the complicated problems of text and authorship that often occur in unedited works of this period. Where I felt that such information would be interesting or essential for readers, I have given it in a note; otherwise I have left it out.

I quote the Bible in the Authorised (King James) version; Shakespeare quotations are taken from the Oxford *Complete Works*, ed. Stanley Wells and Gary Taylor, Milton's prose from the Yale *Complete Prose Works*. With other authors I have tried where possible to use standard editions, but often I have had to quote from an original, badly printed edition. This has inevitably resulted in inconsistencies between old and modern spelling. Except where the appearance of a passage is significant for my argument, I have removed or reversed italics in passages where they were heavily used, and altered spelling and punctuation whenever they seemed erroneous or likely to interfere with clarity. I have not given page references for quotations from single quarto pamphlets or where I have quoted from a brief Preface or Dedication. Many of these are inaccurately or irregularly paginated in any case. Unless otherwise indicated, dates of performance of plays are taken from *Annals of English Drama* by Alfred Harbage, revised by Samuel Schoenbaum. Where I give a precise date for a pamphlet in the Thomason collection, it is the one noted by Thomason himself on the title page.

When a book synthesises the results of research carried on for a variety of projects and over a long period of time, this part of its preface inevitably becomes awkwardly self-referential. An earlier version of chapter 3 appeared, as 'True Tragicomedies of the Civil War and Commonwealth', in *Renaissance Tragicomedy*, ed. Nancy Klein Maguire (AMS Press, New York, 1988). A version of chapter 5 was presented on 13 March 1986 at the

Folger Institute Center for the History of British Political Thought, which
is supported by grants from the Research Programs Division of the
National Endowment for the Humanities (an independent federal agency),
the John Ben Snow Memorial Trust, the George Washington University,
and the Exxon Education Foundation; another version was given at
Merton College, Oxford. Some of the material in chapters 1 and 4 is based
on work done for an edition of *The Four Mistress Parliament Plays* (*The
Journal of Analytical and Enumerative Bibliography*, N.S., I, 1987, pp.
101–70). Material from other sections of the book has formed part of
papers to the Society for Theatre Research, the Modern Language Association, the Folger Shakespeare Library, the first International Conference on
the European Emblem, and graduate seminars at the University of Leicester.

This book has, in every sense, many sources. Its research has been aided
by grants from the Board of Research Studies at the University of Leicester
and by the kindness of the librarians at the Leicester University Library,
the Bodleian Library, the libraries of the universities of Cambridge, Nottingham, Harvard, Yale, the University of Pennsylvania, the Folger Shakespeare Library, the Huntington Library, the Union Theological Seminary,
and, especially, the library of Worcester College, Oxford, and its librarian,
Lesley Montgomery. I am grateful for permission to reproduce the Lely
painting of Charles I and the Duke of York, in the possession of His Grace
the Duke of Northumberland at Sion House. For permission to reproduce
illustrations from books in their collections, I thank the Ashmolean
Museum, Oxford, the Leicester University Library, the Cambridge University Library, and the Libraries of Magdalen College, Oxford, St John's
College, Cambridge, and Trinity College, Cambridge.

I have benefited from the advice and encouragement of A. R. Braun-
muller, James Knowles, D. F. McKenzie, Katherine F. Pantzer (who
helped me track down the early career of Richard Royston), Richard
Proudfoot, Dale Randall, Matthew Seccombe, Peter Smith, and P. W.
Thomas. Sheila Lambert read chapter 1 at an earlier stage, was very helpful
on the subject of printing in the mid-seventeenth century, and saved me
from a number of inaccuracies. Eric Sams gave me some useful information
about ciphers. Claudine Majzels taught me a great deal about looking at
pictures. John Pitcher, Isabel Rivers, and Nigel Wood kindly read and
commented on parts of the book; Robin Biswas read the whole typescript
and was both critical and encouraging. Sarah Stanton and Victoria Cooper,
of the Cambridge University Press, were most supportive and helpful in
the final stages of the project, and I am very grateful for Charles Hieatt's
scrupulous and patient copy-editing.

I

'Secrecie's now publish'd': royalists and the press, 1641–1660

There is an Ordinance framed against printing of unlicensed Bookes, Pamphlets, &c, with Fines, and I know not what punishments against the offenders. Then (Gentlemen) I wish you to buy none that are licensed; for, that will be a sure marke to know all Lies and tame Nonsence.

(*Mercurius Pragmaticus*, no. 2, 21–8 Sept. 1647)

Introduction

This book explores the relation between three events of 1641. The first, and best known, is the abolition of Star Chamber, which resulted, indirectly, in the temporary end of licensing and a great increase in the number of works that came off the press. The second is closely related to it. At some point in the same year, George Thomason, a publisher and bookseller, decided to make a collection of contemporary publications. The project became an obsession with him, and one which he carried on into the Restoration, when he attempted, unsuccessfully, to sell it to Charles II. The most important features of this collection are, first, that Thomason collected *all* available publications, without regard either to quality or party line, and, second, that he normally dated each publication on the day he received it. This means that if one wishes to know what was capturing the public imagination at any point between 1641 and 1660, the material is available for this period as for no other. While the collection is not as complete as Thomason hoped to make it (and some of it went missing in the course of its wanderings, before it was finally bought by George III), it consists, in its present form, of over 22,000 pieces ranging from books to pamphlets, newsbooks, broadsides, and manuscripts (Fortescue 1908, p. xxi; Spencer 1958, p. 102 n. 1). It now forms the enormous British Library collection known as the Thomason Tracts.

The third event has a more tangential relation to the other two. Also in 1641, John Wilkins, a clergyman and future Fellow of the Royal Society, published a study of secret writing called *Mercury, or the Secret and Swift*

1

Messenger. The double meaning of this action was not lost on contemporaries. In verses prefixed to the book, one of Wilkins's friends wrote,

> *Secrecie's* now Publish'd; you reveal
> By Demonstration how wee may Conceal.

It was indeed odd to make secrecy public. One might argue that Wilkins (a Parliamentary sympathiser who was eventually to marry a daughter of Cromwell's) was acting in accord with the spirit of 1641, whose dramatic events had come about partly because of the fear of secrecy, particularly the possibility of Roman Catholic plots framed with the connivance of Charles I, Laud, and Strafford. What Parliament opposed to this secrecy were open forms of protest, the popular demonstration and the petition. In the struggle which had just begun, another Parliamentary weapon would be the publication of intercepted and sometimes deciphered letters, culminating in 1645 with those of the king himself. The printing explosion and Wilkins's book might then seem to be part of the same process of greater openness which is usually associated with the early years of the Long Parliament.

But this is not how Wilkins' friends saw it. What attracted them in his book, at a time when the press was producing more than ever before, was 'how we may conceal'. The paradox can be seen as a microcosm of the period. Thomason's collection includes much which had been secretly published, as it would have been defined as treasonable by one government or another. There are many anonymous and pseudonymous publications, and many which give no imprint, or only a false or nonsensical one ('Printed at Cuckoo time in a hollow tree'). A few of the contents are manuscripts, either because Thomason was copying a borrowed pamphlet or because the work in question was never published. The collection itself, according to Thomason's later statement, had been a carefully guarded secret. His most recent biographer, Lois Spencer, sees no reason to doubt him (Spencer 1959, pp. 13–14). However, there are several unanswered questions about his means of acquiring it. How could the publisher accumulate so much without letting some people into the secret? In 1647 he lent a pamphlet from his already enormous collection to Charles I, then a prisoner at Hampton Court. How did Charles I know that he was likely to have it? Thomason seems to have thought that his activity was risky, and he hid his stacks of volumes under canvas in his warehouse to make them look like covered tables. But most of what we know on this subject is what was written after the Restoration. Thomason and, later, his heirs were desperately anxious to sell the collection, whose acquisition had virtually bankrupted him. Although the bookseller's sympathies had become royalist by about 1647, he had begun as a sympathiser with Parliament and a friend of Milton's. He was a Presbyterian in the sense of being anti-Independent; his friendships and professional connections throughout the 1650s continued to be with other Presbyterians; and when he was imprisoned in 1651 it was for involvement with a conspiracy of Presbyterian royalists (Spencer 1959, pp. 18–21). This background would have done him little good after the Restoration, and it would not have been strange if, like many other people after 1660, he and his family had exaggerated and romanticised any events of the two previous decades which might be construed as assisting the royalist cause.

The questions raised by Thomason's collection also arise for other works of the period. Secrecy is published, indeed, when writers shout from the housetops that they are printing illegally or in defiance of the government. This brings me to the other paradox of this book. It is generally assumed that 'secret writing' is the work of popular and radical groups, and that the printing explosion which followed the abolition of Star Chamber was the point at which these voices at last found an outlet. In fact, from 1642 to 1660 the source of the most deliberately and consciously subversive publications was the royalist party. Because the object of both historical and literary study has always been to pick the winners and explain why they won, comparatively little attention has been paid to the writers of this group. Yet their culture survived despite numerous attempts to discredit it, succeeded in imposing its view of events on the age, and probably helped (more than conspiracies or uprisings) to bring about the restoration of the monarchy. This is one reason for studying it. Another is that it offers an opportunity to modify our understanding of 'subversive' literature in the seventeenth century. Most scholars have been primarily concerned with literature which is subversive in the literal sense of the word: coming from below, whether from the lower classes of society or from suppressed religious and political groups. By contrast, the chapters which follow will be primarily concerned with writers who defied censorship while defending censorship, underdogs whose greatest desire was for the re-establishing of a hierarchy.

It was the coming of printing, Elizabeth Eisenstein (1979) suggests, that led to the view that 'valuable data could be preserved best by being made public, rather than by being kept secret' (vol. 1, p. 116). In practice, however, the existence of licensing regulations made the interplay between publication and secrecy a complex one. When Charles I gave his assent to the abolition of Star Chamber in July 1641, its main effect was to remove the cumbersome ecclesiastical machinery which – among other things – meant that books had to be read and approved before publication by an authorised licenser, usually a churchman. The purpose of licensing had only partly been one of censorship. Its other function was to preserve the closed shop of the Stationers' Company and its copyrights of specific works. Unlicensed printing was a direct threat to the livelihoods of Company members; it was this that they tried to control, not the content of what was printed. In fact, the books most often printed illegally were not subversive texts but the perennial best-sellers – psalters, primers, and so on. One reason for the comparative failure to control illegal printing was that it was relatively easy to acquire and conceal a press. Another was that the overmanned and relatively hard-up Company was somewhat divided in its aims; its less successful members were themselves indulging in unlicensed printing and pinching each other's books (see Lambert 1987).

The end of Star Chamber had an immediate effect on the press: 1642 saw a record number of publications, which would not be equalled until the 1690s (Lambert, quoted in Treadwell 1987, p. 144). Much of what was published was in the form of short works, single sheets and pamphlets which could be handled by the limited resources of the smaller and less established printers (Treadwell 1987, p. 167 n. 8). The Stationers had no desire to see this state of affairs continue. It did continue, however, because between 1641 and 1649 Parliament had too much other business on its hands to enable it to set up an efficient alternative to the old licensing system. A number of attempts were made to regularise the situation: the licensing of newsbooks was made compulsory in March 1642, and temporary licensing machinery was set up in August of that year; on 14 June 1643 the licensing of all books and pamphlets was required by a Parliamentary Ordinance (the term used until the king's execution for acts which were passed without his consent). In September 1647 a new ordinance, largely aimed at royalist publications, gave press control to the army; in October 1649 an Act of Parliament, more efficiently enforced, returned control to the state and succeeded in suppressing all but a few of the most determined opponents of the Commonwealth. In the years between 1649 and 1660 it was this Act, renewed at intervals, which governed the press. Only when the machinery of enforcement broke down, in the last years of the Commonwealth, did the number of publications rise again: 1660 was another peak, second only to 1642 (Treadwell 1987).

It was not only the Stationers who disapproved of the printing explosion. Almost no one was in favour of unrestricted publication. The

London Petition (11 December 1640), largely popular and Puritan, complained of 'the hindering of godly books to be printed', but went on to object to the publication of the works of Ovid and the ballads of Martin Parker. What looked to Milton (*Areopagitica* ([1644] 1959, p. 558) like a 'flowry crop of knowledge and new light' was more commonly seen, as in the conservative Kentish Petition of March 1642, as 'the odious and abominable Scandal of schismatical and seditious Sermons and Pamphlets' (Snow and Young 1969, p. 488). The most immediately obvious effect of the end of licensing was a vast increase in the output of topical literature, especially newsbooks or 'diurnals'. (Diurnals were published weekly; their name refers to their presentation of the news in a day-by-day account of proceedings in Parliament.) Though newsbooks had existed in England before 1641, they had always been confined to foreign affairs. The first one to give English news appeared four months after the abolition of Star Chamber. By December, there were three competing ones (Frank 1961, p. 21), while in 1642 there were at least sixty-four. But competition for survival was intense; the most recent bibliographical study of the diurnals has found that of the year's publications, 'thirty titles appeared in only one issue, and only six in more than twenty issues' (Nelson and Seccombe 1986, p. 14).

Having more news meant, for many, not more but less truth. Printers produced hasty, shoddy work; authors and publishers resorted to sensationalism as a means of ensuring sales. The increase in the number of published works meant that each new one had to fight harder to be read. One way of attracting attention was to claim that one had a secret to tell. Misleading titles abound, sometimes trying to make the book sound more exciting than it is, sometimes trying to lure a hostile reader to look at a piece of propaganda by the other side, sometimes trying to conceal the fact that the work is not so new, or so up-to-date, as it purports to be. The press also lied about its own means of production, with false names and dates on the title page, fake imprimaturs, and counterfeits of official statements of permission to publish. The nickname for diurnal soon became 'lie-urnal'. An anonymous pamphlet of 1641 indicates the problem which faced readers confronted by an overabundance of information and propaganda. The pamphlet's eponymous hero, *The Liar*, makes a series of unlikely-sounding claims – women are preaching, Cheapside cross is down, and so on – which are of course perfectly true. Despite the various punishments inflicted on him for these dreadful statements, he carries on talking. Finally the author breaks in:

Gentle reader, I have heere related under the name of lies nothing but true tales, for if a man doth now speake truth he shall be sure to smart for it now a daies, either heere or in other places; read gentlie, and buy willingly.

The pamphlet's full title – *The Liar: or, a Contradiction to Those Who in the titles of their Bookes affirmed them to be true, when they were false: although mine are all true, yet I terme them Lyes* – is significant. As it indicates, the unprecedented nature of the things that really were taking place in public life made it possible for the wildest statements of the press to win belief. The pamphlet does not take an openly political line, but its implicit ridicule of the events to which it refers indicates a royalist and conservative position (it has in fact been ascribed to John Taylor, a popular royalist writer). Equally characteristic of that position, however, is its stress on the uncertainty of all knowledge: the author hints both at his own danger, which forces him to engage in subterfuge, and at the vulnerability of the reader, unaccustomed to judging between conflicting accounts. Thus, though the pamphlet is unlicensed and illegal, it is not really on the side of illicit publication.

Royalists never embraced freedom of the press as a doctrine; rather, their argument was that the established authority, Parliament, was not a true authority. It is likely that unauthorised publication, as they practised it, was a carefully organised affair. This is difficult to establish, because, although the role of printers and publishers in this period is beginning to be better understood, it still needs much more attention. The fact that many publications have no imprint makes it difficult to analyse the total output of individual publishers, and thus to know how centralised their activity was and how far it was dictated by commercial, as opposed to ideological, motives. Within the Stationers' Company itself, political differences seem to have mattered less than jockeying for position, trying to secure lucrative shares of its stock, and in-fighting between the different branches of the Company. As one might expect, those who had most to lose were the least active. The senior members seem to have tried to stay out of politics as far as possible (Blagden 1958, pp. 14–15). They normally entered at least a proportion of their books in the Register, and sometimes licensed them as well. The less established publishers and printers took more risks, some for ideological reasons, others because they could not afford to refuse any kind of work. In the case of journals and topical satire, particularly, they had nothing to gain by registering their publications (at sixpence a time) in order to establish copyright.

The practice of printing for both sides was obviously common. Even the

Eikon Basilike, the most important work of royalist propaganda in the entire period, includes among its thirty-five English editions of 1649 two by publishers normally associated with parliamentary literature (Madan 1949, p. 42). But it seems to have been felt that publishing should involve more than a purely commercial commitment to an author: hence, the contemptuous reference of a pro-Parliament journalist to 'that Camelion Bookseller, who is of that colour which you aply him next unto' (*Mercurius Britanicus* 11 July 1648), and Milton's disgust that someone who had published Salmasius' *Regii Sanguinis Clamor* should ask to print Milton's reply as well (Spencer 1959, pp. 22–3). In an attempt to give a picture of the royalist literary scene, I shall look at three men whose ideological stance was unquestionably royalist, and who represent three different kinds of 'subversive' publishing. Richard Royston was openly and officially involved in royalist propaganda in London while it was under Parliamentary control; John Crouch and the group associated with him produced a more apparently 'popular' kind of anti-government literature on secret presses; Humphrey Moseley, a highly respectable literary publisher, stayed out of trouble throughout the period, while probably doing as much for the cause as either of them.

Official propaganda and Richard Royston

The first phase of royalist literary activity was completely controlled by the court. The king, from the start, was strongly committed to printing and publishing. He took a printing press with him when he left London for York in 1642, and made sure that copies of his speeches were distributed afterwards for the benefit of those who could not hear them (Thomas 1969, pp. 28–9; Malcolm 1983, pp. 124ff.). The propaganda effort was not wholly in vain: at least one person who chose the royalist side in 1642 apparently did so after reading, among other things, some of these speeches (Hutton 1982, p. 17). One reason for the general belief in the king's authorship of the posthumous *Eikon Basilike* was the fact that he frequently told his close associates of his intention to justify himself in writing. James Howell, the future historiographer royal, obviously knew of this when, in *The Vote*, a poem for New Year 1642, he promised eventually 'To vindicate the truth of CHARLES his raigne, / From scribling Pamphletors' (p. 5). According to George Thomason, the king also knew, and approved, of his collection (Spencer 1958, pp. 114–15; Spencer 1959, pp. 13–14).

During the war, the centre of royalist propaganda was Oxford. Its circle of writers included aristocrats and members of the king's council. On the other hand, it also made extensive use of professionals, some of whom were well-known popular figures such as John Taylor (called the Water Poet because he had once been a waterman) and the ballad-writer Martin Parker. The court sponsored an official newsbook, *Mercurius Aulicus* (the court Mercury), which began publication on 1 January 1643. Under the editorship of Peter Heylin, later largely superseded by Sir John Berkenhead, it drew on official subsidies and the talents of a number of courtiers and scholars. The idea of an official newsbook may have come from France, where the *Gazette* of Théophraste Renaudot, started in 1631 under Richelieu's ministry, was taken up again and given increased prestige by Mazarin in 1643 (Grand-Mesnil 1967, pp. 11–12, 31, 50). This absolutist parentage gives a fair idea of what the court expected a newsbook to be: an official version of the news. Licensing, in fact, was never abolished in Oxford. Berkenhead doubled the role of journalist with that of licenser, a function he had also exercised (as one of Laud's chaplains) before the war. Thus, as Berkenhead's biographer points out, printing in Oxford was actually under tighter control during this period than it had been even during Laud's chancellorship (Thomas 1969, pp. 20–1, 124–5). Among those known to have contributed to *Aulicus* were several churchmen who, like Berkenhead, were Laudian protégés (Thomas 1969, pp. 37–40).

Despite (or because of) its slanted if lively coverage of the news, *Aulicus* had enough influence to be a serious threat to public opinion. The Parliamentary newsbook *Mercurius Britanicus* began printing in September 1643, specifically to counter its effect. Efforts were made to keep copies from reaching London. But a well-organised royalist network succeeded both in smuggling Oxford publications into the city and in producing London reprints of them. *Britanicus* in one of its early numbers reports a rumour that the writer of the London version 'hath his Commission under the *great Seale*' (10–17 Oct. 1643). In fact, he was not a writer but a publisher, Richard Royston, originally from Oxford.[1] *Britanicus* may have been right about his official status, since not only *Aulicus* but a number of other works of this period with Oxford imprints are in fact reprints by the London press, many of them under the auspices of Royston (Madan 1912). London printing helped to supplement the resources of the two Oxford printers, each of whom is said to have had only one press and to have suffered from occasional shortages of paper (O Hehir 1969, pp. 62–6). The purpose of the false imprints must have been partly to conceal the difficult circumstances prevailing in Oxford and partly to protect the London publishers from suspicion. Another reason may have been commercial:

London purchasers might pay a higher price for a book which they thought had been smuggled in, at great risk, from Oxford.

Nothing that is known of the early part of Royston's career indicates why he was to become the most energetic royalist publisher of the next two decades. He was already in his forties when the Long Parliament met, a moderately successful publisher with some interest in 'polite literature'. But he made his views apparent from the first. His first publication after the abolition of Star Chamber was a royalist sermon preached on the anniversary of Charles I's coronation. It was licensed. But he then published *Proquiratio Parainetike, or, a Petition to the People* (dated September 1642), which urged Parliament to trust the king and punish those who had driven him out of the city. This pamphlet was not licensed; according to a note which Thomason wrote on his copy of the pamphlet, it was 'scattered up and down in London' over two days, and finally suppressed as 'scandalous', by order of Parliament. Though Royston put his name on the title page, he was not arrested. That his first acknowledged publication should have appeared so soon after the beginning of open war, and should be so openly anti-Parliament, suggests that he already had some official status as the king's representative in London. Among the printers he employed were Roger Norton, the son of the former King's Printer for England, and James Young, the son of the former Royal Printer for Scotland (Williams 1973, p. 102). These were men with an obvious vested interest in the royalist cause. At the Restoration, Royston was referred to as his Majesty's bookseller. Whether officially or not, this appears to have been his role.

From 1642 on, Royston continued to make a small number of entries each year in the Stationers' Register, mainly works by high church Anglican divines like Henry Hammond and Jeremy Taylor. But his real energies were going into unlicensed printing. Though traffic between Oxford and London was prohibited, publications, like other goods, moved illegally in both directions. Royston employed what were euphemistically known as 'adventurous women' to smuggle copies of *Aulicus* with other correspondence. These women travelled 'like Strowlers begging from House to House, and loitering at Places agreed upon, to take up Books (which Mr. Royston had conveyed by stealth among other merchandise into the Western Barges on the *Thames*, and the Bargemen had put on shore there), and sell them to Retailers well known to them' (Barwick 1724, p. 62).

In 1645, Royston was finally imprisoned for a short period. Considering the extent of his anti-parliamentary activities, it is surprising that this had not happened before. It has been suggested that he was in collusion with the officials of the Stationers' Company (Malcolm 1983, p. 125). Perhaps he also got protection from powerful friends in Parliament and the Westminster Assembly. Though royalists tend to depict both institutions as monolithic structures, they frequently profited from the fact that the members of both were really deeply divided about many issues and contained a number of royalist sympathisers. *The Kingdomes Weekly Intelligencer*, which reported the arrest of 'the great disperser and divulger' of 'Malignant Pamphlets' in its number for 5 August 1645, saw it as a sign that the 'Aulican' party in Parliament was weakening. But Royston was entering books in the Register again within a few months, and even his unlicensed publications often bear his name, defiantly, on the title page. When he was arrested again in 1648, the warrant gave his name as 'alias Allen of St Margaret's, Westminster' (*Calendar of State Papers Domestic* [*CSPD*], xxii, p. 173). Perhaps this alias is another reason why he eluded capture for so long.

His greatest service to the royalist cause was the publication of the *Eikon Basilike*, the 'king's book' of prayers and meditations on events of the 1640s, which was a best seller in its own time and widely regarded as a major contributor to the sentiments leading to the Restoration. Royston always believed it to be a work of the king's own writing. His story, as told (perhaps rather too frequently) in his old age (Barwick 1724, p. 370), was that he had been in correspondence with Charles about the book in the autumn of 1648 (Madan 1949, pp. 163–7). The printing is said to have been done outside London for fear of interruptions. While all later accounts stress the secrecy of the whole process, a number of people obviously knew something about it – for instance, Jeremy Taylor, who is supposed to have suggested the Greek title when he saw the book in proof at Royston's shop (Madan 1949, pp. 141–2). Because of the close watch kept on the presses, and the intrusion of government searchers who in early January destroyed what would have been the first impression of the work, the book did not reach the public until just after the king's execution. The overwhelming demand for copies of the work probably took everyone by surprise. Royston had to use the services of more than one printer. One of them, the schoolmaster William Dugard, actually put his initials to his verses explaining the book's frontispiece, a fact which suggests some confidence in the safety of the undertaking, though in fact it led to his arrest on 16 March. While the *Eikon* itself was not licensed, some of its later contents were, and the rather confused accounts in the press have been interpreted by the book's bibliographer, F. F. Madan (1949, pp. 169–70), as indicating Parliament's own uncertainty as to whether or not to go against public sentiment by banning the book altogether. Both Royston and Dugard must have profited from the divided loyalties of many parliamentarians in the aftermath of the execution. Royston, however, in his post-Restoration account, said that he was imprisoned for a fortnight and pressed by two members of the Council of State to deny the king's authorship of the book (Madan 1949, pp. 152–3). He was called before the Council of State again in May after printing another valuable piece of royalist propaganda, the exchange of letters between Charles I and the Presbyterian Alexander Henderson, which seemed to establish beyond a doubt that, contrary to some of the accusations against him, the king had been a good member of the Church of England and a competent amateur theologian as well (see below, pp. 163–5). Royston had a third confrontation with authority after the passing of the act for regulating printing in September 1649; he was bound over for good behaviour, required to post a bond of £500 with two sureties, and made to promise not to print or sell any unlicensed books (Williams 1973, p. 101). He did not keep this promise particularly well. In 1653 his name occurs as one of eighteen printers arrested for printing pamphlets against Cromwell (Muddiman 1908, pp. 151–2). His publications between that date and 1660 include other royalist works, particularly sermons and anthologies of the writings of Charles I. Many of these were published under his own name or the cryptic 'Vas Regius', which, as Madan points out (1949, p. 167), was easily translatable as 'Roy's tun'.

Royston was well rewarded after the Restoration when he was given a monopoly of printing all the works of Charles I which he had done so much to keep before the public eye. In 1663 Charles II also persuaded the Stationers' Company to admit him to the livery; he was Warden twice during the next decade and Master of the Company in 1673 and 1674. Like other illegal publishers of the 1640s, Royston could be harshly repressive once he himself was in a position of authority, and his conduct as Warden of the Company after the Restoration, which has recently been documented, shows a decided tendency to put profit above ideology (Hetet 1985, pp. 41–3). Moreover, the financial success of the *Eikon* must have been enormous, since, like all 'dangerous' books, it could be more highly priced than ordinary ware.

I find it impossible, even so, to believe that Royston's years of devotion to the royalist interest had only mercenary ends in view. He could presumably have made his peace with Parliament, as did William Dugard, one of the printers of the *Eikon*. Dugard claimed, after the Restoration, that he had been forced to capitulate by extreme hardship: he had suffered a period of imprisonment, his wife and children had been turned out of doors, and he was on the point of being 'tried for his Life by an High Court of Injustice' (Madan 1923, p. 136). His submission was rewarded with the post of 'Printer to his Highness the Lord Protector'. If the Commonwealth was prepared to tolerate and even reward a man who had done as much as Dugard for the royalist side, it would presumably have done the same for Royston himself. A possible motive for his loyalty is indicated in one of the clauses of his will, which states that his copyrights are to be held only by a member of the Church of England (Plomer 1907, p. 159). The importance of loyalty to the church as a motive for loyalty to the king is one which will be apparent throughout this book. Most of Royston's publications place a strong emphasis on the king's role as head of the English church, and his other major publications included collections of works by well-known royalist divines such as Jeremy Taylor. Henry Hammond's *Practical Catechism*, which he published in 1644, was one of his most successful books; it was also particularly admired by the king, who bequeathed a copy of it to his son, Henry, Duke of Gloucester. Some of these high churchmen must have been personally known to Royston; it was from him, for example, that Hammond first heard of the king's death (Madan 1949, p. 165). The story of Jeremy Taylor's seeing the proofs of the *Eikon Basilike* in Royston's shop also suggests a close working relationship between author and publisher. He may have had direct contact with the king at Oxford or elsewhere, and he certainly worked closely with Dr John Barwick, a sort of Cassock Pimpernel whose career shows the extent to which churchmen were prepared to engage in highly risky intelligence work on behalf of the cause. (His life story, written by his brother, is one of the most fascinating of the period.) The status his role gave him may explain why Royston openly acknowledged so many of his works. Royalists who visited his shop knew that they could count on a sympathetic reception and a stock of books with whose views they were sure to agree. Having this kind of reputation with a respectable clientele was probably worth a considerable amount of risk.

John Crouch and the underground press

With the collapse of the royalist cause in 1645–6, and the return to London of many royalists, the clear demarcation between Oxford and London becomes blurred. In 1642–3, when a royalist attack on the city was considered imminent, Parliament had ordered the construction of trenches and fortifications around the city, sealing it off from the rest of the kingdom. Whole families and guilds had taken their turns with the work. Memories

of this embodiment of constructive collective activity must lie behind
Milton's language in *Areopagitica*, with its constant stress on the be-
leaguered 'City of refuge' (p. 553), 'encompast and surrounded with
[God's] protection' (p. 554), and the energetic building activity (pp. 555–7)
which he parallels to the activity of readers and writers. By 1647, London
opinion had ceased to be united behind Parliament. July of that year saw
the first popular demonstration against Parliament by crowds with royalist
sympathies. In September Parliament ordered the trenches demolished. In
a remarkably short time, they were gone and the land ploughed over
(Brett-James 1935, pp. 268–95). It was a recognition that the enemy was
not only outside the city but within it.

The period from the end of 1646 to 1649 saw the development of a
broader-based propaganda idiom than had emanated from Oxford. This
was partly because the king, once he had given himself up to the Scottish
army in May 1646, was no longer in full control of the presentation of his
cause. It was also due to the defection of many former supporters of
Parliament. These were moderates, often 'Presbyterian' in the sense of
wishing a reform of the episcopal structure of the church, who had
expected the civil war to end with the return of the king to his capital and
the establishment of some sort of understanding with Parliament, based on
mutual compromise. Fear of political and religious extremism made some
of them see the king as the lesser of two evils. His seizure at Holmby by
Colonel Joyce and the New Model Army in June 1647 seems to have been
the turning-point for a number of them, a signal that political and religious
radicalism was getting out of hand.

Both *Mercurius Aulicus* and its main London rivals were licensed newsbooks whose publisher was openly acknowledged. The royalist journals of
1647–9 and the pamphlets related to them had to be secret operations. A
number of those who wrote for them had been part of the Oxford circle,
and it is not clear how far they ever really trusted the ex-parliamentarians
who moved into the same employment. *Mercurius Melancholicus*, the first
royalist journal, was started in late August 1647 by a Presbyterian, John
Hacklyt, but also immediately kidnapped by (probably) Parker and Taylor. The two other long-lasting journals followed shortly afterward. *Mercurius Pragmaticus* was the work of ex-parliamentarians – one of them,
Marchamont Nedham, the ex-editor of *Britanicus*, is said to have been
converted after a personal meeting with the king at Hampton Court.
Mercurius Elencticus was the work of George Wharton, an amateur astrologer and member of the Oxford circle. John Berkenhead, Samuel Butler,
and John Cleveland are the best-known of the other writers who are said to

have had a hand in these journals and other royalist publications. That they were successful in avoiding arrest probably means that they sent in only occasional contributions from some 'safe house'.

But any attempt to attribute authorship, at least without the aid of computer tests, soon has to break down. All three journals probably had more than one writer, and they were parodied and pirated to such an extent that their styles often ended up being interchangeable. From the beginning, they found themselves having to tell their public not to trust the 'false' Melancholicus or Pragmaticus, and to pay attention to the day of publication: a false Mercury would sometimes come out a day early and corner the market, or copy the real one and come out a day late to mop up whatever business might still be available. Royalist publications, which did not register their names or those of their printers, were naturally more vulnerable to counterfeits than the newsbooks on the parliamentary side (Nelson and Seccombe 1986, p. 84). Other reasons for counterfeiting may include the teaming up of writers with new printers or publishers, or the defecting of one member of a team. When a new journal was launched anonymously, its enemies frequently leapt into print with identifications of the author, printer, and publisher, as if Mercury, like Rumpelstiltskin, would lose his power once he was identified. Though some of the accusations are probably random ones, these hostile and often unreliable reports are the main source of what little information there is about the shadowy figures of the underground press.

Such a mixed group was bound to suffer from friction. Any attempt to disentangle its history must cope with the volatile nature of both people and events: writers change journals, journals change printers and publishers, and all three engage in elaborate games of deception. Some of these are necessitated by government hostility. The officers of the Stationers' Company who were charged with finding and identifying those responsible for illegal publications approached their task with the same kinds of expertise that are now used by the modern bibliographer: analysis of the type-face and ornaments, the watermarks, and so on (Plomer 1904, pp. 374–403). But, since the producers of illicit literature could anticipate precisely this kind of detective work, they devised ways of fooling the searchers which make the period a bibliographer's nightmare. Printers borrowed and counterfeited each other's type; some probably kept old type-faces and ornaments which they used only for anonymous, unlicensed work. This is one reason why illegal pamphlets are so atrociously printed – a fact which may give a false impression of the amount of trouble that was being taken over them.

Unreliable as they are, the external characteristics which I have just mentioned, taken in conjunction with the cross-references from one publication to another, make it fairly certain that one publisher was responsible for a substantial number of anti-parliamentary works of 1647–9, all of them probably catering for the same group of readers. In May 1648, for example, there were three newsbooks and a number of single pamphlets, including some which name Melancholicus as their author, which were almost certainly the work of a single printing house (Potter 1987, p. 103). Since there is a record of the imprisonment of Edward Crouch as the printer of *Melancholicus*, and he is later mentioned as the printer of *The Man in the Moon*, it is likely that his press was the centre of this underground activity. It also adds weight to the view that he was a relative of John Crouch, who was probably the author as well as the publisher of many of these pamphlets (Werstine 1982, pp. 73–6).

The name of Crouch turns up with surprising frequency in the world of printing and publishing; Crouches were particularly associated with both ballad-printing and scurrilous 'low' royalist propaganda. Humphrey Crouch was a ballad printer; Edward Crouch (of Hosier Lane, Snow Hill) printed royalist newsbooks, and may have been a master printer at the Restoration (Treadwell 1987, pp. 146, 168 n. 14); Nathaniel Crouch was a master printer in that period. One John Crouch was a printer who had been apprenticed to John Bill, the King's Printer, until 1635. One of these may also have been the mysterious 'Swallow' Crouch referred to at this period. It would be interesting to know whether any of them was a son of the Mrs Dorothy Crowch, an alehouse-keeper, who, in 1644, was bound over to the next sessions for letting her son and guests sing songs against Parliament (Rollins 1923, p. 23). Their addresses are significant, since all are in the vicinity of Smithfield, the location of Bartholomew Fair, where ballads had a particularly good sale. Edward Crouch and Edward Blackmore, another publisher with a substantial ballad list, were producing rival editions of *Mercurius Melancholicus* in the summer of 1648 (Nelson and Seccombe 1986, p. 84). Smithfield was also an area traditionally noted for rowdy activities, which, unlike those of the public theatres, were not suppressed by Parliament (Marcus 1986, p. 214).

John Crouch turned out a series of different newsbooks throughout the late 1640s and 1650s; as soon as one was suppressed, he started another with a new title: *Mercurius Melancholicus, Mercurius Bellicus, The Parliament Kite, The Man in the Moon, Mercurius Fumigosus, Mercurius Democritus*. 'News', however, is the wrong word for their contents, which can best be read as satiric fantasy tempered by a talent for verse. He frequently refers to himself or to his various aliases. His works appear to have been among the best known of their kind, and two of his journals, *Mercurius Melancholicus* and *The Man in the Moon*, gave their names to the authorship of a number of other pamphlets, some dramatic or semi-dramatic, some at least partly in verse. Insofar as it is possible to speak of him as a writer with a distinct personality, his output can be seen to move from a particularly intense and mocking kind of anti-government satire into something much more purely scurrilous. This may have been the result of imprisonment. A fellow-journalist, how truthfully it is impossible to know, called him a turncoat, because 'The *Man in the Moon* having throwne him into the Gate-house, his first action after his Infranchisement (by which you may ghesse the constitution of the fellowes soule) was to raile at the present King of *Scots*'; the author went on to describe him as 'a base Illiterate Scribler who lards his leane Pamphlets with the fat of other Bookes; a Rascal that cares not whom he calumniates', and a cuckold as well (S. S. [Samuel Sheppard] 1652, p. 10). It is possible, however, that Crouch and his journals were only the centre of a team of writers. In that case, the *Man in the Moon*'s movement from political to sexual satire might reflect a change not only of persona but of personnel.

It is possible that the Crouch group's takeover of John Hacklyt's *Mercurius Melancholicus* was politically as well as commercially motivated. Hacklyt may not have intended his glum publication to be the first of a series. It reads more like a sermon, highly emotional and rhetorical, and, although it attacks Parliament, its message appears to be that there is much to be said against everyone, including the king. Nevertheless, the pamphlet, or perhaps its Burtonian title, evidently looked attractive enough to inspire a counterfeit almost immediately. This counterfeit, printed by Edward Crouch, seems to have largely taken over from Hacklyt's paper, despite the latter's protests (Rollins 1919, pp. 449–74; Rollins 1923, pp. 7, 26), though Hacklyt continued to bring out numbers of what he insisted was the 'real' *Melancholicus* and he was to be involved in journalism for at least two years more. The journal's name clearly had enough selling power for someone to use it as the *nom de plume* of a number of associated satiric pamphlets. This did not on the whole happen with the other Mercuries; the current writer of *Pragmaticus* disowned as 'a dirty thing' (30 Nov.–7 Dec. 1647) *The Levellers Levelled*, one of the few pamphlets to appear under the name of his journal.

These newsbooks were intended to annoy Parliament, and they succeeded. Largely on their account, a new printing ordinance was passed in September 1647. It was briefly effective, but the three journals were soon to reappear, presumably after having found better concealed printing houses. In the period between this ordinance and the much more successful one two years later, much of the interest of the royalist journals comes from their own accounts of how they had evaded pursuit and capture, and from their rivals' accounts of the arrest of their writers, printers, publishers, and even the women who sold them in the street, who were kept in jail until they revealed the source of their wares. As each capture is reported, other royalists rally round to prove, by the appearance of the newsbook in the following week, that the wrong person is in prison. They seem to have made their greatest impact during the first half of 1648, when the political situation was at its most unstable. There had been popular demonstrations in favour of the king, now imprisoned on the Isle of Wight, and in the spring rebellions against Parliament broke out in Essex, Scotland, and Wales. It was at this point that the search for illegal news-sheets became particularly intense, and the searchers were told to seize 'Pragmaticus, Melancholicus, Elencticus, or any other unlicensed publications', as well as the 'printers, sellers, and authors' (*CSPD*, xxii, p. 19). One of the authors of *Melancholicus* and the printer of *Pragmaticus* were imprisoned in March 1648 (*Perfect Occurrences*, 10–17 March 1648). In April, Edward Crouch, named as the printer and publisher of *Melancholicus*, was committed to prison (*Perfect Occurrences*, 31 March–7 April 1648). *Elencticus*, in March, denied rumours that he had been captured, insisting that the person in jail was the wrong man. Presumably someone else had stepped in to continue the *Mercury* for the original editor. 'I carry a *Presse* in my *Pocket*, and can *Print* in my *Closet*', he proudly declared a month later (*Mercurius Elencticus*, 26 April–3 May 1648). That the royalist propaganda machine was felt to be genuinely damaging is indicated by the fact that Parliament paid John Hall, a young gentleman of Gray's Inn, to attack these newsbooks in a revived *Mercurius Britanicus* (revived even in the misspelling of the name). Hall's main argument was an early version of the loyalist position: everyone should accept the established government rather than plunge the kingdom into new war. His first issue, which complains of the number of writers 'distinguished by their Beards and Cassocks', suggests the extent to which royalist satire was in the hands of clergymen (16 May 1648). His newsbook ran only from May to August, but by then there was less need for it, as the major royalist uprisings had been put down.

Perhaps because of the increasing hopelessness of their cause, the royalist journals show a notable slackening of enthusiasm in the latter part of 1648, and their appearance is more sporadic. Their coverage of the king's trial and execution is particularly disappointing. *Elencticus* and *Melanch-*

olicus did not appear at all in the last part of January, presumably because their printers were being too closely watched. The tone of their numbers for early January suggests that they had no idea how close the king was to the death which they had so often, in their more sensational moments, predicted for him. The current writer of *Pragmaticus*, though he did manage to publish a number dated 23–30 January 1649, obviously had no access to the proceedings in the High Court of Justice apart from what he could read in the official journals.

After the execution, the royalist journals lay low for a while, then turned their attention to supporting Charles II's projected invasion of Britain. A new version of *Mercurius Pragmaticus* appeared again in April 1649, with the addition to its title of the words '(*for King Charls II*)', and, by its third number, had gone back to making jokes about Cromwell's red nose. *Elencticus* reappeared in the following week: 'Gentlemen, you mistake that thinke me in *Prison*: It is the thing I least feare.' *Melancholicus* also continued, but at this point, for some reason, Crouch decided to launch yet another journal.

The Man in the Moon made its first appearance on 16 April 1649. The editor explained his name: it was a warning that, like the moon, he could look in at doors and windows, spying on people's nocturnal activities; moreover, like the man traditionally seen in the moon, he had a dog who would bite. This promise of a mixture of scurrility and satire was faithfully kept. *The Man in the Moon* at once turned out to be the most violent of the royalist Mercuries. In the week in which England was proclaimed a Commonwealth, he warned that he and his fellow journalists were not going to confine their hostile activities to the printed page:

> I know they're *impudent*, and little care,
>   what e're we *say* or *write*;
> But when our *quills* once wearied are,
>   wee'l take our *swords* and *fight*.   (14–21 May 1649)

When the Commonwealth ambassador to Holland, Dorislaus, was murdered there by royalists, some of their sympathisers in England expressed uneasiness about this resort to terrorism, but not *The Man in the Moon*, which produced an unsympathetic epitaph:

> A *rebell* he liv'd, a *rebell* he dy'de,
> And there was an end of a *Regicide*.   (13–20 June 1649)

The increasing violence of royalist writing provoked Parliament into its most successfully repressive legislation. On 17 July 1649 the *Act Declaring*

What Offences Shall be Adjudged Treason defined as guilty of high treason anyone who should 'maliciously or advisedly publish, by Writing, Printing, or openly Declaring, that the said government is tyrannical, Usurped or Unlawful; or that the Commons in Parliament assembled are not the Supreme Authority of the Nation'. This was followed on 20 September by the Printing Act, which finally brought the press under control. The Common Council followed it up on 9 October with an act forbidding the sale of books by hawkers, on the grounds that the practice served as a cover for dispersing 'all sorts of Lybills'.

Each new Ordinance had included a set of severe penalties for those who were caught. Under the one of 1647, heavy fines (or imprisonment) were designated for the author, for the printer, and for the publisher. The hawkers who sold the pamphlets in the street were to be whipped and have all their stock confiscated. The main purpose of the 1649 Printing Act was to enable all previous laws to be put into execution. The penalties for author, printer, bookseller, and street-hawker remained much the same as before; anyone who bought an illegal pamphlet, failed to acknowledge this fact, and say where it was bought within twenty-four hours was to be fined two pounds per item. All newsbooks had to be relicensed. Printers had to enter into bonds for £300 not to print treasonable material or let other people use their equipment without first notifying the Stationers' Company. Offenders were to be barred from ever owning a press again. Presses were not to be set up outside prescribed areas; the government was aware that much of the surreptitious printing had been done in 'by-places and corners, out of the eye of Government'. Magistrates had the power to search the posts for illegally imported or exported books. The effect was immediate. Imprisonment and fines silenced or converted many writers – Nedham, for example. The total number of publications recorded in the catalogue of Thomason's collection of tracts drops from eighty-seven in July to forty-two in September and only twenty in December.

Subversion for the polite reader: Humphrey Moseley

The drop in the level of publication continued into the 1650s; Wing's *Short-Title Catalogue* lists only about 1,000 items a year between 1650 and 1659 (Mason 1974, pp. 219–20). From 1655 to 1659 only two newspapers, both edited by Marchamont Nedham, were officially allowed. In any case, only the most die-hard of royalists could resist the various pressures toward conformity during the two years that followed the king's execution. There were periodic banishments of known royalists and Catholics from London (Hardacre 1956, pp. 78–9). Then came the Engagement (an oath of loyalty to the Commonwealth), which was first imposed in February 1649 on all officials of the Council of State, in October on 'most of the literate population', and then, on 1 January 1650, extended to all male persons aged eighteen or over (Wallace 1968, pp. 43–9). Above all, the defeat of Charles II's invading army at Worcester in 1651, reinforced by the failure of successive royalist uprisings, made compromise with the *de facto* government look like the most sensible course of action. The Act of Oblivion (1652), which offered pardon and relief from the sequestration of estates (Hardacre 1956, p. 93), was part of the Commonwealth policy of making life under its rule as easy as possible for ex-royalists, thus removing the temptation to rebellion. With regard to the press, the licensing authority usually distinguished between open and oblique opposition. Thus, it prosecuted publications defined as blasphemous (mostly those of the sects), but largely ignored the numerous poems, plays, and romances with a strongly anti-government line.

This is presumably why, by contrast with the breathless, hand-to-mouth existence of Royston and the Crouch group, the publisher Humphrey Moseley had a prosperous and relatively uneventful career. Though younger than Royston, he was already rising in the Stationers' Company at the start of the war, and none of his subsequent activities seems to have threatened his position. He is remembered as the most prestigious literary publisher of the time, and one who, by the time of the Restoration, owned the copyrights of most extant dramatic works. Nevertheless, he was firmly royalist throughout his career, and consistently advertised the fact in the prefaces to his publications. In bringing out a book of sermons in 1641, he took the opportunity to express his admiration for the 'venerable Hierarchie' of Bishops and to lament 'the disease of these times' (Reed 1930, pp. 73–4). He had no difficulty in obtaining an official imprimatur for John Raymond's narrative of a journey through Italy, published in 1648. Probably the licenser did not see the preliminary material. The book was dedicated to Prince Charles and prefaced by a letter to the author from his 'most ingenious Friend', 'J. B.'. J. B. was John Berkenhead, the former editor of *Aulicus*, and, not surprisingly, his letter is nothing less than a polemic against the present state of England: it tells his long-absent friend that he has come home to still stranger sights than any he has seen abroad: 'you'l see *Great Brittaine* a *Floating Island*, and the most vertuous *Monarch* under Heaven cast into a small Isle as on some plank in a great Ship-wrack ... Sir, when you behold a Kingdome without a King, a Church without Clergy, a University without Scholars, you'l grant wee

have a *thorough Reformation*' (Raymond 1648). Berkenhead prefaced
remarks to two other books by Moseley (Thomas 1969, pp. 192–3), notably to what he described as the 'corrected impression' of *Cooper's Hill*
(1655). Comparing this version of Denham's already famous poem to what
he claims was an earlier and less accurate transcript, 'J. B.' draws attention
to 'that excellent Allegory of the Royall Stag', supposedly truncated in the
earlier version. In fact, as the most detailed analysis of the texts of *Cooper's
Hill* has shown, the 1655 edition is *not* a correction of the original text of
1643. It is a revision in which Denham has, first, greatly expanded the
episode of the stag hunt (probably intended originally as an allusion to
Strafford's death) and made it more obviously applicable to Charles I, and,
second, rewritten the passage about Henry VIII's dissolution of the mon-
asteries so that it can be taken as an allusion to Cromwell's effect on the
English church (O Hehir 1969, pp. 227–56). It is evident that the author
and supposed editor must have colluded with the publisher, since Moseley
owned the copyright of the poem, which he had brought out in an earlier
version in 1650. The deception here being perpetrated has a double motive:
from Moseley's point of view, the claim that the text was a more authentic
one than hitherto was obviously a strong selling-point; for Berkenhead and
Denham, it was a way of drawing the reader's attention to the importation
of a new political meaning (for instance, by describing the passage about
the stag as an 'Allegory') while pretending to be restoring a purely literal
one.

Moseley's editions of Beaumont and Fletcher (1647) and William Cartwright (1651) had an unprecedented number of commendatory verses.
There were thirty-four – one for each play – in the Fletcher volume; in the
Cartwright volume Moseley went still further, with fifty-two verses – one,
he explained, for each week of the year, or shire of England. These
prefatory pages offered Berkenhead and other writers a platform from
which they could praise great literature of the past, drawing attention at the
same time to the cultural degeneration which they blamed on Parliament
and the war. As Louis B. Wright said in his important study of 'The
Reading of Plays During the Puritan Revolution' (1934), the Beaumont
and Fletcher edition is 'almost a literary manifesto of Cavalier writers'
(p. 82). The Cartwright edition is Oxford's revenge on those who had ejected
so many of its fellows and scholars in the Visitation of 1648. Cartwright,
whose early death had spared him from seeing this desecration, is praised
by fellow-Oxonians and clergymen as a symbol of all that was best in their
past. Like Royston, Moseley exploits nostalgia for the Church of England,
depicting Cartwright, in the portrait-frontispiece, in a clergyman's gown

rather than a gentleman's cloak. The clergyman Jasper Mayne, living under sequestration, complains that his ability to write a commendatory poem has been destroyed by 'Times which made it Treason to be witty'; Moseley himself, in his dedication 'To the Reader', explains that the small print of the book is designed to keep its price low, since 'it is such weather that the most ingenious have least money' (Cartwright 1651). It is no wonder that the verses written for Moseley's volumes 'praise the publisher himself rather than the authors of the books they precede' (Reed 1930, p. 69).

An incidental effect of press control seems to have been the channelling of political satire into the apparently more acceptable genre of the dirty story, as in Crouch's later newsbooks. Much political satire had already taken the form of absurd accusations about the sexual misdemeanours of Commonwealth leaders and their wives. By telling the same sorts of story about anonymous but vaguely puritanical figures, the author could simultaneously offer satire and pornography to his public. An interesting glimpse of this kind of book trade is given in Cosmo Manuche's play, *The Loyal Lovers* (1652), supposedly set in Amsterdam but clearly depicting the English social scene. It opens with an exiled royalist examining the wares of a 'book-crier'. He turns down the pious work that he is first offered, insisting, 'Pray let me have more facetious language, and less of your spirit.' The book-crier replies,

Sir, I know your minde, And shall endeavour to pleasure you presently. Let mee see, here is A true, perfect and exact account of Justice *Dapper*, and his Clark's Sodomitical revenue, to the great disabling and impoverishing the Active, and well-affected Females.   (I.i.sig. A3)

The royalist, though outraged at the price being charged, is otherwise delighted to buy the book. The logical result of so many years of secret publication was that pornography could now be enjoyed with a clear conscience.

Economics versus ideology

But how different, after all, were propaganda and pornography? Were Crouch and the other members of the royalist publishing network simply running a commercial enterprise, where the danger and the profit went together? Was theirs, in fact, a genuinely dangerous activity?

The penalties mentioned above sound discouraging. As we have seen, Royston was imprisoned several times; his 'adventurous women' cannot always have evaded detection; the authors and printers of the underground newsbooks were constantly in and out of jail. In pre-war years they might perhaps have been pilloried; to that extent, things had become more civilised. Similarly, although the number of book-burnings increased under Parliament, there was no more bodily mutilation of the authors such as had occurred before the war (Farrar 1892, pp. 94, 98). But those actually involved in anti-government activity have no way of knowing how puni-tive that government will turn out to be in the eyes of history. Some indication of their own sense of danger may be seen in the extent to which they feel obliged to conceal their identity. Writers, for instance, are slightly more likely to acknowledge their works than are printers and publishers. It was, after all, easier for writers to keep hidden or, as a last resort, to go 'beyond the seas'. Imprisonment may not have been so harsh a punishment for them as for printers, who were utterly deprived of their livelihood by it. *The Man in the Moon* complains bitterly about the hardship which impris-onment caused to the family of his printer, Edward Crouch, whose wife worked as a Mercury Woman, or hawker of pamphlets. Writers, by contrast, were often able to carry on writing and publishing from prison.

Still, there are more reasons than one to explain anonymity or the lack of it. A work by a known author was considerably more saleable and authori-tative than an anonymous one. This must certainly have been true of the professionals John Taylor and Martin Parker, whose reputation made their works stand out from the crowd of pamphlets and ballads of the period. Parker, indeed, attacked anonymous writers in *The Poet's Blind Mans Bough, or Have among you my blind harpers* (1641), claiming that

What ever yet was published by mee,
Was knowne by *Martin Parker*, or *M.P.*

To some extent, the situation changed in later years: with so many anony-mous works on the market, a nonentity might profit from being taken for a better-known writer, and Parker and Taylor no longer had as much to gain by acknowledging their pamphlets.

Some writers clearly felt that they were taking a risk by putting their names to their work. Edward Simmons, whose *Vindication of King Charles* appeared in 1647, says in his 'Epistle to the Reader' that he had at first intended to publish anonymously. Having spent the two previous years abroad, he seems to have been surprised to find so much royalist writing being openly produced in England in 1647. He was not altogether happy to see 'wickednesse rather scoffed at, then pursued with such grave and home rebukes as the case requireth it', but the existence of such works encouraged him to acknowledge his own, as he had always done while the king was in power, rather than 'be reckoned in the number of *night-birds* that love darknesse'. His was, however, a piece of undisguised royalist prose. The situation of those who wrote imaginative literature was perhaps less predictable. Royalist poets sometimes express fears for themselves, but perhaps these reveal only their own temperaments. John Quarles' *Fons Lachrymarum*, a collection of royalist verse, was published in 1648, complete with his name, his printer's, and his publisher's, but his prefatory epistle asked the reader's indulgence for typographical errors: 'Had not the perverseness of these times debarred me from coming to the Press, the Printers Mistakes had not been so numerous.' This presumably means that either he or the printer was in hiding. Nevertheless, all three of the parties involved seem to have felt that the advantage of putting their names to the work (the author was the son of the well-known poet Francis Quarles) outweighed the possible dangers. The fact that both Simmons and Quarles decided to leave the country in 1649 (though Simmons was captured in disguise and died at Gravesend) may have been an emotional response to the king's execution, or it may mean that they now felt themselves to be in danger as they had not been before. The execution and the Treason Act clearly made a difference to the poets' sense of their own safety, and I shall look in chapter 4 at some of its effects.

Whatever the motives behind other works, it is likely that those involved in the publication of the underground newsbooks were at least partly in it for the money. It is possible that Crouch and others like him got some official financial backing, or benefited from unofficial patronage; the verses by 'W. M. B.', prefixed to the second part of [Crouch's?] *Newmarket Fair*, praise the effect of Part One on Royalist morale and conclude,

> Mean while thou hast the wishes of my heart,
> This *Gold* to boot, to write thy *Second Part*.

Since Crouch's pamphlets were positively courting punishment, their tone would be easier to understand if he were being encouraged by someone higher up in what remained of the royalist propaganda organisation. But even unsubsidised printing of illegal works could be profitable. As Roger L'Estrange (1663) put it after the Restoration, 'The *Gayn* of Printing some Books, is Ten times Greater, if they *Scape*, then the *Loss*, if they be *Taken*' (p. 30).

Uncertainty about the size of the reading public makes it hard to know just how profitable this kind of publishing was. It is sometimes assumed that literacy was higher among parliamentarians (because of the Puritan emphasis on Bible reading) than among royalists. Recent research, however, seems to indicate that the relation of literacy to Puritan sympathies is not so great as one might expect. David Cressy, whose *Literacy and the Social Order* is the most thorough survey of the subject, was unable to find that the mere fact of a Puritan preacher's being in a village made any significant difference to its level of literacy (Cressy 1980, pp. 82–5). The literacy level was highest in London, where the newsbooks were produced. Print runs of 9,000–10,000 are mentioned for some publications of the 1640s (Thomas 1969, p. 52). Joseph Frank (1961) calculates that if the population of London was 500,000, and if half the adult males could read, there might have been a market of some 60,000 potential buyers, four or five of them probably to each journal (p. 57). Margaret Spufford (1981) thinks that chapbooks might have been sold in alehouses, and that perhaps a stock might have been kept there for patrons (pp. 109–10); the same thing might have happened with some journals. *Aulicus* is said to have had as many as 3,000 copies printed at a time, some in Oxford and some in London. In the case of the royalist journals of the late 1640s, the readership may have been smaller because they could not be sold openly; on the other hand, the danger involved in possessing this illegal literature may have meant that more readers bought individual copies and that they were willing to pay higher prices for them.

In any case, as Anthony Cotton (1971) pointed out, the newsbooks must have made a profit: 'only that would have excited so much competition' (p. 6). He calculates that even a sale of 250 copies at one and a half pence each would have covered a fee of half a crown for the author and made a small profit for the bookseller. The Mercury Woman, who sold pamphlets in the street, generally supplemented what the bookseller paid her by charging customers more than the official price (pp. 8–9). John Hall gives a deliberately grotesque image of young Inns of Court men buying their copies of *Mercurius Elencticus* from a female book-hawker: 'But who would think so admired an author as *Elencticus* should be found lurking under a womans petticoats? Commonly the young Gentleman, who *softly* enquires for him, feels and findes him in her *placket*, and when he hath got him, hastily pockets up his *two penyworth of lyes*, least another standing by, might chance have the first sight of them' (*Mercurius Censorius* 1–8 June 1648). This suggests a small circulation among a readership that could be targeted. It is not impossible that some of the rivals and counterfeits of the period were the product of collusion between publishers, counting on their public's willingness to buy anything that looked controversial (Potter 1987, pp. 106–7). A number of bound sets of royalist Mercuries, dating from the seventeenth century, have survived (Nelson and Seccombe 1986, pp. 94–5). There was clearly a polite readership somewhere, not to mention collectors like Thomason, who could be counted on not only to buy the counterfeit but also to look out for the real one in order to make their collections complete.

The implied reader

It would be interesting to know more about this readership. Joyce Malcolm (1983) has argued that the king's absolute control over his instruments, in the period up to 1646, prevented royalist propaganda from having any appeal outside a limited and elite circle (pp. 152–63). It is evident, though, that some of the publications turned out by his supporters were intended to reach a much wider audience. The implied author of some of this literature is a man of the people – Taylor and Parker are the two best-known examples – but it is possible that, as the other side argued of Taylor, their names were sometimes put to pamphlets by other people (see *DNB*: 'John Taylor'). Thomason ascribed to Taylor a pamphlet in verse, *Ad Populum, or, a Lecture to the People* (1644), which in fact is the work of an Oxford don, Peter Hausted, and is said to have been read and approved by the king himself (Madan 1912, p. 345). I wonder if Thomason had read the poem before making his note on its title page. It is only ostensibly an attempt to reach popular support; the 'people' whom it addresses are rural peasants, not urban artisans, and the poet's nostalgic evocation of the world they had lost inevitably recalls Jonson's *To Penshurst* in its picture of mindless fecundity and happiness. Was it not better, he asks,

> When no grimme Saucy Trooper did ye harme,
> Nor fiercer Dragon, when no Strangers Arme
> Did retch your yellow Bacon, nor envy
> The Richnesse of your Chimneyes Tapestry,
> When good Dame *Ellen* (your beloved Spouse)
> Bare to the elbow in the Dairy-house,
> With fragrent Leekes did eat the Cheese she wrought,
> Not sent it to the Garrison for nought.
> O those were Golden dayes!   (p. 3)

The author's implied reader may be a peasant, but his real reader obviously is not. It is for the latter's benefit that, when the poem contrasts the realities of war with the 'harmlesse Playes' that preceded it, he adds a marginal gloss explaining that this means 'Christmas games i th Country'. Glorification of the golden past competes with ridicule of the people who enjoyed it, the country girl gaping at her lover or the goodwife reeking of her leeks and cheese. The pre-war era was a time of 'Shorter Sermons, Longer Prayers'; what seduced the people away from their happiness was meaningless language:

> But see what love of Liberty affords,
> And the strange Lusting after new-coynd Words! (p. 3)

> But these your Apples were, yee would be wise
> Though with the Hazard of your Paradise. (p. 4)

> Ye'ave almost your whole wish: and, faith, confesse,
> What have yee got? Come, be ingenious.
> Would yee not give the best horse in your Teame
> The three yeares past were but a fearefull Dreame? (p. 9)

This patronising tone is obviously intended only to reinforce the views of readers considerably more sophisticated and affluent than the ones the poem purports to be addressing. In this version of events, the war was caused by purely verbal differences; pre-war England was a paradise; the population as a whole was now longing for a return to the old ways.

A readership which shared these views certainly existed. Martin Parker's most popular political song, 'When the King Enjoys His Own Again', assumes that everyone will be attracted to the image of a properly ordered society with the ruler and his aristocratic court sweeping their way through a splendidly furnished palace:

> Though for a time you see Whitehall
> With cobwebs hanging over all,
> Instead of silk and silver brave,
> As formerly it used to have,
> And in every room the sweet perfume
> Delightful to the princely train,
> But all this shall end, when the times they shall mend
> And the king enjoys his own again.

'Popular' forms like the ballad were not exclusively popular in their appeal. Much cavalier poetry employs a popular style, and the theme of the aristocrat enjoying exile from his own class is an important part of the romantic tragicomedies which will be discussed in chapter 3. The Earl of Newcastle and his distant relative, Sir Francis Wortley, were both admirers and patrons of the Jonsonian tradition in drama and of writers like Taylor. Wortley, who was in the Tower from 1644 to 1649, spent much of his time writing royalist satires and panegyrics in popular verse and prose. His

Loyal Song of the Royal Feast (1647), celebrating Charles I's sending a gift
of venison for the benefit of the impoverished royalist prisoners in the
Tower, concludes with a reminder that it is intended for singing as a ballad:

> Old Chevy Chase was in his minde
>   If any sute it better
> All those concerned in the Song
>   Will kindly thank the Setter.

In his broadside, *Mad Tom a Bedlam's desires of peace* [27 June 1648],
Wortley, adopting the persona of a social outcast, wished well to both the
unlicensed press and the ballad:

> Bless the Printer from the Searcher
> And from the Houses takers [Parliament's informers],
> Blesse *Tom* from the slash, from *Bridewell*'s lash,
> Blesse all poore Ballad-makers.

Once Parliament had begun to transform the face of England and old
English customs, the Stuarts naturally became identified with the same
golden past that had previously been associated with Elizabeth I.

   The less attractive side of this nostalgia is its obsession with preserving
the social hierarchy. The persona adopted by an anonymous defender of
Charles I after the publication of his correspondence in 1645 suggests that
remarks were thought to carry more weight if they came from a person of
substance: he would rather, he says, have the king's epistolary skills 'then
to be Lord of that Manor that makes me neighbour to you; and yet you
know it is a very faire one' (*A Letter* 1645, pp. 2–3). The pamphlets which
acknowledge their author only as 'a Person of Quality' make the same
assumption. Some of those written between 1646 and 1649 go still further
as they feel more threatened by what must have seemed the imminent
breakdown of all social boundaries. The royalist newsbooks often address
their readers as 'Gentlemen', and *The Famous Tragedy of Charles I* (1649)
has a Prologue to the Gentry, which distinguishes their 'refined Soules'
from 'the Monsters of the times'. It goes on to suggest, probably inadvertently, that the tragedy of England lies less in the act of regicide than in
the truly heinous crime to which this will lead, the loss of proper class
distinctions:

> For having kill'd their KING, where will they stay
> That thorow GOD, and MAJESTIE, make way,
> Throwing the Nobles, and the Gentry downe
> Levelling, all distinctions, to the Crowne.
> So that (which Heaven forbid) should they reduce

> Our *English* world, to their confused use,
> 'Twill be admir'd, more then a prodegee
> To hear an Herald, state a pedigree,
> An 'twill be thought, a sharpe, and bitter blur
> To salute any, by the title (*Sir*).

The attitude is taken to absurd lengths in one of the elegies in *Lachrymae Musarum*, the collection of elegies on Lord Hastings which appeared in the summer of 1649. The writer (Bold) allows himself to imagine Hastings's arrival in a heaven that is blissfully like pre-war England:

> Fly then from *Babylon* up to *Sion*; there's
> In Heaven both Monarch, and an House of Peers;
> Yea, there are Bishops too, with grave aspect,
> The Churches Nobles, all with glories deckt:
> And there's an Academ, though here's none now,
> Where high degrees are given to such as thou.   (p. 34)

It was just this concern with social stability that made some royalists willing to accept Cromwell's government. Waller's 'Panegyric to My Lord Protector' (1655) includes among the benefits of his reign the fact that his

> extraction from an ancient line
> Gives hope again that well-born men may shine.   (lines 125–6)

Some readers probably did find such attitudes offensive. John Hall, in 1648, attacked the royalist conspirators for their contempt of 'the Vulgar, which in their esteeme is so far inferiour to themselves' (*Mercurius Britanicus* 11 July 1648). However, when it came to personal abuse, any accusation, including financial embarrassment, was good enough to level at the enemy. Hall, like most parliamentary journalists, generally describes the royalist pamphleteers as a collection of drunks whose 'news', such as it is, is mostly made up in the tavern. The royalists retort with the same accusation: that the author of *Britanicus*, if not exactly poor, is at any rate writing for money – a weekly stipend of £5. Moreover, his pamphlet is sold in the streets by 'a poore sneaking Tobacco-stopper'. 'Art thou,' the author of *Mercurius Elencticus* asked indignantly, referring to the rest of Hall's respectable and mainly royalist literary coterie, 'a fit associate for such Ingenious and candid soules as Col. Lovelace, Captaine Sherburne, Mr Shirley, or Mr Stanley?' (15 June 1648). Hall, or his defender, in *Mercurius Censorius* (1–8 June 1648), retorted that the royalist writers were 'fed with the excess of that money which a sort of needy Gentlemen, your Patrons, should have spent upon their Whores'. Clearly, each side saw its opponents much as Pope saw the Grub Street of *The Dunciad*. The assumption was that no one who wrote for money could be relied on: 'cleane linnen, clothes and meat are so requisite, that a man for them must not make scruple to play the fool in print' (*A True Diurnall* 31 May 1647). When *Mercurius Melancholicus* first appeared, a rival Mercury told the public that its author was a 'frenzie Priest' living 'against the Grate in Little Brittaine, whose breath smels stronger then the Common-shore' (*Mercurius Morbicus* 20 Sept. 1647). Of course, this pamphlet is an attempt to beat the royalists on their own ground, so it is not surprising to find it reproducing their snobbery. It does suggest, however, that a genuinely egalitarian tone is not necessarily going to be found more easily among parliamentarians than among their opponents. By the late 1640s, in any case, both sides were doing their best to present themselves as the party of social order. The voice of the ordinary man, as it is heard in pamphlets of this period, is often a persona created in order to express a plain, blunt man's desire for peace and stability: in royalist terms, this means restoring Charles I or Charles II to his proper role; in parliamentary terms, it means accepting the present government and keeping quiet.

However, there was a brief period during which royalists and levellers shared, if not similar views, at least a common satiric idiom. The way had been prepared for this somewhat uneasy alliance as early as 1647, when Lilburne, who had been pilloried under Charles in the pre-war years, informed Parliament that he now regarded their tyranny as far worse than the king's (McCormack 1973, p. 175). The levellers were the one group which, throughout the period, was consistently committed to openness of publication and debate. They sought publicity constantly, making capital out of every arrest, publishing the accounts of every argument, every trial. One of them, possibly Overton, wrote that 'this persecuted means of unlicensed Printing, hath done more good to the people, then all the bloodie wars' (Overton [?] 1646, p. 26). Most of the royalists, apart perhaps from Nedham, had no time for them in 1647; *The Levellers Levelled* (1647), a pamphlet-play which depicts Lilburne as John O'London, a mixture of Catiline and Jack Cade, is a fair reflection of their view. But some of them had obviously read Overton's racy attacks on the Presbyterians, mostly published 1645–6, which took over the language of the Elizabethan Marprelate tracts and aimed it lower: Martin Marprelate becomes Martin Claw-Clergy or Martin Marpriest, with Sir John Presbyter and Sir Simon Synod as his chief victims. Royalist pamphlets of 1647–8 borrow some of these characters for their own purposes.

The alliance between royalists and levellers grew somewhat closer in 1648–50, though it was based more on mutual enemies than on mutual friendship. One of the Crouches may have acted as Overton's printer or publisher while the latter (a printer himself) was in prison. In August 1649, with the Act against Scandalous Pamphlets looming before him, Crouch brought out a satire on Cromwell's relations with the levellers, called *A New Bull-Baiting*. The title is probably an allusion to a recent pamphlet by Richard Overton, *The Baiting of the Great Bull of Bashan*. In this sequel, four levellers bring Cromwell in to be baited and a number of other 'dogs' – opponents of Cromwell ranging from Prynne to the Man in the Moon himself – attack him with such comments as 'he brewed *smal-beer* in the Isle of *Ely*, till he had six Wenches with Child at one time'. The pamphlet does not express unqualified admiration for the levellers, but it is willing at least to use them as mouthpieces for the attack on what it takes to be a greater enemy.

If Marie Gimmelfarb-Brack (1979, p. 410) is right, however, Crouch also betrayed Overton. At one point in an Overton pamphlet (*Overton's Defiance of the Act of Pardon*, July 1649), the tone suddenly changes to one so flippant as to suggest self-parody. She thinks that this anomalous passage must have been added by Crouch while the work was being printed. This kind of tampering did occasionally occur (Clyde 1934, p. 133). At the same time, however, Gimmelfarb-Brack finds such a close resemblance between Crouch's writings and Overton's as to make him a 'double stylistique' (p. 11). One explanation for the resemblance may be their common source. Just as they were prepared to make common cause politically with the levellers, when it suited them, the royalists took over a great many leveller themes and techniques in their writing. Or, to put it more accurately, both groups of writers drew on a common satiric tradition, already used in the Elizabethan Marprelate controversy over church government, which goes back at least as far as Lucian. All-purpose satiric situations (the mock-trial, mock-testament, characters vomiting up ill-gotten gains or giving birth to symbolically appropriate offspring), already used for attacks on Strafford and Laud, were revived yet again with different victims, probably by some of the same writers who had used them earlier.

For instance, the anti-Laud pamphlet-play, *Canterbury's Change of Diet*, sometimes attributed to Overton (Wolfe 1947–8, Heinemann 1978, Gimmelfarb-Brack 1979), contains a scene where Laud, at a banquet, finds that his finicky appetite can be satisfied only with the ears of Burton, Bastwick, and Prynne. In *News from Hell, Rome, and the Innes of Court* (M., J. 1642) the Pope is shown at a great feast to which King Lucifer has helpfully sent a few contributions, including a lot of English bishops; it looks, the Pope says, like 'a most LAUDable dish of meat' (p. 17). The same motif was turned against Cromwell in *Epulae Thyestae, or The Thanksgiving Dinner*, written in 1649 by a royalist prisoner in the Tower. He depicts the leading parliamentarians feasting while the country starves:

> First Course is *Bishops Lands*; a stately Dish,
> Quoth OLIVER, and *Cook'd* unto my wish.

They quaff '*Charls* his bloud, a crimson wine', and drink confusion to his whole house:

> The Health goes *round, Round* through the Cursed Hall,
> And no Man sees, THE HAND UPON THE WALL.

The period after the king's execution did see a few royalist–leveller conspiracies. But the fact that the same satiric modes can be used by writers of opposed political views makes it difficult, I think, to identify a genuinely 'popular' idiom, or to know whether the royalist and the leveller were aiming at the same readership.

Cultural subversion

Another point which royalist and leveller writers have in common is that the words 'seditious', 'treasonable', and 'dangerous' are frequently used about them. But it has been argued that such writings 'were not the prelude to action; they were a substitute for it' (Wedgwood 1964, p. 212). So one final question remains about the royalist publishing effort: how subversive was it?

The surviving literature of the period includes some examples of what by any standards is subversive publishing. Rabble-rousing was a device used successfully on the side of the Long Parliament, in its early years, to coerce the king and his party. The commonest way of doing this was to scatter single sheets about the street at night; an anonymous well-wisher to Parliament is supposed to have sent three successive letters to Pym simply by dropping them in the street (Snow and Young 1969, p. 40). Such gestures were also made on the royalist side; on 19 April 1648, the Speaker told the Lords that someone had been taken spreading abroad 'a seditious paper, to stir up the People to rescue Sir John Gayer as he was to come to this House this Day' (*House of Lords Journals*, X, 208). Thomason's collection contains a seditious paper (E. 392.7), which he says was 'scattered upon and downe the streete in the night June the 11th 1647'. It consists of a handwritten message: 'For the renowned Apprentices of this famous citie Speed Speed Speede, Hast hast Hast Horse and away the day is our owne my Boyes God bless King Charles'. The other side of the page urges all apprentices over the age of fifteen to consent to the king's coming in, which will make them 'for ever thrice happy'. The document cannot, by itself, have had much effect, since it fails to tell its readers where to go or what to do when they get there. Some copies of books printed in 1648 contain a single inserted leaf which parodies the usual order for printing a fixed number of copies, and goes on to urge

> that all who love their king and Countrey, and hate Rebellion and Treason, doe forthwith make all provision and speed that may be to rise, and take by force or otherwise, all Garrisons they can in all parts of the Kingdome, and summon in the Countrey to them, for the speedier suppression of these abominable malicious Rebels, and Traitors, this prevailing Party in the Parliament Houses, and their Army. *(Craftie Cromwell*, pt I, pp. 177–8)[2]

Most writers, whatever their actual intentions, usually disclaim any desire to cause riot and civil war. The opposite is true of the royalist journals, particularly in the first half of 1648. It is not only that they publish constant reports intended to stir up rebellion: the king is on his way; the prince is about to land somewhere with foreign troops; great royalist victories have taken place in distant parts of the realm; reports of parliamentary victories are false; absent parliamentary generals are dead. They constantly proclaim their intentions of committing treason at the first opportunity. *Elencticus* protested (19–26 Jan. 1648) that 'if that *Musty fiction* of *surprising* the *Tower* and *Pick-Purse-Hall*, had harboured but the least shew of *Reality* in it, the Members should have found me up to the very *Eares* in the *Designe*.' *Craftie Cromwell*, pt I (10 Feb. 1648) is prefaced by an address 'to the Inslaved Commons of England' urging them to restore the king. *Mercurius Melancholicus* (27 March–3 April 1648) reports various 'Dangerous Plotts' and adds, 'what pitty 'tis none of them took'. For good measure, he urges his reader to join the Scots and Welsh rebels.

How seriously is one meant to take all this? Perhaps the ballad verses on the title page of part II of *Craftie Cromwell* are a clue to the author's real intentions: 'Sit round,' he tells his readers, 'and let us Treason talke / Against the Houses twaine'. The setting envisaged for this dangerous behaviour is obviously a private one, since the verses continue, 'Here wee can freely sit and sing'. 'Talking treason' and singing drinking songs with an anti-government refrain – or ballads about the 'blackbird most royal' (Charles II), or Henry Lawes's setting of Psalm 137 about the Israelites in exile, with its obvious relevance to royalists on the continent – such were the sorts of private ritual that helped royalists survive what Earl Miner (1971) has called 'the cavalier winter'.

That so many of the satiric pamphlets were in dramatic form is the result of another much-disliked feature of parliamentary rule, the refusal to reopen the public theatres, initially closed (in September 1642) on the grounds that the times were unfit for public sports. Thus, on each occasion when the ordinance against stage-plays was re-imposed, royalist news-pamphlets appeared in the form of miniature plays, with prologues claiming that they were offering these as alternatives to the forbidden drama. The first of these, Samuel Sheppard's *Committee-Man Curried*, appeared just in time to coincide with the renewal of the legislation against stage-plays in July 1647. The new and stiffer Declaration against Stage Plays, in preparation in January 1648, was met by the two-part *Craftie Cromwell*. This Declaration was probably the chief inspiration behind a series of highly dramatic Mercuries who address their readers like a theatre audience. *Mercurius Aulicus*, for instance – now revived with a new author – has a startlingly theatrical manner, stage-directions and all:

Sound Drums and Trumpets, Enter *Aulicus* doing *Penance* in a *White Sheet* for his tardiness.　　　　　　　　　　　　　　　　　　　　(30 March – 20 April 1648)

Whether these quasi-dramas ever were performed is debatable. Only one is specifically said to have been acted, and that was after the Restoration (see below, p. 112). Cosmo Manuche's *The Loyal Lovers* (1652) depicts two royalists giving an amateur performance for a few of their friends in the private room of a tavern; the piece is a farce about the punishment of the parliamentary chaplain Hugh Peter by a butcher whom he has cuckolded. This sort of thing may sometimes have happened in real life. But many of the supposed plays are really no more than conventional dialogues; they have no proper stage directions and show little attempt to visualise the action in theatrical terms, though they sometimes end in an anti-parliament song which the reader is invited to join in singing. I think that they are more likely to have been read aloud.

Cultural rebellion was probably widespread, whether it took the form of celebrating Christmas in private houses, singing ballads, or engaging in amateur theatricals. As there was little danger in most of it, it says little about the political intentions of those who practised it. Attending surreptitious performances in the public theatres was the most dangerous activity, but the spectators risked only embarrassment and fines. There is very little evidence of anti-government feeling actually manifesting itself in public performance, and much of what there is comes in untrustworthy royalist publications. An example of what might be called a one-man 'malignant' performance is, however, reported in a somewhat more reliable source, the pro-parliamentary *Perfect Occurrences* (16–23 June 1648):

Malignants are so bold that one came with a stoole upon his head to the Exchange in *London*, and there set it down, stood by it, and made Proclamation, thus.

   Ho Yes *If anyone can tell of any good deeds that the Parliament hath done this seaven years, let them come hither, and I will sit downe and heare them.*

If *The Man in the Moon* can be believed, a couple of fairground performers in Smithfield commemorated the first anniversary of the king's execution by a skimmington ride in which they impersonated Fairfax and his wife (23–31 Jan. 1650).

   Even if he was making up this story, it is interesting that *The Man in the Moon* should choose to invent a demonstration which arises out of a folk custom. Crouch was in fact, perhaps because of his background of ballad-selling, particularly given to the use of popular motifs like the fairground setting with its crier of allegorical wares. Overton had written a satire called *Lambeth Fair* in 1641; a number of royalist works, many of them apparently from the Crouch group, follow a similar pattern: *The Kentish Fair*, which deals with the royalist uprising in Canterbury 1647–8; *Newmarket Fair*, which depicts the Commonwealth selling off the late king's possessions (1649); *A Bartholomew Fairing* (1649). Some of the other pamphlets treat the pamphlet as a booth to which they are charging admission ('Tis but three halfpence in,' the prospective reader of *Mrs Parliament Brought to Bed* [1648] is told encouragingly). *The Terrible, horrible, Monster of the West* (1650), almost certainly by the author of *The Man in the Moon*, takes the form of the show of a monster at a fair. The cast includes two scolds who fight among themselves, an old shepherd, Carolina, his friend Rusticus and the shower of the monster, Toby Tell-troth. Carolina laments that a 'monstrous Wolf' has 'Kill'd the *chiefe shepheard of Arcadia*', while his friend, in stage rustic, adds, 'A vengeance take 'um, that made it zo.' They settle down to watch the show. It soon turns out that the monster is Parliament. Toby Tell-troth's speech is a fine summary of all the traditions it has devoured, and includes Crouch's own persecutions among its crimes:

It came to the Citie, and there it devour'd S. *Pauls* Church, eat the very Scaffolds and bones of the dead, Stones, Altar, Church, Steeple, Organ-Pipes, and all, and yet as hungry as ever. It came to *White-Hall*, and there it chopt up the Head of the *Owner*, our ever sacred King, banqueted in his bloud, eat up all his Revenues,

Honors, Manors, Hereditaments, Forests, Parks, Chases, Trees, Venison, and all;
and yet not satisfied, but it gobled up all the Kings, Queenes, & Princes goods, not
sparing the very *Hangings*, but devoured all ... It went to *Black-Fryers* and the
Fortune Play-houses, and there it eat up the Benches, Galleries, Stages, nay their
very Hell and Heaven to boot ... It went to Hang-mans *Acre*, and there it eat up *the
man in the Moone's* presse, Letters, Books, and all ... It made account to swallow
Lieutenant Col *Iohn Lilburne*, but he was too hard to be digested.

I quote at greater length than usual, because this pamphlet is particularly
scarce. Carolina's response, 'The men at *Westminster* will suppresse this
Sport', turned out to be so true that Thomason himself failed to get a copy
of it. Toby's speech ends, 'God save King *Charles* the Second', and the
epilogue reminds the gentlemen who have viewed the monster that their
king is coming and needs their support:

> If (like Saint George) you doe not kill this Beast,
> England (wrong'd Virgin) will want Peace and Rest.

Here, it is evident, Crouch is using every possible weapon in favour of the
royalist cause: popular culture, the popular hero Lilburne, the evocation of
a pastoral England. By the end, the fairground monster has become the
dragon slain by St George. The reader, in one interpretation, is being
invited to take part in a mummer's play; in another, he is being urged to
engage in conspiracy and rebellion.

This chapter has dealt with works that were published illegally, in the
special circumstances of the 1640s and 50s. Royalist hostility to the
Commonwealth remained a constant factor in literary publishing up to the
Restoration, but, as has already been made clear, royalists had no enthusiasm for freedom of the press except where they believed that the established authority was an unsanctioned one. After the Restoration, the
toughest proposals for press control came from Sir Roger L'Estrange,
whose knowledge of the methods of clandestine publishers must have been
drawn from his own experience. Readers' willingness to pay more for a
pamphlet which had been illegally printed was based on the assumption
that this illegality was somehow a guarantee of truth. While some of what
was published gave information that could not be obtained elsewhere,
much of it was subversive not because of its content but by the very fact of
its publication against the will of the government. For example, the fact
that the reading of plays had a mildly subversive meaning under the
Commonwealth was part of its attraction. Writing in 1654 of *Alphonsus,
Emperor of Germany*, Moseley comments that some of his readers will
have been lucky enough to see it 'with all the elegance of Life and Action on

the *Black-Friers* Stage', and adds that 'The Design is high, the Contrivement subtle, and will deserve thy grave Attention in the perusall' (Reed, pp. 96–7). The comment (though not a very good description of the play) is typical of Moseley's particular kind of propaganda: it appeals to nostalgia for a pre-war England which was also a Stuart England; it assumes a shared set of values on the part of his readers; and it whets their appetites for finding hidden meanings in polite literature. It was thanks to people like him that a large part of the reading public, whatever its political views, was able eventually to see the Restoration as something which it had always supported in its heart.

2

'Our cabbalistical adversaries': secret languages

Keyes for this Cypher you can never get,
None but S. *Peter's* op's this Cabinet.
(Cleveland, 'The King's Disguise')

Ciphers and decipherers

The previous chapter has shown that a large part of what was 'published' in the 1640s and 1650s was at the same time 'secret', in that it was produced and distributed by clandestine means or used to convey a message hostile to authority. I now want to examine the concept of secret language itself. Encoding and decoding are terms often used in contemporary critical theory as metaphors for writing and reading, and it is generally accepted that *all* communication involves the exercise of these skills. But the civil war was a period when encoding and decoding had more than a metaphorical meaning. They were widely practised among many of the same people who were also involved in more apparently literary communication. How far, then, are we dealing with differences of degree, as opposed to kind? I shall approach this problem through a study of the actual practice of enciphering and deciphering, then through other kinds of secret language, including those which replace the verbal with the visual and those which depend on more complicated kinds of 'key'.

As a starting point, it may be useful to return to the kinds of secret writing mentioned in *Mercury* (Wilkins 1641) which takes the concept in a very wide sense. Wilkins's examples include ways of concealing a message, such as shooting letters in arrows and writing in invisible ink; ways of communicating more quickly (birds, speaking tubes, smoke, trumpets, and bells); separate languages like canting; and visual codes: shorthand, hieroglyphics, emblems, even pictures and musical compositions. The most basic distinction, and one which will be important for my purposes, is between the kind of encoding which is self-evidently secret and the kind which is so secret that it conceals even the fact that it *is* a code.

38

Wilkins claimed in the dedication to *Mercury* that he had written his book only for the sake of the bookseller, since 'the vanity of this age is more taken with matters of curiosity, then those of solid benefit'. Yet the 'solid benefit' of this work must also have been obvious in 1641. Ciphers had been used seriously in England under Elizabeth, by Walsingham's intelligence team (Kahn 1967, pp. 118–23). Jonson's Sir Politick Would-be was a satire on those obsessed with secrecy, and in his poem 'The New Crie' he ridicules the 'statesmen' who read 'Porta' and try to practise secret writing. 'Porta' is the famous *De Furtiva Literarum Notis* (1563) of Giovanni Battista Porta, one of Wilkins's chief sources. However, the civil war made the ability to use ciphers a practical necessity in a way that Jonson clearly felt it was not. Ciphers became so much a part of the consciousness of the period that, as John Wallis wrote in his *Discourse* on the subject, 'now there is scarce a Person of Quality, but is more or lesse acquainted with it' (Davys 1737, p. 12). That persons of quality would be those who particularly needed not only to convey but to conceal their meaning is an interesting assumption, and one which this chapter will be examining.

The interception and opening of private correspondence was the most obvious example of secrecy becoming public, especially since such correspondence was frequently published to score a propaganda point. When Parliament controlled London and most of the ports, it was inevitable that most of what was intercepted would be by royalist writers, and, therefore, that royalists should resort to enciphering much more than parliamentarians. This in turn meant that the mere use of a cipher was likely to make a letter suspect to Parliament, and to encourage the image of royalists as devious and 'cabbalistical' (as they were called in the preface to *The King's Cabinet Opened* in 1645). In April 1643 Parliament ordered that anyone who wrote in cipher or any other unknown character should be punished as a spy (*Mercurius Aulicus*, 15–21 Oct. 1643).

James Howell lamented anonymously in 1644 that the 'Barbarism' of this intercepting and opening of Letters had 'quite bereft all ingenous Spirits of that correspondency and sweet communication of fancie, which hath been always esteemed the best fuell of affection, and the very marrow of friendship' (Howell 1644, sig. T1).[1] In fact, members of the Long Parliament at first felt a certain delicacy about opening private letters. On capturing a packet of royalist correspondence early in 1642, they carefully forwarded one writer's letter to his parents unopened, while opening those written by two men to their brothers (Coates, Young, and Snow 1982, p. 58). They had difficulty, too, in deciding what was and was not private. Letters to women usually came into the former category, but it was at first difficult to decide whether the Queen should be treated as an ordinary woman. In February 1642, the House of Commons was faced with a packet of intercepted letters from a man whom nobody trusted, Lord George Digby. They first decided to open all the letters except the one to Henrietta Maria, but then, after hearing a report on the others, voted to open that one too. The House of Lords, to demonstrate its superior sense of honour, refused to join them in the act (Coates, Young, and Snow 1982, pp. 367, 379).

A number of cipher keys have survived. British Library MS Egerton 2550 is one example. It is clear from these that really elaborate codes could not often be used, due to the speed with which letters needed to be enciphered and deciphered. There was probably not much occasion for such arcane methods as invisible ink (but see Spencer 1959, p. 20n). Although Wilkins illustrates a music cipher, which was copied in Bishop Godwin's novel *The Man in the Moon*, no example of such a cipher has so far been detected (Davies 1967). (I suspect that a study of Henry Lawes's compositions might reveal an element of royalist coding.) Ordinary correspondence generally relied on simple letter and number substitutions; sometimes only the names of persons were replaced. A letter of 1644/5, addressed to Sir Edward Nicholas, refers to the King and Princes of Portugal as 'blade' and 'scabbard', King Charles as the 'barber', the King of Spain as a 'goldfinch', and Parliament's ships as 'pigeons' (*CSPD* vol. XLIII, pp. 260–2). Charles II figured in royalist ciphers of the 1650s as 'Mr Kerby', 'Mr Cross', 'Heer van Lorne', 'Mr Bridgeman', and even 'Mrs Brown' (Underdown 1960, pp. 341–9; Townshend 1924, p. 207). Decipherers were so scarce that even quite simple codes could be effective: in 1692, when an ambassador requested a simple cipher for ordinary use, those which the cryptologist Wallis suggested were absurdly easy. He maintained nevertheless that they would be sufficient to deter the casual intercepter, adding that the exiled James II was using 'Ciphers not better than these' for his correspondence in England (Smith 1917, pp. 82–96, 95).

Official ciphers usually involved the substitution of two- and three-figure numbers for letters, often with several equivalents for each, and with other sets of numbers to stand for proper names and commonly used words. The weakness of this type of cipher was that the words and phrases were often listed alphabetically, to make the key easier to use: this also made it easier for the decipherer, since guessing one name accurately gave a clue to all the others. Some ciphers therefore included 'irregulars', words and phrases listed out of alphabetical order. There were also a number of 'nulls': numbers to which there was no letter equivalent, intended merely to confuse. One page of Egerton MS 2550 (no. 38, labelled 'new cipher'), shows that someone was experimenting with a much more complex type, now called the Vigenère after its first inventor. It uses two alphabets, one of them based on a key-phrase which indicates the order in which the two alphabets are to be shuffled. Long key-phrases, though hard to crack, were also hard to remember, so famous sayings or lines from well-known literary works were often used for this purpose (Kahn 1967, pp. 147–54). Despite its difficulty, it eventually became generally known; in 1655 a version attributed to Cardinal Richelieu was published in *Wit's Interpreter, or the English Parnassus*, a collection supposedly meant for fashionable readers. The book assures them that Richelieu had considered this cipher 'so rare a secret, and of such dangerous consequence if ill imploy'd, that it was death in his army to have it or to make any use of it' (Cotgrave 1655b, p. 124).

John Wallis, the first acknowledged professional decipherer, was, like Wilkins, a clergyman and mathematician and eventually became a Fellow of the Royal Society. His short *Discourse* on deciphering, not published until after his death, gives an interesting account of his career. His first cipher came to him almost by accident in 1643 when he was chaplain to the Countess of Warwick. It was an easy alphabetic substitution, and he deciphered it within a few hours. Even this feat was regarded as extraordinary, and he was sent a second one which involved nearly 800 characters and took him three months. With no precedents to help him, he seems to have worked by random hypothesising (Davys 1737, pp. 11–13). Whatever method he did eventually evolve, he never explained it, since he realised the advantage of guarding his reputation for almost miraculous expertise.

The very existence of a science of cryptology was not taken seriously, at least on the royalist side, until very late. Hence, even when a packet of royalist correspondence was seized in 1658, the authors did not think themselves in danger, since 'every different Person's Letter was written in a distinct Cypher, and that contrived with great Thought' (Barwick 1724, p. 251). Until someone showed them their own letters in a deciphered state, the conspirators simply did not believe that it was possible for anyone to perform such a feat. Even Edward Hyde, writing later to one of them, declared that he had never believed the claims of any self-styled decipherers (Barwick 1724, p. 504). Wallis himself seems to have played something of a double game, since, although he deciphered the intercepted correspondence, it appears never to have reached the office of John Thurloe, the head of the intelligence service. Perhaps Wallis was deliberately shielding the group, which included Dr John Barwick, a fellow clergyman; perhaps, by this time, he was also aware of the possibility of a restoration of the monarchy and wished to hedge his bets.

When Wallis's successor John Davys published the *Discourse*, with his own *Essay on the Art of Decyphering* (1737), he included not only examples of ciphers complete with solution but also others in an undeciphered state, challenging the reader to solve them. His purpose was partly to make sure that no one underrated his profession. By giving the information, he pointed out, 'we have enabled our Readers the more *readily* to judge, whether the Letters are rightly decyphered; but have we informed them, *how* we did it?' (p. 29). He meant that the perception of method was the key to understanding the art of deciphering, as opposed to merely admiring the miraculous skills of the decipherer. Davys, like Wallis, may have enjoyed concealing his methods so as to benefit from the rarity of his talents. But when he advises the aspiring decipherer to study other ciphers of the same country and period as the one currently being worked on he shows a sophisticated awareness that successful deciphering involves treating the cipher as a language complete in itself (p. 41).

Universal sign systems: concealing and revealing

The seventeenth-century fascination with schemes for a universal language looks at first sight like the antithesis of the search for the perfect code, since its declared object was to improve and widen communication. But every language looks like a secret code to the person who does not know its rules. The desire for universal enlightenment expressed by the proposers of such schemes is rarely free from a secret elitism (Knowlson 1975, p. 87).

Some of those who supported language reform in the mid-seventeenth century argue that most disagreements between people are purely seman-tic; others feel that a universal language will make it possible to arrive nearer to the true nature of things. The assumption, obviously, is that different languages represent more or less adequate translations of a single fixed meaning. This is why scientists, in particular, often express a dissatis-faction with language, or with the time needed to learn the languages in which most intellectual activity takes place, because this inevitably meant the domination of arts subjects in the early years of education. Some of the more reformist-minded parliamentarians wished to see education given a practical and commercial turn. John Dury's proposals of 1649/50 condemn 'the Curious study of Criticismes, and observation of Styles in Authors, and of straines of wit, which speak nothing of Reality in Sciences'. He intended that all children at his proposed Reformed School should be taught drawing as part of their education: between the ages of nine and eleven they were to copy pictures and figures, while in the final phase they would be studying 'Schemes and Pictures, to represent Hieroglyphically those things that have no visible shape' (Dury 1649, pp. 49, 53–66). Wilkins, the author of *Mercury*, was in 1668 to publish a scheme for a *Real Character and a Philosophical Language*: that is, a new alphabet which would answer to the nature of the things depicted in a less arbitrary way than the alphabets in current use.

Shorthand was seen by some as a possible universal language. Indeed, Wilkins and some other members of the Royal Society were later to adopt it for this purpose (Matthews, in Shelton 1642, p. iv). It was already, according to Wilkins, widely used by 1641, 'it being usuall for any common Mechanick both to write and invent it' (Wilkins 1641, p. 98). Timothy Bright, the author of the first known shorthand system, was already, in 1588, pointing to secrecy as one of its advantages (Knowlson 1975, p. 19). Shelton himself claimed that his system had enabled some Englishmen abroad to read Bibles and other books in shorthand, 'without danger of bloudy Inquisitours' (Shelton 1642, sig. A4). As a cipher, it was not very difficult; Wallis says that it took him about an hour to master it (Davys 1737, p. 16). But the number of competing systems and the fact that users often adapted these for their own purposes made it possible to be used for a private code.

The same mixture of revelation and concealment can be found in the fascinating works of the physician John Bulwer. He is best known today for his two studies of gesture, *Chirologia* and *Chironomia* (published together in 1644); the book's illustrations, depicting expressions and hand gestures, have been used as evidence for the style of Elizabethan acting (Joseph 1951; Knowlson 1975, pp. 87, 211–23). Though Bulwer does indeed draw some of his examples from actors and orators, what primarily interests him is not the encoding of emotion but how to decode it when it betrays itself. Drawing on written accounts of the gestures used to accompany various emotions, on the evidence of pictures and statues, and even on personal observation of the 'horse-rhetoric' of horse dealers in Smithfield, which he found significantly different from the 'fish dialect' of Billingsgate (Bulwer 1974, p. 85), he described what he called the 'hieroglyphics' of human gesture. The result inspired one of his friends to write enthusiastically that 'Chirologie redeems from Babel's doom' (Bulwer 1974, pp. 10, 12). Bulwer's *Philocophus: or the Deafe and dumbe Mans Friend* (1648) is the earliest English work to describe the teaching of speech to the deaf and dumb. He also wrote on the language of the muscles of the head, and in 1653 published an imaginative study of artificial adornment (*Anthropometamorphosis: Man Transformed, or, the Artificial Change-ling*), with illustrations comparing the apparently bizarre practices of primitive societies with some of those taken for granted in contemporary England. Though he saw his efforts as a continuation of Bacon's opening up of new frontiers, he was never able to get support for his practical suggestions, like that of a special academy for teaching speech to the deaf, and seems to have remained largely unknown outside the small circle of admiring friends who wrote verses for his books.

Bulwer's work is remarkable not only in its anticipation of the twentieth-century interest in non-verbal communication and (in *Anthropometamorphosis*) the semiotics of fashion, but also because it is a particularly good illustration of the way in which a study intended to enable communication can also be used to conceal. The 'chirograms', or illustrations of specific gestures, which illustrate *Chirologia* and *Chiromania* not only show the gestures that signify each emotion but also, as a caption points out, 'are so ordered to serve for privy cyphers for any secret intimation' (Bulwer 1974, p. 114). The *Philocophus* frontispiece offers a series of pictorial solutions to the communication difficulties deriving from physical handicaps. It depicts the senses descending on to a stage like masquers to a ball, suggesting the way in which the theatre can often make one sense work for another: an 'anagram' of the senses, one of Bulwer's friends called it in his prefatory verses. Yet, like an anagram, the picture itself is utterly baffling at first sight (Corbett and Lightbown 1979, pp. 202–17). Though most of the stress in the book is on the way in which lip-reading has helped the deaf, Bulwer also comments with approval on the practical political advantages which it might offer. Charles I, on his visit to Spain in 1624, had shown considerable interest in a deaf and dumb man who had been taught to speak:

the subtilty of this Art was worthy of the Curiosity of a Prince; It being likely his Majestie (who is knowne to be an excellent Motist [a decipherer of movement], as his judgement in Pictures and Statues witnesseth: and who was ever vigilant for the advance and security of government) might apprehend this Art possibly to be translated into a use of State, and to the advantage and improvement of king-craft.
(Bulwer 1648, pp. 149–50. See also Corbett and Lightbown 1979, p. 214)

Bulwer's analogy between Charles's interest in lip-reading and his art-collecting may seem to blur an important distinction, since sign language is a restricted, referential code, while art criticism is an open, aesthetic code. Bulwer, however, is probably thinking largely of the iconographical aspect of the study of painting and statues, which he develops into the suggestion that the king might have learned from it how to decode physiognomy, perhaps even to lip-read treasonable mutterings.

Ambiguous Hieroglyphics: the 'Popish picture' and other devices

Henry Vaughan (in 'The King's Disguise'), called Charles I a 'Hieroglyphick King'. The term has an obvious appropriateness, as Stephen Kogan (1986) has shown, for a king who loved masques and the visual arts as well as the mystique surrounding the symbol of kingship. 'Hieroglyphics', a term often used as a synonym for emblems, were for some theorists the obvious model for a universal language. However, both masque designs and the more static imagery of pictures suffered in this respect from the fact that their meanings were not more but less fixed than those of words. The copious notes that Jonson felt it necessary to publish with his masques, the verses explaining the meaning of emblematic frontispieces, the fact that the emblem and impresa had to be made up of both words and pictures, neither independent of the other, all show that pictures only *seem* to speak a universal language. That the masque design or the portrait frontispiece should be compared to the body and the explanatory verses to the mind further suggests what Hamlet says, that external qualities cannot denote one truly, but 'that within which passeth show' is, by definition, at the mercy of the interpreter.

Even when the subject matter of a picture was clear, there could be considerable uncertainty over the response it was meant to elicit. This uncertainty was the basis of the deep suspicion of religious art in this period. Iconoclasm was based on fear that the sign would replace the signifier, that the owner of a religious painting might worship the image rather than what it represented. But there was a different danger, of which the iconoclasts themselves seemed less aware. The icon might be worshipped not in place of the divinity but as an image of the ruler who was also the image of the divine on earth. This appears to have been its function for the Christian emperors of Constantinople, whose coins 'usually have the Emperor's portrait on the obverse and the head of Christ on the reverse, to emphasize the intimate connection' (Runciman 1975, pp. 78–80). Even the iconoclastic emperors allowed their own portraits on coins, 'with a simple cross on the reverse' (p. 89).

A curious episode of 1644 illustrates the difficulty of handling the two-edged tool of iconography. In January of that year, a ship on its way from Dunkirk to Spain went aground on the south coast of England. Some of Sir William Waller's troops, hoping for prizes or the right of salvage, seized its contents and brought them to Arundel Castle, pending a decision on the status of the ship and its goods. The case was not settled until 4 October, at which time Parliament ordered the contents to be delivered to the Spanish ambassador (*HCJ* III). However, the governor of Arundel Castle had already taken matters into his own hands. *Mercurius Britanicus* (10–17 June 1644) reports that he had sent word by express to the Houses about the 'Popish pictures and superstitious Imagery' found among the goods. In particular, he describes one large picture in some detail: it was supposed to represent the king of England offering a sceptre to the queen, who 'declines it and offers it to the Pope'. The picture was interpreted as showing Charles's subordination to his wife, through which '*Pope and Queene* share the *Sceptre* of *England* between them' (p. 307). The picture was brought to London and displayed in the Star Chamber in early July. It must have been an impressive piece; *Mercurius Civicus* (11–17 July) calls it 'huge', another writer (*The Sussex Picture* 1644, sig. A2) 'stately'.

The motives behind this exhibition are not hard to guess. The year 1644 had begun with a bonfire of pictures and 'popish trinkets' at the site of Cheapside Cross (Gardiner 1897, vol. I, p. 273). By the summer, anti-popish feeling was at its height, as was hostility to both the queen and Archbishop Laud. The queen, who had stayed at Exeter until her child was born, was about to take shipping for France. Laud had just been brought to trial on charges which included the attempt to reintroduce popery into the country. Among the evidence brought against him were pictures found in his rooms, 'as, the inspiring of divers popes and cardinals by the Holy Ghost, resembled in the form of a dove' (Whitelock 1853, vol I, p. 259).

Within three weeks, a short pamphlet had appeared, obviously intending to counteract the claims about the 'Popish' picture. *The Sea-Gull, or the New Apparition in the Starchamber at Westminster* (dated 8 July by Thomason), was published anonymously, but can be shown to be by Daniel Featley, a churchman recently expelled from the Westminster Assembly and imprisoned for corresponding with the royal party. William Leo, who preached Featley's funeral sermon, mentions having seen the pamphlet in manuscript when he visited the divine in prison (Leo 1645, p. 24). Featley gives a detailed account of the picture, its artist (Gerard de la Valle, based in Antwerp), and its destination (a church in Seville). He then demonstrates a remarkably good grasp of iconography, pointing out that the figure supposedly representing Charles I is wearing the costume of an ancient Roman captain, that the churchman is clearly a bishop and not the Pope, that the distinctive spire in the background shows the scene to be

Cologne, and that, in short, the subject is an episode from the life of St Ursula, whose martyrdom, with that of her followers, is depicted in the background. The sceptre being offered her is merely 'Master Painters Embleme, to shew the commanding power of Beautie' ([Featley] 1644, p. 5). His pamphlet provoked contrasting reactions in the parliamentary press. *Mercurius Civicus*, utterly convinced, paraphrased his account in the following week (11–17 July 1644), explaining that it did so 'out of love to truth, and for a just vindication of his Majesties Person'. A pamphlet called *The Sussex Picture, or, an Answer to the Sea-Gull* followed on about 29 July. Its title page offers a crude woodcut version of the central, and controversial, part of the picture: a bishop standing between a king and queen. The author reminds readers of the message which they should have received from the 'stately Picture': 'Thou hast beheld therein the weaker sexe triumphing over the stronger, and by the help of a Miter, thou hast seen a scepter doing homage to the Distaffe.' Yet, though he half-acknowledges that the reader will have 'seen' these things only with the help of a careful political explanation, he nevertheless defends his appropriation of the meaning of the picture, whatever its original iconography may have been:

we onely expose the Picture to view, and permit it to speak for it self, and if it speak otherwise then the Author intended it should speak, we quarrell not with the Inventor, neither ought any to quarrell with us thereabout.　　　(sig. A2ᵛ–A3)

Opposing to intentionalism the concept of 'invention' (finding out, rather than creating, meaning), he disingenuously states that the picture can 'speak for itself', but then proceeds to use specialised knowledge of his own to counter the specialised knowledge on which the royalist writer had drawn for his 'correct' interpretation. His approach is eclectic; at one point he situates the subject matter in its supposed historical context: the figure in a mitre *could*, he argues, be the Pope rather than a bishop, since at the time of the St Ursula legend the Pope was only the bishop of Rome. Later he treats the picture as a satirical allegory, noting that the presence of the numerous virgins might be intended to show that 'the see of *Rome* ha's owed much of late yeers to the industrie, and art of women' (sig. A4). After all, he concludes, 'An *English* Tragedie may be acted by *Germain* Mimicks, and there is a declining Church in *Britain*, as well as there is a crooked Steeple at Cologne' (sig. A4).

The most surprising thing about this whole episode is the seriousness with which it was taken. Featley's reply is very likely to have been officially sponsored (how else did he happen to be so well informed about the picture?). It is significant that his usual publisher was Richard Royston. Royston also published the funeral sermon by Leo in which Featley's authorship of the pamphlet is mentioned, and he may well have been responsible for *The Sea-Gull* too. It is hardly surprising that the royal party should be anxious to scotch an explanation which depicted the king as weak, uxorious and papistical. No one, however, seemed concerned to ask the obvious question: if the subject matter of the picture was what had been claimed at first, what would have been the motive for painting it and sending it to hang in a Spanish church? The level on which the debate was conducted by both sides suggests uncertainty about the autonomy of the picture, comparable to that which had led to the destruction of religious paintings earlier that year. How was one to know whether the sceptre was being literally or symbolically given to the woman, or, if the latter, what it symbolised? Could the picture really 'speak for itself', conveying a secret meaning unknown to the original painter? Painting clearly did not work like the hieroglyphics envisaged as part of Dury's educational system.

The pamphlet controversy over the 'Popish picture' coincided with a more spectacular demonstration of the ambiguity of visual language. Emblems and devices were used on both sides of the war, though the royalists liked to think of them as specifically their own, something that distinguished them from the vulgar. As Thomas Blount puts it in *The Art of Making Devices* (1646), a translation from the French of Henri Estienne, 'by how much this way of expression is less usuall with the common people by so much is it the more excellent' (2nd ed., 1648, p. 13). Indeed, Estienne suggested, God may have been the first author of devices, in his two trees in the Garden of Eden and the motto '*Ne Comedas*' (p. 16). One of their commonest uses during the civil war was on military banners. Including a list of these in his book was Blount's own idea; he gives examples from both sides, and it is clear that both sides took them seriously.[2] When forty-eight royalist colours taken in the Battle of Marston Moor (2 July 1644) were displayed at Westminster, the parliamentary press made the most of the ambiguity of their symbolism. The defeat at Marston Moor was generally seen as a victory over the 'popish' troops of the Marquis of Newcastle and Prince Rupert. Thus, *Mercurius Britanicus* satirically suggested that the banner depicting a crown above a mitre meant 'Poperie riding into the kingdom on *horseback*' (8–15 July 1644). Rupert's own device had been a hand reaching from a cloud holding a sword with the inscription '*Fiat justitia*'. Naturally, *Britanicus* pointed out that this had come true in an ironic sense:

it is evident to all the world that a sword out of a cloud hath done *justice* upon that bloody *Prince*, and thus they might read their misery in their own *Hieroglyphicks*.

Richard Vines, who preached one of the sermons of thanksgiving for this victory, also made much of the captured banners, which may have been on display to his congregation as he spoke:

The Oracle with which he consulted that devised that motto *Fiat Justitia*, was too cunning for him ... and so it pleased God that the tables should be turned and the motto should become ours. (Vines 1644, p. 13)

Although both sides had made use of symbolism in their choice of banners, the parliamentarians now saw in those of their adversaries not only presumption but even a sinister belief in the oracular value of their own mottos. The 'double sense' which (as Macbeth noted) is characteristic of diabolical prophecies is here invoked to explain the fact that pictorial language can have more meanings than one.

Arbitrary codes

Implicit in any controversy about iconography is the question of whether meaning is inherent or constructed. For polemical purposes, writers on both sides allow themselves to move between the two theories, attributing motives to their enemies where it is convenient or else ascribing to God himself whatever meanings they have been able to detect. The popularity of some minor genres of the period seems partly related to the fact that they involve 'inventing' only in the sense of finding what is already there. An example of a code devised by God himself would be the numerological symbolism which led to so much scrutinising of dates and counting of words. Thomas Fuller's *Church History of Britain*, while expressing scepticism about the practice, nevertheless reported that someone who had counted the words in the Solemn League and Covenant of 1643 discovered that they came to 666, the mark of the Beast (Fuller 1845, vol. VI, p. 259). The use of etymology, as practised in this period, was often a branch of fiction. It is Fuller again, and again pretending to be noncommittal, who records the interest in finding the etymological origins of the words 'roundhead' and 'malignant'. The latter, he suggests, may come either

from *malus ignis*, 'bad fire,' or *malum lignum*, 'bad fuel;' but this is sure, betwixt both the name made a combustion all over England ... However, the royalists plead for themselves, that *malignity* properly denoteth activity of doing evil, whereas they, being ever since on the suffering side in their persons, credits, and estates, conceive the name improperly applied unto them, which plea the parliamentary party smile at instead of answering, taking notice of the affections of the royalists, how malignant they would have appeared if success had befriended them.

(vol. VI, p. 241)

The search for origins has become a search for meaning in a wider sense.

It is in this light that one can best understand the popularity of such forms as the anagram and chronogram. The chronogram is the rarer of the two, probably because the Roman numerals on which it depends were already becoming less common in the 1640s. It is a verse (often in Latin) in which the letters which happen also to be Roman numerals are used to form a significant date, such as that of the first session of the Long Parliament or the execution of Charles I. Often, the important letters are printed in larger type, or in capitals, to draw the reader's attention to the device. The date is important not in itself but because of what it signifies; the sentiments expressed in the Latin phrase, which themselves require the decoding of translation, are 'shown' to be evoked by the events to which the date refers.

Similarly, the object of the 'inventor' of an anagram was not simply to recombine the letters of a particular name; the new word or words were supposed to form a meaningful comment on that name. Many anagrams were taken seriously enough to be copied into commonplace books. They sometimes consisted of a series of well-known names, each with only one, obviously significant, anagram. Though no English anagrammatist can compete with the Frenchman who composed 400 anagrams on the name of the king of Great Britain, each of which tried to score a point against 'la Religion prétendue réformée' (Nicéron 1638, p. 117), the 1640s saw some feats of verbal ingenuity. Multiple anagrams on Parliament were especially popular: 'I part al men', 'I pm rent al', 'I rap tal men', 'in part lame', 'a trap. il men', etc. (MS 'Assheton's Memoranda' (c. 1642), pp. 126–7; *Mistress Parliament Her Invitation*, 1648, sig. A3). Neither side had a monopoly of the form. In 1648, Henry Walker, a Parliamentary journalist who had studied Hebrew, treated the readers of his *Perfect Occurrences* to a series of weekly anagrams in that language, each of which paid a compliment to some distinguished parliamentarian. The royalist press naturally responded with a series of uncomplimentary Latin and English anagrams on the same figures. The controversial Independent preacher John Saltmarsh was anagrammatised by one writer as 'Al's Trash', according to *Mercurius Civicus* (11–18 June 1646), by another, in *The Presbyterians Letany* (1647), as 'Smart lash'. Much was made, even before the events of 1648–9, of the

fact that 'Charolvs Stuartvs' could (with a little shuffling) be anagrammatised as 'Christus Salvator' (Parry 1981, p. 252).

The concept of the anagram is sometimes used analogically, as in the
mock love poems which misplace the terms appropriate to praising various
features of the woman's face until she is reduced to absurdity (as in
Donne's 'The Anagram': 'For though her eyes be small, her mouth is
great,/Though they be Ivory, yet her teeth be jeat', etc.). But it is more
commonly used as a cipher which draws attention to the arbitrariness of a
sign system – the order in which letters are arranged. '*England*,' James
Howell wrote in 1644, 'may be termed now, in comparison of what it was,
no other then an *Anagram of a Kingdome*' (Howell 1644, sig. T1ᵛ). For
anyone obsessed by the idea that the world was turned upside down, the
anagram was the perfect literary form. Unlike most ciphers, it does not
make clear which is the plain text and which the coded text. Is 'Saltmarsh'
the meaning of 'Al's Trash', or is 'Al's Trash' the meaning of 'Saltmarsh'?
The new order, presumably, is at least as true as the original one.

Social codes and translation: Lord George Digby

The fact that some forms of literature can be seen as codes was noted in
Wilkins's *Mercury*. He suggested that metaphors, allegories, fables, parables, and oracles,

so farre as they concerne the ornament of speech, doe properly belong to *Rhetorick*,
but as they may be applied for the *secrecy* of speech, so are they reducible unto this
part of *Grammar*.   (Wilkins 1641, p. 15)

So far, this chapter has been mainly concerned with the use of devices for
concealing and revealing secret meanings, with examples from ciphers, sign
language, iconography, and numerology; in the case of the anagram, I have
finally approached something like Wilkins's concept of rhetoric. His discussion of the relation between ornament and secrecy is interesting because
it indicates how literary evaluation can depend on the sense that one is
reading a coded text. Secrecy, he argues, may be an added ornament to
rhetoric if, as with the parable of the vineyard which Nathan told David by
way of upbraiding him with his treatment of Uriah, it enables a moral point
to be made more effectively under the guise of a story. Where the moral is
too effectively concealed, however, a story can appear merely grotesque
(pp. 15–17). Wilkins attributes the obscurity in the works of ancient
writers to their imitation of the ways of God, who had concealed so many

of the secrets of nature. The hierarchy implied by this theory is one in which not only literal meaning but more subtle matters like the sense of tone and aesthetic evaluation will be accessible to readers in proportion to their worthiness. The analogy is no longer simply that of the cipher, with its one-to-one correspondences, but with the art of translation, where the 'best' meaning may sometimes be the least literal.

This type of free translation/adaptation was becoming commoner in the period. Theo Hermans has noted that the belief in the superiority of imitation to translation was based on a metaphor of class and competition: the imitator was an equal of the original author, and sought to excel him, whereas the translator was only a humble follower whose project by definition was an inferior one. The word-for-word translation was described as 'servile', the less accurate one as 'free' (Hermans 1985, pp. 122–8). Thus, it may be significant that the writers who claim most 'freedom' for themselves are the royalist translators. What Denham admired in Fanshawe's translation of *Il Pastor Fido*, as he said in his verse epistle to the writer, was that it read like an original, and could have passed for one (Denham 1928, pp. 143–4). As so often when one writer praises another, Denham was singling out what he had attempted to do in his own translations. The idea that 'the letter killeth but the spirit giveth life' (2 Corinthians 3:6) is a submerged metaphor in Cotton's poem on Edmund Prestwich's version of *Hippolytus*, where he imagines the translator, like Aesculapius with Hippolytus himself, breathing life into a dismembered corpse:

> Hippolitus that erst was set upon
> By all, mangled by misconstruction,
> Dis-member'd by misprision, now by thee
> And thy ingenious chirurgerie
> Is re-united to his limbs, and grown
> Stronger as thine, than when great Theseus' son.
>
> (Cotton 1923, p. 402)

Michael Wilding suggests that Milton's image in *Areopagitica* of attempting to reassemble the broken pieces of Truth, like Isis with 'the mangl'd body of *Osiris*' (Milton 1959, p. 549), arises out of his recollection of the non-metaphorical mutilations which Burton, Bastwick and Prynne suffered under Laud, a dismembering which is then transmuted into 'the positive values of separation and division' through the concept of 'harmony in variety' (Wilding 1986, p. 16). By contrast, the royalist Cotton is concerned to 'cure' separation and division. Translation, in his example, stands for transcendence, the healing wholeness that removes controversy and contradiction rather than using it as a basis for construction. The preface to Denham's *The Destruction of Troy*, a translation of part of the second book of the *Aeneid*, draws several comparisons with changes of costume:

And as speech is the apparel of our thoughts, so are there certain Garbs and Modes of speaking, which vary with the times; the fashion of our clothes being not more subject to alteration, than that of our speech.   (Denham 1928, p. 160)

Though the image of language as the dress of thought is commonplace, Denham might even have been thinking of the striking modernisation of Sophocles' *Electra* by Christopher Wase, whom he had known as a fellow-protégé of the fifth Earl of Pembroke. Wase's translation, published in 1649, was dedicated to Charles I's young daughter Elizabeth. It adapts the 'manners' of the tragedy to seventeenth-century usage: for instance, Clytemnestra's first words to Electra are 'you now it seems are gadding forth agen' (Wase 1649, p. 21), and 'unanointed head' is translated as 'hair uncomb'd unpowdered' (p. 18). Wase justifies his modernisation on the grounds that his work is intended for women, but it is by no means simply a piece of polite condescension. In making Sophocles up-to-date, the translator also makes him highly political. Italics act as a signpost to the more topical references. The heroine, Electra, is called the Princess Royal; the Chorus are her maids of honour; and Orestes identifies himself to his sister by showing her their father's seal. The religion of the characters is obviously Christian; there is a reference to 'root and branch' destruction, and Clytemnestra is keeping a thanksgiving day, in the manner of parliamentarians. Charles I is obviously the murdered Agamemnon, and the analogy between the house of Atreus and the House of Stuart probably extends to the sacrifice of Iphigenia, a counterpart of Charles's consent to the execution of Strafford. The ritual of Greek tragedy could be applied to England's history, and Charles I, in the role of the dead Agamemnon, could be vicariously mourned and avenged. Wase's friends declared in their dedicatory poems that the translator, in co-opting Sophocles to his cause, was bringing the equivalent of foreign aid, but they also noted his cleverness in escaping punishment:

> For 'tis but Sophocles repeated, and
> Eccho cannot be guilty or arraign'd.

Translation had a double satisfaction for a royalist writer. Not only was it relatively safe, it was proof of the essential applicability and truth of words

from the past, a belief which lay behind the nostalgia for the rituals of
monarchy and the Church of England.

The choice between the letter and the spirit was particularly important in
the interpretation of Scripture, the most important kind of translation and
the paradigm for all interpretative activity. An anonymous writer in 1645
argued that Scriptural texts, on their own, were as meaningless as the
separate features of a face: what made a likeness, or an interpretation, 'that
which Painters call the Aire in every Face', was 'the Generall aire, the Scope
and Harmony of the Whole Text, with that which went before, and that
which followes' (*Consideration touching the late treaty for a Peace at
Uxbridge* 1645, p. 13). What is meant, evidently, is something like context,
or, again, the 'spirit'. Hobbes in *Leviathan* takes a similar line on 'the
word', which he understands within the concept of discourse:

When there is mention of the *Word of God*, or of Man, it doth not signifie a part of
Speech, such as Grammarians call a Nown, or a Verb, or any simple voice, without a
contexture with other words to make it significative; but a perfect Speech or
Discourse, whereby the speaker *affirmeth*, *denieth*, *commandeth*, *promiseth*,
threateneth, *wisheth*, or *interrogateth*. In which sense it is not *Vocabulum*, that
signifies a *Word*; but *Sermo*, (in Greek λογος that is, some *Speech, Discourse*, or
Saying.   (Hobbes 1968, p. 451)

Hobbes's contention that the word has meaning only in discourse is a
counterpart of his stress on the essential meaninglessness of many individual words. One of his most famous contentions is that excessive use of such
words, and perhaps poor translation from the classics, was the chief cause
of the civil war: 'men have undertaken to kill their Kings, because the
Greek and Latine writers, in their books, and discourses of Policy, make it
lawfull, and laudable, for any man so to do; provided before he do it, he call
him Tyrant. For they say not *Regicide*, that is, killing of a King, but
Tyrannicide, that is, killing of a Tyrant is lawfull' (p. 369). In insisting that
England is not classical Greece or Rome, Hobbes is pressing for historical
sense as opposed to the airy updating which Christopher Wase had
adopted for his own polemical purposes.

The question of letter versus spirit has wider implications when what are
being interpreted are the words and acts of living human beings. By way of
illustration, I propose to look briefly at the career of Lord George Digby, a
man whose whole life was bound up with intrigue. His father, as English
Ambassador to Spain under James, had been at the centre of a vast labyrinth of codes. He himself, for much of his life, was in charge of sending
letters in cipher. He was also virtually bilingual as a result of spending the

first thirteen years of his life in Spain, and, like others who had lived too long in Catholic countries, was distrusted by his contemporaries. At the beginning of the Long Parliament he at first sided with the reformers, but when he voted against the death sentence on Strafford his role changed with great rapidity from that of Parliament's hero to one of its most hated enemies. His colleagues were first outraged by his eloquent speech in defence of the man whose prosecution he had initially supported, and then by its publication, supposedly without his consent: the speech was publicly burned by the hangman. Then a letter of his to the queen was intercepted and opened by the House of Commons. It revealed that he had welcomed her on her arrival in Holland, from 'a country not worthy of her'. Not surprisingly, Parliament took this to show 'much venime and rancour' to his country. In an attempt to mollify public feeling, Digby published in 1642 an *Apology* for his conduct. His main point was the need to understand the special tone which he had been adopting in his correspondence. Thus, with reference to the passage that had given particular offence, he writes, 'I . . . must appeale to those who are best acquainted with the Civility of language, whether the addresse might not be comely to any Lady of quality, who should upon any not pleasing occasion, leave one Country for a while to reside in another' (Digby 1642, pp. 11–12). It was not a very successful argument; obviously, there was no way in which Digby could avoid admitting, on the one hand, that he had merely been flattering the queen, or, on the other, that he had meant his unpatriotic expressions literally. Implicit in this defence, however, is the concept of a language of politeness, suitable for women, which need not be literally true.

After throwing in his lot with the king at Oxford, Digby became one of the contributors to *Mercurius Aulicus* and other works of royalist propaganda. When Lord Falkland was killed in action in 1643, Digby replaced him as Secretary of State. Falkland, according to the account written later by his friend Edward Hyde, was a man of strict honour who always refused either to employ spies or open intercepted letters (Hyde 1888, vol. III, p. 185). Digby, by contrast, revelled in intrigue. It was in his new role as Secretary that, two years after the *Apology*, he was the centre of an even more embarrassing episode, again involving his correspondence. This was his attempt to persuade the Parliamentary commander of Abingdon, Major General Browne, to betray the town to the royalists. It was felt, with some justice, that Browne might not be totally committed to the cause (he did in fact become an active royalist after the king's execution). Digby sounded him out indirectly, then in a letter. Browne immediately saw what he was being asked to do and proceeded to show the correspondence to his council. They agreed that Browne should string Digby along as much as possible, gaining time in which to fortify the town. Browne therefore kept replying, in a cipher sent him by Digby, with carefully ambiguous phrases. He combined protestations of loyalty to the parliamentary cause with polite expressions which could possibly be taken by Digby and the rest as hints that he was willing to be persuaded. When he felt that his defences had been sufficiently strengthened, he dropped the pretence. 'My Lord,' he wrote to Digby, as he explained what he had been doing, 'let this Letter be the Cipher to all my former' (Browne 1644, p. 34).

Browne's interpretation of the whole episode is summed up in this phrase. Digby, he implies, was overreached precisely because, not being familiar with the language of honesty, he inevitably read it wrongly. Like the key to a cipher, Browne's final letter was intended to make Digby aware of the true meaning of all the previous letters: that their apparently hollow professions of loyalty to the parliamentary cause were sincerely meant, and that only so duplicitous a nature as Digby's could possibly have put any other interpretation on them. In this well-publicised case, each man was able to blame the other for not having fully understood his tone. What Digby had argued in his *Apology* – that few men's private correspondence could bear being studied out of context by unsympathetic readers – can be read in terms of the clash of opposing political and literary discourses where shared values matter more than precise word-by-word equivalents. Scripture could be given a variety of allegorical or contextual readings, but one of these contexts had to be an assumption that the speaker of the word was a figure of infinite goodness and wisdom, and no interpretation which conflicted with this belief would be allowable. What Digby is really asking for himself is a similar act of trust in the goodness of his own real meaning. By stressing the importance of general context over precise vocabulary, the writer is inviting his readers to escape from a world of nit-picking particularity to one of general truths. But it is evident, also, that in catching the spirit of a work, a translator may be allowing himself not merely freedom but tendentiousness and gross inaccuracy. In its most extreme form, this can mean ignoring the literal meaning of what is there in the interest of the supposed personality of the author, perhaps imposing on him a unity and consistency which he does not in fact have. After the Restoration Digby ended his literary career by translating plays from the Spanish. The only one which survives, a piece originally by Calderon with the significant title *Elvira, or the Worst not Always True*, is a very free adaptation.

Digby was only one of a large number of royalist writers who were involved in work with ciphers during the 1640s and 1650s. One would naturally like to know what effect this experience had on them. Annabel Patterson (1984) had suggested, in the case of Cowley, that the author's later work reflected 'the habits of mind encouraged by such tasks' (p. 149). But there was nothing particularly literary about the enciphering and deciphering on which Cowley, Denham, and their colleagues were engaged. The interpretative codes which readers apply to their reading of literary texts are learned unconsciously, and most people were not even aware of them until the advent of recent critical theory. The arbitrary element in ciphers means that they cannot be learned in this way, though an experienced cryptographer like Wallis could acquire enough familiarity with the different available types to puzzle out the rules of a private language. The 'polyalphabetic' code would be a better model for the semiotics of literature than the simple substitution code, since it requires the user to know when a particular interpretative strategy is or is not appropriate, but the rules for applying the two alphabets are themselves arbitrary. In any case, this cipher was not in general use. What Denham and the other royalist writers were doing was something much more purely mechanical: they converted words into numbers and vice versa, and were helpless without the keys to their numerous ciphers, since a cipher whose key could be remembered would have been too easy to crack. The fact that several of these men were also experienced translators may, however, have fostered a sense that the process of decoding was only half complete when a text had been literally rendered. In 'To Sir Richard Fanshaw', Denham praised his friend's translation of *Il Pastor Fido* for its willingness to take freedoms with the original, even to improving it in places where it was flat: this, he felt, was 'True to his sense, but truer to his fame' (Denham 1928, p. 143). In Digby's case, there were obvious reasons why the writer should prefer to be judged on his 'fame' rather than his 'sense' – that is, by an ideal concept of his character rather than by his precise words or actions. Bearing in mind this concept of translation as transcendence, I shall now turn to the central royalist text, that of Charles I.

The king's cabinet

One of the dedicatory verses to Wilkins's *Mercury* comments on the embarrassment of kings whose correspondence is made public:

> Nor are Kings Writings safe; To guard their Fame,
> Like *Scaevola*, they wish their Hand i th' Flame.
> Ink turns to bloud; they oft participate
> By wax and Quill sad *Icarus* his fate.

His remarks turned out to be prophetic. The publication in 1645 of Charles
I's private correspondence was to be one of the most damaging events of
the war for the royalist cause. This happened despite the fact that both
Charles I and Henrietta Maria knew from an early stage that they needed to
write with one eye on the possible hostile intercepter. In 1642, the queen
commented several times on the possibility of her letters being opened and
printed: 'You see that I do not even fear lest this should be opened,' she
declared in 1642, after urging the king to stand firm; besides, she added for
the benefit of the potential eavesdropper, they would not be likely to print
it in any case, 'for what they find just and good they hide, and what is
thought bad is printed' (Green 1857, p. 109). A short ciphered passage in
one letter informs him that he is about to read a 'decoy': 'All that follows is
on purpose in case this letter should be opened' (p. 131). She lays traps for
the intercepter, for instance attempting to cast suspicion on Pym by
mentioning money which he is supposed to have promised her (p. 141). In a
letter from Paris in 1644, she gave the king a symbol which she said she
would use 'when I desire any thing in earnest', a statement which makes
one aware that not everything in her letters can be taken at face value; court
language is a code within a code (*The King's Cabinet* 1645, p. 32). The
couple went through four different ciphers within a three-year period
(*CSPD* vol. XLIII, p. xi). Eric Sams, who deciphered a number of these,
notes that the 'longwindedness' of the correspondents and their repetition
of key phrases like the affectionate 'dear heart' or 'mon cher coeur' facilitated the process of code-breaking (Sams 1985, pp. 89–90, 92). The length
at which the king and queen wrote to each other was probably the result of
their conviction that the ciphers would be impenetrable as long as the key
was kept safe – a view in which they were justified, since some of their
letters were not deciphered until this century. Even while living in virtual
captivity, first with the Scots and then the Army, the king seems to have
been able to keep up a voluminous correspondence and to handle a new set
of ciphers (e.g., Dyve 1958, pp. 49–96).

In spite of these precautions, or rather, because they did not follow them
consistently enough, the interception of the royal correspondence frequently had disastrous results. A letter which revealed the double game
that the king was playing in his response to Parliament's articles of cess-
ation was published in March 1643. The phrase about his 'fine designs' on

his adversaries was particularly damning and was constantly quoted there-
after when other royalist intrigues were discovered (Gardiner 1897–8, vol.
I, p. 99). He had already written to the queen, after the interception and
publishing of an earlier letter, in words which he must have intended to be
public: 'others presse me as being brought upon the Stage, but I answer that
having profest to have thy advice it were a wrong to thee to doe any thing
before I had it' (*The King's Cabinet*, p. 39).

After the capture and publication of the letters taken at the Battle of
Naseby, a legend grew up that Wallis had deciphered them. He always
denied any involvement, claiming that they had needed no deciphering,
only the occasional translation from the French (Wallis 1698, letter, 1685).
He was probably telling the truth. The fact that some parts of the published
letters were left in cipher when they were printed probably means that no
one had the necessary expertise to deal with them. The reason so little help
was needed was that the king, although he sent letters in cipher, kept the
unciphered drafts among his papers. Some of the enciphered letters which
he had received were also found with the deciphered text written between
the lines. Matters were made still easier by the fact that the cabinet also
contained the keys to other ciphers (*CSPD* vol. XLIII, p. v). But the fact that
the letters were *believed* to have been in cipher was important to the way in
which they were read. Like the hieroglyphics on the royalist banners, it
was assumed, the secret language of the 'cabbalistical adversaries' had been
turned against them.

The king himself made no attempt to deny the letters (it would have been
useless anyway), though he did comment, in the same tones as Digby
before him, 'I would fain know him who would be willing, that the
freedom of all his private Letters were publickly seen, as mine have now
been' (to Edward Nicholas, 4 Aug. 1645, in *Reliquiae* 1650, p. 224).
Realising that the letters spoke for themselves, and that they were bound to
be damaging to the king's reputation, Parliament went to great trouble to
avoid accusations of forgery by placing the originals on show in a room in
Westminster for anyone who cared to examine them. Transcribed and
translated versions were then published in a book called *The King's Cabinet Opened*. Their contents were all that any parliamentary supporter
could have hoped. Not only did they make plain that Charles had been
saying different things to different opponents throughout the war, but he
was shown not even to like or trust many of his own supporters: he had
complained to the queen of the dull company at his Oxford court (9 April
1645), called its Parliament 'our Mungrell Parliament here' (13 March
1644), and warned Jermyn to manipulate the news more effectively in his

dealings with the French court: 'for as I would not have them thinke that all assistance bestowed upon me were in vain soe I would not have them beleeve that I needed noe helpe, lest they should underhand assist any Rebells to keepe the ballance of dissention amongst us equall' (24 April 1645). With regard to marriage proposals for Prince Charles and the daughter of the Portuguese king, he intended to 'give such an answer as shall signifie nothing' (30 Jan. 1644). At crucial junctures in his affairs, he was writing to the queen about the disposal of court offices and minor intrigues among his followers. Here was all the deviousness and 'king-craft' of which his father before him had been accused. Most damning of all was his willingness to promise concessions to the Roman Catholics in England and Ireland, in exchange for their support. The annotations published with the letters made as much capital as possible out of Charles's supposed subordination to his wife, partly because this lent credence to the view that he was soft on Catholicism. The first note to the letters points out that 'the Kings Counsels are wholly managed by the Queen; though she be of the weaker sexe, borne an Alien, bred up in a contrary Religion, yet nothing great or small is transacted without her privity & consent' (p. 43). For further reinforcement of the message, three London clergymen gave public addresses on the subject.

It is easy to imagine the significance for hostile and neutral public opinion of the publication of *The King's Cabinet Opened*. But what of its effect on the royalists who had just suffered defeat in his cause? There was an immediate outpouring of pamphlets arguing both that the letters were not genuine and that, even if they were, they still did not reflect badly on the king. Some writers adopted a worldly stance, arguing, for instance, that no one should be attacked for inconsistency, since circumstances do change (*A Satyr* 1645, p. 9). But this pragmatic approach was suitable only for politically sophisticated readers. Attacking the hypocrisy of the king's enemies, and their misogyny, was a more successful tactic. There were a number of gallant defences of the queen, and some apologists virtually argued that the king's letters should be read as part of the discourse of love rather than that of politics. As with Digby's early defence of himself, the oblique and tactfully subdued implication was that no one really means what he says to a woman. In the most inept of all attempts at justification (*A Letter* 1645, pp. 2–3), an anonymous author, presumably in order to counteract the charge that the king was too uxorious, makes a point of claiming to have been impressed by his 'masculine' style. This is typical of his attempt to shift attention from content to form, or the king's personality. Even this author, however, despite his carefully established qualifications for understanding the language of true gentility, cannot do much about Charles's willingness to negotiate with the Roman Catholics apart from referring to a friend who, in some mysterious way, has satisfied him on this point. What is being invoked here is the concept of *arcana imperii*: the king is right, but his rightness can be discerned only in the light of knowledge so secret that even his defender cannot mention it.

This notion of state secrets was of course a familiar one, and generally accepted. In *Basilikon Doron* James I had said, 'a king will have need to use secrecy in many thinges'; Henry Peacham, who turned some phrases from the work into emblems, illustrated this one with a picture of a bird holding a key in its mouth (Peacham, *Heroica Emblemata*, Book 3, no. 4) – presumably that of the cabinet in which the king would have locked his most private correspondence. As Annabel Patterson has shown, 'cabinet' and its synonyms, along with the concept of the key which opens it, were already 'key words' before the civil war (Patterson 1984, pp. 7–8). When Charles I's captured correspondence was published under the title *The King's Cabinet Opened* the editors were alluding to such 'secret' works of fiction as Barclay's *Argenis*, where the solution to the complications of the romance turns out to lie in a cabinet, and where the romance itself (a *roman-à-clef*) similarly requires a 'clavis', or key, to be supplied by later commentators. They may also have wished to remind their readers of the 'casket letters' which had incriminated Charles's grandmother, Mary Queen of Scots. The title became famous and inspired many others pretending to offer secret discoveries: *The Queen's Closet Opened* (1655) is a collection of recipes and beauty treatments; *Cupid's Cabinet Unlocked*, a collection of love poems, is a rare and undated part-publication tentatively attributed to Humphrey Moseley (Wells and Taylor 1987, pp. 135–6). Titles of this kind have been found well into the Restoration.

The preface to *The King's Cabinet Opened* also makes use of another image for an embarrassing revelation: 'Now by Gods good providence the traverse Curtain is drawn, and the King writing to *Ormond* and the Queen, what they must not disclose, is presented upon the stage' (p. 4). The phrase about bringing someone on the stage is one which Clarendon singles out as belonging to this period; the idea of drawing the curtain goes with it (Hyde 1857, vol. I, p. 143). Lord George Digby's unsuccessful attempt to persuade Richard Browne to betray Abingdon had already been described by the governor in terms of a ludicrously inadequate performance: 'we ... perceived other faces peeping behinde the Arras, waighting for the Cue to bring them out', and Digby himself, with his 'properties' on, was ready to enter on to the stage (Browne 1644, pp. 12, 18). An attack on the royalist

Earl of Ormond in 1646 is called *Ormond's Curtain drawn*. Drawing the curtain, like opening the cabinet, thus seems to offer the reader a chance to exercise impartial judgement, rather like the invitations offered the spectators at the beginning of a play ('View but his picture', 'Behold and see'). However, 'discovery', in this context, is generally damaging. To be discovered is to be found out; all secrets are bad secrets.

The royalist reply was that such discoveries were in the eye of the beholder: there was a way of reading the letters that made sense of their apparent duplicity. The contortions involved in decoding an already decoded text in a manner compatible with devotion to the king created a positive need for someone who could yoke heterogenous ideas by violence together. This is why John Cleveland found his perfect subject in 'The King's Disguise', a poem about Charles's escape from Oxford in 1646. The poem focuses not on the reasons for his behaviour but on a single startling visual image – the king dressed like a servant, in black, with his hair chopped short – which, like the 'Popish picture', says many different things depending on how it is viewed. Cleveland starts, however, by asking whether he should be viewing it at all. The paradox is the same one that informs Donne's 'Good Friday 1613. Riding Westward', where the poet explains why he cannot allow himself to behold the crucifixion:

> Yet dare I almost be glad I do not see
> That spectacle of too much weight for me.
> Who sees God's face, that is self life, must die;
> What a death were it then to see God die?

Cleveland's opening lines express similar reluctance to behold a monstrous sight:

> And why so coffin'd in this vile disguise,
> Which who but sees blasphemes thee with his eyes?
> My twins of light within their penthouse shrinke,
> And hold it their Allegeance to winke.   (lines 1–4)

When Cleveland actually describes what he sees, we understand what sort of 'blasphemy' is involved in looking at Charles. It is laughter. The disguise is an absurd one, and the poet makes the most of it:

> Thy visage is not legible, the letters,
> Like a Lords name, writ in phantastick fetters:
> Cloathes where a Switzer might be buried quicke,
> As overgrown as the Body Politique.
> False beard enough, to fit a stages plot,
> For that's the ambush of their wit, God wot.   (lines 63–8)

The first part of the poem is devoted to developing the paradox that the king, by voluntarily assuming this uncouth and humiliating disguise, has become a traitor to himself, performing all the sacrilegious acts of which Parliament had already been guilty. Thus, his clothes are compared to a hypocritical clergyman and a desecrated church; his features are 'under Sequestration' (line 36), like the property of royalists; the 'accurst Stenographic of fate' has turned the 'Princely Eagle' into a bat (lines 47–8); and the whole effect is 'a Libell' (line 71) as bad as the one Nedham had recently written in *Mercurius Britanicus*. What lies behind this is never openly said, but made abundantly clear by the references to legibility, letters, writing and stenography: Charles's letters have indeed, like his disguise, libelled and betrayed him. When the letters were put on public display, as a guarantee of their authenticity, *Mercurius Aulicus* (13–20 July 1645) warned royalists that the intention might be to trap them into identifying themselves. Some royalists may therefore have refused, as Cleveland loyally refuses, to 'see' the evidence against the king. Blaming him for putting himself into an absurd disguise for his own safety is Cleveland's way of blaming him for destroying his own image in the letters:

> Oh for a State-distinction to arraigne
> *Charles* of high Treason 'gainst my Soveraigne.   (lines 5–6)

Just as Donne's poem finally shows that an apparently outrageous act ('I turn my back to thee') is an appropriate one in context ('but to re-ceive/Corrections', lines 37–8), so Cleveland finally inverts his central image to argue that the apparently degrading disguise is really, like the parables and proverbs of the Bible, a symbol of the divine royalty. Then he turns to *The King's Cabinet*:

> Hence Cabinet-Intruders, Pick-locks hence,
> You that dim Jewells with your Bristoll-sense:
> And Characters, like Witches, so torment,
> Till they confesse a guilt, though innocent.
> Keyes for this Cypher you can never get,
> None but S. *Peter*'s op's this Cabinet.
> This Cabinet, whose aspect would benight
> Critick spectators with redundant light.
> A Prince most seen, is least: What Scriptures call
> The Revelation, is most mysticall.   (lines 105–14)

Cleveland's endless abundance of odd images makes everything interchangeable with everything else. The letters in the king's cabinet are jewels made to look false when they are put beside the glittering but false 'Bristol stone' of the commentators; similarly, the king himself is a jewel within a cabinet that such men can never open. The 'cabinet', I take it, now means not only the absurd disguise but the entire physical reality of the king, including perhaps the speech impediment which *Britanicus* in its 'libel' had dared to hint at, and which Cleveland sees as yet another bar between the 'true' king and the understanding of his subjects. The king's handwriting writhes and twists under the gaze of the transcriber or decipherer, as if the separate letters of the alphabet, not their meaning, were being accused. Cleveland's language also twists and turns in its determination to prove that, despite all the evidence to the contrary, the mystical ruler of royalist devotion is still real. The 'discovery' of the king's papers turns out to be like the Scriptural Revelation: dark language hiding a dazzling reality. Cleveland has transferred the discussion of Charles's *words*, the letters, to the visual plane: the alphabet comes alive, the disguised figure becomes an emblem or cipher. But, like these visual images, the disguised king is static and timeless; the letters, with their specific bases in temporal events, can be discounted in the analysis of the eternal verities embodied in the figure of the ruler.

The king's second escape in disguise was from Hampton Court on 11 November 1647. He left behind him a letter addressed to the two houses of Parliament, explaining that he was motivated by fears for his own safety; he had received warnings of an intended assassination attempt. The letter concluded, 'Let me be heard with Freedome, Honour and Safety, and I shall instantly breake through this Cloud of Retirement, and shew my selfe really to be *pater Patriae*' (*The King's Most Gracious Messages for Peace* 1648, p. 81). It was probably this letter which inspired the broadsheet poem *C. R. in a Cloud* (1647), which Thomason acquired only six days after the escape. Though obviously influenced by the Cleveland poem, it stresses the comic and grotesque aspects of the king's situation to a still greater extent. The opening lines compare the king to Jupiter, whose 'escapes' were famous (a manuscript play of 1620–40, adapted from Thomas Heywood's mythological dramas, is called *Calisto, or, The Escapes of Jupiter*). For some reason, the author decides to stress the most tactless aspects of the comparison:

> It is no strange thing
> To heare that the king
>   Hath made his escapes;
> For *Jove* did the same,
> And got him a name
>   (For shifting and Rapes)

Cheerfully, he then explains that Charles is not acting on the same motives as Jupiter: his Juno's not a shrew, and he can't rape women by turning into a shower of gold, because he hasn't got any. All he wants is liberty ('Won't you have Princes free?'). So he is urged to

> keep in thy Cloud,
> And there safe thee Shrewd,
>   Nor break, but as Day,
> The mid Region be
> Thy Artillerie
>   Where Clouds bear the sway.

The true king, the sun enveloped in a cloud, is contrasted with his opponents, especially Independents like Henry Marten, with their 'new-found lights'. The poem thus ends with a familiar royalist motif. Yet its tone could hardly have been less irreverent if it had been written by Marten himself. Only the ending rules out the possibility of reading it as an anti-royalist satire. If Cleveland's poem is an equivalent of the now-famous duck-rabbit which can be seen as either one thing or the other, but not both at once, this author's attempt to deal with the two opposing reactions to Charles's predicament can be compared with a rather bad picture of a duck followed by a feeble attempt to argue that it is really a rabbit after all.

Lely's portrait of the king with his second son, the future James II (plate 1), was painted some time between the king's coming to Hampton Court (24 August 1647) and his escape from there to the Isle of Wight (11 November 1647). Richard Lovelace wrote a poem on it, probably in the same period, since he makes no mention of the king's second escape. Although this is a famous piece of ecphrastic poetry, neither it nor the picture seem to me to have been fully explicated, and I should like to end this chapter with a look at the way in which they combine visual and verbal codes. While Lely's Charles is not literally in disguise, his defeated and imprisoned state is an equivalent of the cloud and darkness described in the two poems just quoted. For Lovelace, however, the 'clouded Majesty' at once reveals the king behind the disguise; the royal images of sun and eagle, inverted and travestied in 'The King's Disguise', are restored to their original power. In commanding the hypothetical viewer to 'See!', the poet immediately takes the opposite line from Cleveland's initial appalled refusal to look at the disfigured image:

1   Sir Peter Lely, Charles I with James Duke of York

See! what a *clouded Majesty!* and eyes
Whose glory through their mist doth brighter rise!
See! what an humble bravery doth shine,
And griefe triumphant breaking through each line;
How it commands the face! so sweet a scorne
Never did *happy misery* adorne!
So sacred a contempt! that others show
To this, (oth' height of all the wheele) below;
That mightiest Monarchs by this shaded booke
May coppy out their proudest, richest looke.

Whilst the true *Eaglet* this quick luster spies,
And by his *Sun's* enlightens his owne eyes;
He cares his cares, his burthen feeles, then streight
Joyes that so lightly he can beare such weight;
Whilst either eithers passion doth borrow,
And both doe grieve the same victorious sorrow.

These my best *Lilly* with so bold a spirit
And soft a grace, as if thou didst inherit
For that time all their greatnesse, and didst draw
With those brave eyes your *Royall Sitters* saw.

Not as of old, when a rough hand did speake
A strong Aspect, and a faire face, a weake;
When only a black beard cried Villaine, and
By *Hieroglyphicks* we could understand;
When Crystall typified in a white spot,
And the bright Ruby was but one red blot;
Thou dost the things *Orientally* the same,
Not only paintst its colour, but its *Flame*:
Thou sorrow canst designe without a teare,
And with the Man his very *Hope* or *Feare*;
So that th'amazed world shall henceforth finde
None but my *Lilly* ever drew a *Minde*.   (Lovelace 1930, pp. 57–8)

What fascinates Lovelace, like Cleveland, is a paradox. But the one he finds in the picture is human and psychological rather than emblematic: the emotional charge which it creates between king, prince, and spectator, while apparently suppressing all emotion. The 'lines' referred to in line 4 are those of the painter and those of Charles's face; Lovelace reads between them, and in his own lines supplies the oxymorons which reconcile the appearance and the reality of the picture. Being an 'eaglet', the prince can look on the sun without being blinded, so he can see what we are being asked to see, and Lely himself, 'for that time', sees it too: it is as if the painting were seen through Charles's eyes. Suppressing his own role as the interpreter who directs our eyes, Lovelace compliments the artist not on creating meaning but on perceiving it; perhaps he also hints at a new Trinity in this fusion of the artist's 'spirit' with the mutual understanding between Father and Son. The artist's control over his medium reflects his sitters' control over their emotions, and thus justifies what might otherwise seem a rather stiff composition. The sympathetic painter or observer can interpret what both must *really* be feeling and admire them for not showing it.

The last part of the poem draws a contrast between Lely's picture and portraits in which character and emotion are spelled out in 'hieroglyphics', and where the effect is of juxtaposition rather than (a key word of the period) transcendence. Lovelace might be thinking of the old-fashioned iconic royal portraits of Queen Elizabeth I, or perhaps of emblematic art in general. The point of the tradition to which Lely belongs is precisely that the king needs no crown to reveal his innate royalty. But the most widely circulated visual images, and those which had the greatest effect on public opinion, were the woodcuts and engravings in books and broadsides, not the paintings of Van Dyck, Dobson, and Lely which usually represent the period to posterity. It is ironic that the best-known and most influential of all the images of the king was to be an example of the emblematic school which Lovelace is denigrating here, William Marshall's frontispiece to the *Eikon Basilike* (plate 2). I shall discuss this famous picture in more detail in the final chapter, which focuses on the king's execution and its aftermath. At this point I wish only to suggest that the contrast between the iconographic methods of Lely and Marshall is not so great as appears from the disparity between their talents and between the mediums in which they worked. The symbolic language of the emblem is largely the same as that of the Lely painting: the image of light shining in darkness ('clarior ex tenebris') is precisely that which Lovelace had discerned in Lely's work. The same is true of the other royal and Christian paradoxes of the emblem: the palm tree which grows the more for being weighed down, the rock unmoved in the stormy sea, and the crown of thorns which will become a crown of glory. The difference is that in Lely, as interpreted by Lovelace, one of the pairs of opposites is seen as transcending the other (the king's dazzling regality shines through the depths of sorrow), whereas Marshall, like Cleveland (and, in intention at least, the author of *C. R. in a Cloud*), places the two concepts side by side, exploiting the grotesqueness that results from their coexistence.

It is also possible that the Lely painting contains another emblem. This has not been commented on before, partly because most reproductions, including this one, are not able clearly to show the significance of the objects being held by the king and prince (see detail in plate 3). The best description is given in the *Anecdotes of Painting* by Horace Walpole, who had obviously seen the original: the King is holding a letter from the Prince of Wales, addressed 'Au roi monseigneur', and the Duke of York is giving him a penknife to cut the strings (Walpole 1862, pp. 443–4). The pose is similar to the one in a pre-war painting by Van Dyck, later engraved, in which Henrietta Maria, holding an olive branch in one hand, offers her husband a laurel wreath. This kind of action is a natural way of creating rapport between the sitters in a double portrait. Of course, there is a great difference between giving someone a wreath and giving him a penknife, and the solemnity of both parties seems almost disproportionate to this simple action. But in 1647, only two years after the king's private correspondence had been made so embarrassingly public, the delivery of an obviously personal letter to a man in captivity is a momentous occasion.

The Explanation of the EMBLEME.

Ponderibus *genus omne mali, probris, gravatus,*	Though clogg'd with weights of miseries
Vicq; ferenda ferens, Palma *ut* Depressa, *resurgo.*	Palm-like Depress'd, I higher rise.
Ac, velut undarum Fluctûs Ventiq; *furorem*	And as th'unmoved Rock out-brave's
Grati Populi Rupes *immota repello.*	The boistrous Windes and ragging waves:
Clarior è tenebris, *cælestis stella, corusco.*	So triumph I, And shine more bright
Victor et æternùm-felici pace triumpho.	In sad Affliction's Darksom night.
Auro Fulgentem *rutilo gemmisq; micantem,*	That Splendid, but yet toilsom Crown
At curis Gravidam *spernendo calco* Coronam.	Regardlesly I trample down.
Spinosam, *at ferri facilem, quo* Spes mea,(Christi	With joie I take this Crown of thorn,
Auxilio,)Nobis non est tractare *molestum.*	Though sharp, yet easie to be born.
Æternam, *fixis fidei, semperq;*-beatam	That heav'nlie Crown, already mine,
In Cælos *oculis* Specto, *Nobisq; parataa.*	I View with eies of Faith divine.
Quod Vanum est, sperno; quod (Christi Gratia *præbet*	I slight vain things; and do embrace
Amplecti studium est; Virtutis Gloria *merces*	Glorie, the just reward of Grace.

Τῷ Χρ̄ς͂ σέλι ἠδἴχνοτ τὸν ὠδἴνα, θεῖ τῇ Κάρτωκ .

G.D.

2 William Marshall, frontispiece to *Eikon Basilike* (1649)

The fact that he needs a penknife ought to mean that the letter has not previously been opened. But how can he be sure? The knife stands for his right to privacy.

It has been suggested that Lovelace, who was apparently something of a painter himself, might have seen the picture while it was still being worked on in Lely's studio. This seems quite possible. For one thing, he writes only about the expressions of the sitters, which would presumably have been painted first, not about their pose and its significance. On the other hand, it is also possible that the meaning of the attitude adopted by the king and the prince was not fully understood by either poet or painter; it may have been a private code devised by them. Lovelace saw Lely's painting as a study in the concealment of feeling, but it can also be seen as a defence of concealment in general. As Cleveland had written, 'A Prince most seen, is least'. The biblical assertion that 'the heart of kings is unsearchable' (Proverbs 25: 3) had become an essential royalist tenet.

This study of royalist codes began with those which have explicit meanings, looking then at those which involve a double process of interpret-

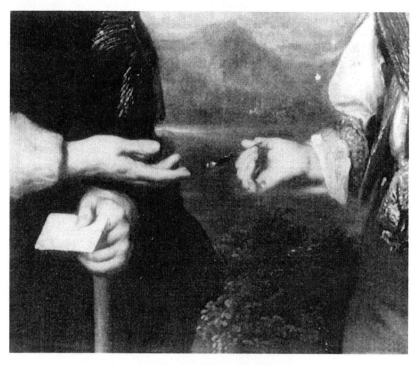

3   Detail of Lely painting (plate 1)

ation, from symbol to word, and from word to spirit, and finally at those which rebuff all attempts at translation. Language and character, in this final category, are indistinguishable. It remains to consider what happens when this aesthetic of mystery is extended to the handling of plot, as in the royalists' favourite literary form, romance. The king, like God, is not only mysterious himself; he also moves in mysterious ways.

3

Genre as code: romance and tragicomedy

Designs of War and Peace are better hinted and cut open by a Romance, than by downright Histories.

(Humphrey Moseley,
Preface to a translation of Madeleine de Scudéry's *Artamenes*, 1653)

The arch-traitor Cromwell, and two of his choicest instruments, Bradshaw and Ireton, finished the tragedy of their lives in a comic scene at Tyburn; a wonderful example of Justice.

(Edward Nicholas, *CSPD* vol. xxx; quoted Nicholas 1955, p. 301)

The realism of romance

A curious letter, preserved among the State Papers for 1644, begins,

Fidelia to Philitia. I know you are impatient to hear what becomes of our friends at *Oxford*, especially Silvander, who is in a kind of *prison* there. For Polimuse, though his Lordship deserves a speedy punishment, yet it is deferred.

(*CSPD* vol. xxiii, p. 657)

The annotators of this letter obviously took it seriously as a cipher: they suggest that Silvander is Charles I and Polimuse the Duke of Hamilton. The message might have been a coded one; on the other hand, it might have been the work of real people using romance names for their own amusement, as the French *précieux* did. It is sometimes hard to tell the difference. The first step in any correspondence between royalists was an exchange of ciphers, but the practice of exchanging secret signs also served a romantic purpose. Cotgrave's *Wit's Interpreter* (1655b), a collection of poems, dialogues, letters, and other *jeux d'esprit* for fashionable people, contains a section on ciphers, offered as a means by which absent lovers can communicate in secret. During the 1650s Sir John Berkenhead was known as Cratander, the hero of Cartwright's *Royal Slave* (Thomas 1969, p. 137), to such friends as Katherine Phillips, who was herself generally known as 'the

matchless Orinda'. The latter was certainly a coterie name, but Berkenhead's may have been something more, since he seems also to have acted as
a royalist agent. Were the royalists using romance for a serious purpose, or
were they merely indulging in a collective fantasy?

The latter was certainly the view of their oppenents. John Hall's anti-
royalist *Mercurius Britanicus* (1648) constantly uses the language of
romance to support his contention that his opponents are the victims of a
dangerous delusion. He attacks one man whose 'life hath been nothing but
a mad *Romance*' (16 May 1648), comments on 'that late fine *Romance* of
the Isle of *Wight*, a business that carries as much probability as any thing
that we read of *King Arthur* or the *Knight* of the *round* table' (27 June
1648), and asserts that those who attempt to involve the Scots on the
royalist side are undertaking 'rash, heady and desperate adventures, which
are as improbable as any thing we have read of in *Bevis, Amadis, Palmerin*,
or the *Knight of the Sun*' (13 June 1648). This language recurs so often in
pro-Commonwealth newsbooks and pamphlets throughout the next
years, particularly in conjunction with Charles II's attempts to reclaim his
throne, that it almost seems to have become the official line on the subject.
To treat invasion and conspiracy as fantastic 'Chimaera's of the old
Romances' (*The Life and Reigne of King Charls, or the Pseudo-Martyr
Discovered* 1651) was to appropriate the urbane and gentlemanly tone
which the royalists liked to think peculiarly their own. *Hudibras*, which
turns the Don Quixote myth back against the parliamentarians, was to be
the ultimate royalist revenge.

One of the main contentions of this book, which is also my justification
for the eclectic range of examples in the previous chapter, is that life
imitates literature at least as much as literature imitates life. The habit of
seeing events in literary terms was common to both sides in the civil war, as
was the attempt to 'place' those events by assigning them to the correct
genre. There were some forms which both sides tried equally to appropriate: the ballad and emblem, for example, because of their associations with
the popular sentiment which both sides claimed to represent. Pastoral and
epic were disputed territory for the opposite reason. For instance, John
Corbet's *True and Impartiall History of the Military Government of the
Citie of Gloucester* (1647) declares in its dedication that 'The Action of
these times transcends the Barons Warres, and those tedious discords
between the Houses of *Yorke* and *Lancaster*, in as much as it is undertaken
upon higher Principles, and carried on to a nobler end, and effects more
universall' (sig. A2ᵛ). More modest than Milton was later to be in his
comparison of his subject matter with that of Homer and Virgil, Corbet

was apparently placing his in the context of the English heroic poems on the subjects he mentions, as practised by Daniel and Drayton. But there were some literary forms which belonged specifically to the royalists, and which were equally specifically the targets for satire by parliamentarians. These were plays, whose performance had been forbidden by ordinance since August 1642, and romances. Simply to write in either form was to make a statement about one's relation to the party in power. Many royalists managed to do both at once, since the most popular plays of the period were dramatised romances or romantic tragicomedies.

The precise definition of romance tended to vary according to the demands of controversy. When used pejoratively, the term usually means the incredible tales of quasi-supernatural deeds that had even sunk to the level of the chapbook. When taken seriously, romance means either the contemporary French novels or, more likely, those which were thought to be 'about' recent history: Sidney's *Arcadia* and John Barclay's *Argenis*. It was generally believed that, as William Dugard wrote in the preface to a new edition of the *Arcadia* in 1655, Sidney had been 'shadowing moral and politick results under the plain and easie emblems of Lovers'; numerous keys had attempted to explain the topical meaning of his romance. But it was Barclay's *Argenis*, first published in Latin in 1621, that made the form a recognised vehicle for political allegory and comment. Along with generalised political maxims and depictions of various kinds of good and bad ruler, courtier, adviser, and subject, it offered some portraits which even an uninstructed reader could recognise as based on real examples. A key, first published with the work in its English translation of 1628 by Robert le Grys, explained most of the identifications, though it recognised that a simple one-to-one relationship did not always exist. For instance, it had already been suggested that the heroine's two suitors might be seen as different aspects of the same person, the future Henri IV; this, Le Grys felt, would create 'so many absurdities, or rather impossibilities . . . as I should never be able to disintangle my selfe' (Barclay 1628, p. 487).

A romance by a Roman Catholic writer who devotes some space to ridiculing the doctrine of predestination inevitably required selective reading and annotating: the 'clavis' is sometimes quite evasive, particularly in its notes on figures in the Roman Catholic hierarchy. But Barclay's firm commitment to absolute monarchy was apparently felt to outweigh his religious views. Annabel Patterson and Paul Salzman, who have written excellent accounts of seventeenth-century romances, suggest that there were political motives behind James I's commissioning a translation of the book (unfortunately lost) from Ben Jonson in 1623, as also in Charles I's commissioning the one by Le Grys in 1628 (Patterson 1984, pp. 183–4, Salzman 1985, pp. 151–2). Kingsmill Long's translation of 1625 may also have been motivated by the topical appropriateness of the romance's ending, in which a son of Hyanisbe (Queen Elizabeth I) marries the daughter of the French king. If a successor of Elizabeth I could be called her son, the story could be seen as a graceful allusion to Charles I's marriage to Henrietta Maria. By 1628 war between France and Britain was making nonsense out of the policy behind that marriage, and the 1628 translation may have been intended to remind the two kingdoms of their mutual interests.

Our desire to interpret literature in terms of a political code usually follows from the failure to crack its aesthetic code; we cannot be sure that the meaning most interesting to us was equally interesting to its original readers. How the seventeenth-century romances were read must always be a puzzle, though one to which there are clues. For instance, the margins of the British Library copy of Barclay's *Argenis* in its 1625 edition indicate that at least one reader took considerable interest in the political aspect of the book. He or she has set pointing fingers near the most obviously political passages, with marginal notes like '*A Discourse between POLI-ARCHUS and HYANISBE, touching Tribute and Impositions of Kings vpon their Subiets*' (p. 527), and the headings of their various arguments as 'Mixed monarchy', 'Monarchy absolute', and 'A Republique' (pp. 300–4). There is a good deal of underlining in the section where King Meleander enlarges on the need for princes to be fully informed in secret by their ambassadors (pp. 337–9). Political theory was not the annotator's only interest, however; the margins also draw attention to the 'description of an Elephant' (p. 309), to a medical discussion about the best cure for over-heated blood (p. 326) and to the use of ice-boxes in Africa as a way of enjoying fruits out of season (p. 348). Some of the underlining, indeed, is little more than an acknowledgement of the truth of moralising general-isations. Anyone who had the patience to look up all surviving copies of the book in search of other marginalia might be in a position to say more about reader response in the seventeenth century. The interest of this particular example lies in the annotator's evident view of the romance, not as an escapist fantasy, but as a realistic genre from which much can be learned.

The Caroline court has often been seen as an elaborate system of flattery, cut off from any knowledge of the real world: the compliments of the Court poets, it has been claimed, 'had the effect of inducing a self-com-placent and congratulatory attitude in the king and in some of his closest friends' (Wedgwood 1960, pp. 30–1). Annabel Patterson (1984) provides a useful corrective to this view in her chapter on 'The Royal Romance', which sets Charles's chivalric romance and Henrietta Maria's pastoralism in a political context and recognises its sophistication. Both the *Arcadia* and the *Argenis* depict more bad rulers than good ones; moreover, the most sympathetic characters in these books frequently find themselves, through the exigencies of the plot, in opposition to the absolute monarchy in which they and their author apparently believe. Musidorus and Pyrocles are (unjustly) accused of murdering the ruler of Arcadia; Amphialus is forced, through his mother's actions, to make war on him. Despite its frequently iterated advocacy of absolute monarchy, Barclay's *Argenis* portrays a hero, Poliarchus, who for much of the time is out of favour with the king and forced to live in hiding. Both Sidney's Basilius and Barclay's Meleander are weak kings. The fact is both politically important (both writers insist on the need for a strong monarchy) and crucial to the narrative structure, since much of the plot results from decisions taken in error by these rulers or taken behind their backs by dangerously powerful courtiers. The fact that some of the harshest portraits of incompetent kingship occur in the romance did not prevent it from being the most popular royalist form. Nor, I think, does it mean that romance authors were secretly attempting to subvert the society for which they wrote. They stress the king's enormous power for good or ill, but do not go on to argue that this power should therefore be limited; the consequences of such limitation are always shown to be disastrous.

A characteristic of seventeenth-century romance, as Patterson points out (1984, pp. 180–90), is that it often includes among its characters one or more writers, often somewhat comically presented, whose occasional verses (in both senses of the phrase) provide a running commentary on the action, sometimes even an alternative account of it. As a result of something in the air of the country, the entire population of Arcadia consists of compulsive poets. In the *Argenis*, Barclay uses the character of Nicompompus as a mouthpiece for, among other things, his view of his own role in the court setting. Thus, when some exceptionally flowery verses on a prince are read out, everyone laughs at the exaggerated flattery apart from Nicompompus, who argues that poetic genius often 'wanders from the truth, and indeed so much the more freely, because when she knowes, that whatsoeuer she faineth, is not beleeued, it rather is matter of innocent mirth, then of impudent lying' (1628, p. 235). As with some of Jonson's verses to his patrons, this comment suggests a highly sophisticated awareness of the element of game in court writing, the importance of rules, and the problem of distinguishing playfulness from insincerity.

Charles's court was, in any case, a sober place. His coronation had set the tone. The text chosen for the sermon at the ceremony in February 1626 had been Revelation 2:10: 'Be thou faithful unto death, and I will give thee a crown of life' (Wedgwood 1964, p. 15). The new king disconcerted some people by wearing a white suit instead of the conventional purple. It was apparently intended to symbolise 'that Virgin Purity with which he came to be espoused unto his Kingdom'; it was doubly appropriate, since he chose to be crowned on Candlemas Day, the feast of the Purification of the Virgin (Wordsworth 1892, pp. v, 6). Both the white suit and the sermon were later to be taken as prophetic of his 'martyrdom', but it would probably be better to see them as a fusion of religious seriousness with the behaviour of a romance hero.

Romance, however, also enabled the narration and thus the assimilation of potentially embarrassing events. The most obvious example was its idealisation of the relationship between Charles I and Henrietta Maria. No one could have been unaware that he had shown no interest in marrying her until after the breakdown of negotiations for the hand of the Spanish Infanta. As is well known, Middleton's highly successful *A Game at Chess* (1624) used allegory to transform the Prince's unsuccessful journey to Spain with Buckingham into a witty attack on the villainy of the Spaniards and a celebration of the heroism and intelligence by which, supposedly, the two English heroes had escaped the evil designs of their adversaries. Far from suppressing the sense that Charles was marrying, so to speak, on the rebound, court mythology incorporated it into the story. Charles and Buckingham had visited the French court on their way to Spain, and the Prince, in the first of the many disguises that he was to wear, caught a glimpse of Henrietta Maria taking part in a dance. He made the most of the episode in the letter with which he opened the marriage negotiations with France: 'my happiness has been completed by the honour which I have already had of seeing your person, although unknown to you; which sight has completely satisfied me that the exterior of your person in no degree belies the lustre of your virtues' (Green 1857, p. 5). Court poets later exploited the romantic possibilities of this story, and the king's secret passion for the French princess was invoked to explain why he had no better success with his courtship of the Spanish one. A French writer, looking back on the episode shortly after the king's execution, assured the queen that the entire Spanish journey had been only a pretext for seeing her, and that the fame of the prince's exploits became a subject for poets all over Europe (Cailloué 1649b, p. 4). Examples of the kind of thing he meant can be found in two of Waller's poems, which attempt to lift the episode to the dignity of epic. Charles is likened to Aeneas in his storm-tossed career; Waller has tact enough not to pursue the analogy to the point of turning the Infanta into an abandoned and despairing Dido, but he profits from the sense that the hero's destiny calls him to another bride. In 'Of the Danger His Majesty (being Prince) Escaped', Waller imagines the prince's roman- tic feelings when the ship, on its return journey, is in danger of shipwreck. Like Aeneas, he remains calm, but

> if any thought annoys
> The gallant youth, 'tis loves untasted joys,
> And dear remembrance of that fatal glance,
> For which he lately pawned his heart in France:
> Where he had seen a brighter nymph then she
> That sprung out of his present foe, the sea.
>
> (Waller 1901, lines 99–104)

Waller also imagines the French princess hearing the fame of the British prince and feeling a concealed passion for him. In 'To the Queen, Oc- casioned upon Sight of her Majesty's Picture', Waller reworks the idea, making the conflict take place in Charles himself, while he is watching her at the French court. At crucial moments in classical epic, the hero is sometimes enveloped in a cloud or given added lustre by some god. Both happen in quick succession to Aeneas when he first arrives at Carthage and astonishes Dido by suddenly appearing in a blaze of splendour. (The Lovelace poem discussed in the previous chapter may be drawing on the epic tradition as well as on recollections of Waller.) The disguised prince is compared to the clouded Aeneas, wondering whether to break forth or not:

> There, public care with private passion fought
> A doubtful combat in his noble thought.
> Should he confess his greatness, and his love,
> And the free faith of your great brother prove;
> With his Achates breaking through the cloud
> Of that disguise which did their graces shroud;
> And mixing with those gallants at the ball,
> Dance with the ladies, and outshine them all?
> Or on his journey o'er the mountains ride?   (lines 45–53)

While the notion of the disguised hero may be epic, the idea that he might reveal himself through his *dancing* – a compliment to Charles's starring role in so many court performances – transforms the genre from Virgilian epic to romance.

Another variation on the myth is so obliquely expressed that it seems never to have been recognised. Walter Montague's *The Shepherds Paradise*, performed in January 1633 by an all-female cast of the queen and her ladies, is now remembered chiefly because it contributed to William Prynne's punishment for writing *Histriomastix*, with its reference to actresses as 'notorious whores'. However, it is equally important for its elaborate and public transformation of the king's unsuccessful Spanish journey into a statement about his courtship of Henrietta Maria. Bellesa, the character played by the queen, is of foreign birth, a fact which is mentioned several times (no doubt to excuse her accent). She has come to the Shepherds' Paradise in disguise, because, although she is contracted to Prince Basilino, she has learned that he loves someone else, and wants to avoid embarrassing him or demeaning herself. Basilino and a friend, having finally gained the king's permission to travel, come to the same place, also in disguise, after his rejection by his first love. He falls in love with the disguised Bellesa and discusses his predicament with her in the third person. It is his view that 'our minds are but love's pupills at the first. Which fit themselves but to proceed and take degrees, and so our second love is a degree wherein our soules attaine to experience that imploys it selfe in loves refinement' (Montague 1659, p. 62). She calmly agrees: 'I do confesse the Prince for many reasons might not only be allowed but wished a second, and succesfull love: that he may know our Sex have joyes that may outprise his sufferings' (p. 63). Under all the flowery language, this is a surprisingly frank recreation of what had actually happened eight years before. It was possible to acknowledge it, because it was also a recognised tragicomedy plot. Perry Gethner's cataloguing of the various formulae used in French tragicomedy shows that one of the 'Most Common Scenarios' of plays with kings among their characters is the one he calls 'Reason lost and regained', in which the ruler falls in love with the wrong person, or is estranged from the right one, but undergoes a drastic metamorphosis enabling a happy ending to take place (Gethner 1987, pp. 187–8).

The dominant roles that Henrietta Maria played in Montague's play and the court masques indicate the importance of women in romance, and thus in court culture. Sometimes they are active in the plot, sometimes their passive courage is celebrated, sometimes they are called on to exercise their acknowledged gift for dissembling. In *Salmacida Spolia* (1640), the last court masque, Henrietta Maria played an Amazon. Her letters to her husband during the 1640s suggest that she saw herself as one of those heroic female warriors who are minor figures in the classical epic but central to the Renaissance one. It was the visibility of women on the royalist side, as much as their actions, that inspired hostility from parliamentarians. Thomas May's *History of Parliament*, 1647, commented contemptuously on the large number of women present at Strafford's trial, obviously on the side of the defendant (1854, p. 91). It was Charles's supposed subservience to 'female advice', as revealed when his letters were published after Naseby, that later aroused the most unfavourable comment. The author of *The Life and Death of King Charles, or, the Pseudo-Martyr Discovered* advises royalists not to care for a king who cared so little for them, being 'overpowred with the Inchantments of a Woman' (1650, p. 214). This is itself the language of romance being turned on the romantic hero (as in Milton's 'fondly overcome with female charm'). In defending the role of women and of the private life, romance allows the major religious differences between the king and queen, and the hostility between their two countries, to be glossed over by the myth of a love which transcends conflict. Those who attack romance want that conflict to be fought out openly, not transcended.

The aesthetic of tragicomedy

Like Lovelace, in the poem examined in the last chapter, Waller's poems and Montague's play depicted the royal couple wearing disguises which both did and did not conceal the true majesty beneath. This attitude to the 'naturalness' of hierarchy is also part of a larger aesthetic principle which has been emerging from a number of the attitudes already discussed. It is the contrast between the literal translation and the 'free' one, between the fragmented emblematic art and the synthesis of the painter who makes 'the thing orientally the same', as Lovelace put it. The notion that the real nature of things shines through their aesthetic representation, rather than being superimposed on them through the addition of symbolic devices, is potentially a programme for psychological realism. Indeed, without some such programme, this kind of art is meaningless. Yet both romance and tragicomedy are mixed genres which embrace diversity as a structural principle. The romance narrative is interspersed with letters, verses, and descriptions of masques or other events, often separately indexed for the benefit of the reader who might want to create a new kind of text on subsequent readings. Tragicomedy, the dramatic manifestation of romance, is a self-conscious hybrid.

It is necessary, however, to distinguish the juxtaposing of the two forms and the true mixture of the two. It was this distinction which was the basis of Guarini's influential discussion of the new genre in the *Compendio della Poesia Tragicomica* published along with his *Pastor Fido* in 1602. A mixture, the poet insisted, was not a coupling of heterogenous forms but a blending or tempering of extremes in order to create a third, distinct form. His analogies for tragicomedy were the republic (a tempering of the extremes of monarchy and democracy) and the well-balanced humours of the healthy human body. Like other Renaissance theorists, he took Aristotle's metaphor of *catharsis* to apply not only to tragedy but also to comedy: thus, if the former purged pity and terror (that is, in his interpretation, the unhealthy extremes of both), the latter was a purge for melancholy. It is clear from the *Compendio*, however, that Guarini, despite his ostensible admiration for the ancients, actually felt that both their comedies and their tragedies were limited by the violent and primitive religion which had produced them. Christianity, he argues (Guarini 1914, p. 245), already contains the rules for a virtuous life; spectators do not need to be frightened into respect for the gods by seeing their terrible power displayed in a story such as that of *Oedipus*.

His own play, therefore, is a reversal of the *Oedipus Tyrannus*, with the workings of a benevolent Providence replacing those of a blind Fate. Whereas the prophecies and oracles of Sophocles are inescapable, those of *Il Pastor Fido* are only conditional, and can be averted by the virtuous actions of human beings. At the climax, the shepherd Mirtillo is saved from execution when a series of elaborately interlocking revelations culminate in his being recognised as the son of the priest who was lifting the axe to sacrifice him. Mirtillo had been lost in infancy, and the servant who went in search of him had lied about his whereabouts because of an oracle declaring that, should the child ever return home, 'he should be like to die / By's Father's hand' (Fanshawe 1964a, v.v.4908–9). The discovery of Mirtillo's true parentage makes possible the fulfilment of another oracle. Arcadia has been suffering under a curse which, according to Diana, will be lifted only by the marriage of 'two of race divine' and the sacrifice of a faithful shepherd. At the point where Mirtillo's identity is revealed, he has already fulfilled the second part of the oracle by offering to die for his beloved Amaryllis, falsely accused of infidelity and thus sentenced to death under Arcadian law. Since he has turned out to be 'of race divine', he is now able to marry her and make the prophecy complete.

Guarini's analysis of his own work in the *Compendio* stresses that its two plots are so inextricably linked that the same discovery serves to resolve both at once. Thus, although the subplot relationship of Silvio and Dorinda depends partly on a psychological change in the young man's character, it is the discovery of Mirtillo's true identity which frees Amaryllis and Silvio from the marriage which is being forced on them, thus enabling the two couples to recombine and marry for love. Guarini's images for his plot are curiously suggestive: it is like the single thread which led Theseus out of the labyrinth (p. 284); it is also seductive, like the beautiful woman who teases one with a glimpse, now of her face, now of her bosom, thus luring one on to wish to see more of her (p. 277). In the play, the shepherds see the discovery of Mirtillo's birth as itself a monstrous birth, though it turns out instead to be a miraculous one. Like the sun through the clouds, comedy breaks through the gloom of potentially tragic situations, revealing the reality of divine providence in human affairs. The ruler's own divinity also breaks through, despite the errors caused by his mysterious birth or the disguise he has assumed. Thus, as in the Lovelace poem on Lely's painting, an aesthetic principle is also a political one.

Despite the attention given to the definition of tragicomedy by Guarini, and by Fletcher in his preface to *The Faithful Shepherdess* (c. 1609), the use of the term in seventeenth-century England is by no means straightforward. 'Tragicomedy' can mean a play containing both tragic and comic elements, or a mixture of high characters with low actions. It can also be used, metaphorically, as a description of the mixed nature of public events. By the mid-seventeenth century, although it still retained all those senses, it had social as well as aesthetic connotations. This is partly because of its association with the sophisticated theories of Guarini and other continental writers, and partly because it had been the favourite mode of the courtier playwrights of the immediate pre-war era. Whereas Berkeley, Carlell, Davenant, and Thomas Killigrew published plays which were designated on the title page as tragicomedies, and the term was also used for *The Two Noble Kinsmen*, first published in 1634, it was not applied to any of the works of Brome or Shirley, writers for the popular theatre. As late as 1647, the Beaumont and Fletcher Folio was called simply *Comedies and Tragicomedies*, although many of its contents were retitled tragicomedies in the second, post-Restoration edition. On the other hand, William Cartwright's works, which had strong royalist associations, were published in 1651 as *Comedies, Tragi-comedies, with Other Poems*. The term had obviously become fashionable, and a good selling point among the readers who might be expected to buy playbooks. Hence, Cosmo Manuche published two 'tragicomedies' in 1652; Shirley's *Six New Plays* (1653) included three 'tragicomedies', and even *The Witch of Edmonton*, first performed in 1621, appeared in 1658 as 'A known true Story. Composed into A Tragi-Comedy by divers well-esteemed Poets'. John Tatham's *Love Crowns the End*, called 'A Pastoral' in its first edition of 1640, became a 'tragicomedy' when it was reissued with another play in 1657. Particularly significant is one work which did *not* call itself a tragicomedy, Richard Flecknoe's *Love's Dominion*. Flecknoe published it in 1653 as 'A Drama-tique Piece, Full of Excellent Moralitie; Written as a Pattern for the Reformed Stage'. His avoidance of the world 'tragicomedy' is probably deliberate. In 1653 he was treading very warily, in the hope of getting permission to produce the play in England, and he took the precaution of dedicating it to Cromwell's daughter, Lady Claypole. After the Resto-ration, the play, revised and retitled *Love's Kingdom*, was published as 'a Pastoral Tragicomedy'.

The plays that actually received surreptitious performance are known, in most cases, only because the performance was interrupted by government soldiers. If they are typical of what the public most wanted to see, then they add to the evidence that tragicomedy was regarded as a particularly royalist form of drama: they include Beaumont and Fletcher's *A King and No King* in 1648 and Thomas Killigrew's *Claracilla* in 1652 (Hotson 1928, pp. 26, 49–50). John Evelyn recorded that he 'saw a *Tragie-Comedie* acted in the Cock-pit' on 3 February 1648, at a time when the latest and strictest Parliamentary Ordinance against plays was being prepared for publication (Evelyn 1955, vol. II, p. 539). In a private performance of 1654 Dorothy Osborne acted the heroine of William Berkeley's *The Lost Lady*, first performed and published (as a 'tragicomedy') in 1638 (Osborne 1928, pp. 172–3). In a letter of 23 April 1654 the son of Edward Nicholas expressed his disapproval of the acting of *A King and No King* by the Princess Royal's household in Holland, and his father agreed that it looked 'As if Cromwell himself had made choice of and appointed it of purpose to have thrown scorn on the king' (Nicholas 1955, p. 267). The fact that Nicholas responded primarily to the title's satiric implications for the situation of Charles II, whereas the Princess and her household were presumably untroubled by them, shows the difficulty of generalising about the interpretation of codes.

The illegal performance of *Mucedorus* in 1653 deserves separate con-sideration, because it inspired some interesting comments on the signifi-cance of the genre. The play was performed by a group of amateur actors who took it on tour in Oxfordshire, playing, as far as can be guessed, to a socially mixed audience. Apparently the old piece, vaguely based on the *Arcadia*, was still a crowd-puller, more than fifty years after its first performance. At seven o'clock on a Sunday night, while nearby Oxford was keeping a day of fasting and prayer, at least three hundred people gathered to see it in a room at the White Hart Inn at Witney, Oxfordshire.

The play opens with a dialogue between Comedy and Envy, who differ considerably over what kind of play should be performed. Whereas Comedy wants to tell a happy story, Envy insists on warlike sounds and battles. The arbitrariness of the action is thus explained, as in some other sixteenth-century entertainments, by the conflicting effects on the plot of two arbitrary powers. 'I'll interrupt your mirth,' Envy promises, 'And mix your music with a tragic end.' The hostility between Comedy and Envy must have had a topical edge in the Witney performance, since the reason the play was being given at an inn was that the local authorities had refused the actors permission to use the town hall. In the play as written, Comedy triumphs. Despite the obstacles put in his way by Envy, the disguised prince eventually marries the princess whose life he has saved. At Witney, the story never got this far. About two-thirds of the way through the performance, the floor collapsed beneath the spectators, leaving several dead and many injured.

The occasion afforded an excellent opportunity for the Presbyterian minister John Rowe, an Oxford Fellow and Lecturer at Witney. Shortly after the disaster he published a pamphlet called *Tragi-Comaedia*, consisting mainly of the sermon which he had preached at the time. His introductory narrative has been of great interest to theatre historians because it gives a full account of the production, including a diagram of the hall in which it was performed.[1] Rowe had also taken the trouble to read the play, from which he quoted the lines spoken by Envy that had turned out to be prophetic. In choosing a title with theatrical associations for an attack on the theatre, he was following the example of Beard's *Theatre of God's Judgments* (1597) and Prynne's division of his *Histriomastix* (1633) into 'acts' and 'scenes'.

Rowe's definition of tragicomedy was clearly not the same as, say, Guarini's. His primary reason for using the word seems to have been that 'the Comedy being turned into a Tragedy, it had a sad *Catastrophe*' (Rowe, 1653, sig. ¶¶ᵛ). In other words, it had become a 'tragic comedy' like Fernando de Rojas's *Celestina* (translated by James Mabbe in 1631), which begins in pleasure but ends in grief and retribution. Rowe probably also knew that Plautus had defined the genre in the prologue to *Amphitryon* as a comedy in which kings and gods appear. He had no doubt that God had indeed appeared in Witney, making it 'a publick theatre whereon he would manifest his holynesse, justice, & other Attributes to the world', and he warned his congregation, 'If you do not repent, some worse thing will come upon you. It may be the Lord will send a Fire next to consume your houses.' Rowe's God was a jealous God, and the part He had played in

Witney sounds rather like that of Envy. While the players, and the play, were attempting to imitate divine providence in the workings of their romantic plot, the true Author of all events had created a tragic parody.

Rowe's sense of tragicomedy as the tension between the world of the play and the world outside the play helps to explain the otherwise puzzling use of the term to describe other, very different works of the period. The earliest political satire to call itself a tragicomedy is Richard Braithwait's *Mercurius Britannicus* (1641). Its title associates it with the news-sheets and implies that it will be up-to-date, while the phrase on its title page, 'A Tragi-Comedy, At Paris', might mean either, as Martin Butler (1984) suggests, that it had been performed there, or that Braithwait had been influenced by the French tradition of satire in play form; the *mazarinades* of the Fronde include short semi-dramatic satires which have much in common with those of the 1640s in England. Braithwait's play, first written in Latin, deals with the aftermath of the Ship-Money controversy in a highly sophisticated imitation of classical tragedy, with a Chorus and a Ghost (that of Coriolanus, who represents Strafford), but, as it was written *in medias res*, it is unclear whether the ending will be tragic or comic: Heraclitus and Democritus, who act as commentators, represent the two extremes of response. The author's own attitude was clearly mixed. The play is written in only four acts, but the first English edition ends with an Epilogue explaining that 'the next day (by Joves permission) the fift Act shall bee acted upon Tyber, I should say Tyburne, by a new Society of Abalmaites.' As in Rowe's pamphlet, the reader is reminded of the ironic contrast between the ending in the play, and the ending, still to come, in the world outside. It is God who will determine the ending – and thus, also, the genre of the play.

Fanshawe and Il Pastor Fido

While no other tragicomedy of the period is deliberately left incomplete, there are many which require to be completed by the reader's awareness of their context. As has often been noticed, pastoral language and settings are frequently turned into an allegory of pre-war England – a 'world without the world', as Fanshawe put it in his 'Ode' of 1630 – whose inhabitants, like Virgil's farmers in the *Georgics*, lack only the sense to appreciate their own happiness (Fanshawe 1964b, p. 6). In a privately performed masque of 1640 by Mildmay Fane, Earl of Westmorland, the character representing England bears a shield depicting 'a Shepheard Swaine asleepe whilest his flocks are feeding about him representing Security with this word –

4   Jean-François Nicéron, perspective picture showing how facets of different heads of former popes were combined to make up a composite head of the present one; from *La Perspective Curieuse* (1638)

ffoelices Nimium, Bona si sua Norint' (Fane 1938, lines 155–9). Like Braithwait, Fane was expressing ambivalent political feelings. If the Virgilian tag is an indictment of an ungrateful and complaining nation, the over-secure, careless shepherd may be meant for Charles I. Another of Fane's masques of the same year, *Candy Restored*, depicts an afflicted country which, thanks to Dr Psynodarke (Parliament), is instantly transformed from wasteland to forest and pasture (Fane 1938). A stage device designed for use in masques (revolving wings) becomes a symbol of the quick change needed in the 'real' world. In its presentation of polarised oppositions which are then resolved, or dissolved, without conflict, the masque appeals to the same desires and needs that are fulfilled by tragicomedy.

Fanshawe could hardly have failed to read Guarini's *Compendio*. Politically speaking, he is unlikely to have been sympathetic toward the Italian poet's analogy between the balancing of the extremes in tragicomedy and that in the republic. But he might well have been attracted to its implied third world of an Arcadian kingdom in which class distinctions were as blurred as literary genres. The golden age may have been a time of equality, but, as Guarini understood it, some shepherds were much more equal than others. In the dedication to his translation of *Pastor Fido*, Fanshawe refers to a picture in Paris made up of small faces (the ancestors of the Chancellor) which, through a perspective glass, revealed itself as 'a single portrait in great of the *Chancellor* himself, the Painter thereby intimating, that in him alone are contracted the Vertues of all his Progenitors; or perhaps by a more subtile Philosophy demonstrating, how the *Body Politick* is composed of many *naturall ones*' (Fanshawe 1964a, pp. 3–4). What Fanshawe was describing was not a composite picture like the famous frontispiece to Hobbes's *Leviathan*, but the type of 'Perspective Curieuse' devised by the Jesuit Jean-François Nicéron. Nicéron's rather crude drawing (plate 4) shows how one such perspective worked. The picture visible to the unaided eye depicted the face of Christ surrounded by the faces of various former popes. When the spectator looked through a special glass, facets of each portrait (here indicated by dotted lines) combined to become the face of the current pope, occupying precisely the part of the picture formerly occupied by Christ (Nicéron 1638, pp. 115–18). The political/religious message of this picture is obvious, and Fanshawe understood it perfectly: as he wrote, the individual faces existed only for the sake of their role in the composite picture, 'first and chiefest in the Painter's designe'. Nicéron's art symbolises, not the tempering of monarchy and democracy which Guarini describes, but the absolutism which absorbs and transcends all the power of its separate components.

Some aspects of the *Compendio*, however, would have been congenial to Fanshawe's political views. Guarini had implied that tragedy, far from being the perfect form of which tragicomedy represents a corruption, is really a crude and violent solution to the difficulties which tragicomedy resolves in a more civilised way (Guarini 1914, pp. 245–6). It was probably while he was working on his translation of *Il Pastor Fido* that Fanshawe wrote his poem 'On the Earle of *Straffords* Tryall'. Though he presents Strafford as a self-sacrificing tragic hero, Fanshawe also makes it clear that he becomes this only when circumstances alter the genre of the play in which he is performing. What fascinates Fanshawe, more than the Earl's courage at his execution, is his skilful handling of his celebrated trial, in which he insisted on meeting his adversaries' charges point by point. This long and patient unravelling of their 'plot' makes him a counterpart of the tragicomic writer who refuses to fall back on the facile device of a *deus ex machina* (in this case, the king's promise of protection):

> As artless Poets *Jove* or *Juno* use,
> To play the Mid-wife to their labouring Muse.   (1964b, lines 7–8)

By contrast, Fanshawe suggests, Strafford had played by the rules, and therefore behaved like a supremely conscientious artist:

> No, he affects a labour'd Scene, and not
> To *cut*, but to *untye* the Gordian Knot[;]
> Then if 'twill prove no *Comedy*, at least
> To make it of all *Tragedies* the best.   (lines 9–12)

The image of the Gordian knot is an important one in this period. Alexander's action in cutting it is sometimes seen as an example of the admirable decisiveness and practicality of the man of action. Fanshawe, like many royalists at the end of the war, is reacting against military values. He links the 'untying' of the knot to the concept of the dramatic *dénouement*, the process by which a complex action is brought to an aesthetically satisfying ending. Guarini had taken particular pride in threading his plot through a labyrinth and solving it all with a single 'discovery'. Jonson's *Volpone* works a similar effect when Volpone removes his disguise; his action is greeted with the comment, 'The knot is now undone by miracle' – not only a cry of relief but the author's comment on his own skill. For Fanshawe, then, the play which Strafford had tried to create is associated with the noble or royal craftsman imitating the secret purposes of God; the cruder kind of tragedy is a second best, forced upon him by his unsubtle and villainous opponents. Thus,

> for his lifes *last act*,
> *Times* shall admiring read it, and *this age*,
> Though now it hisse, claps when he leaves the Stage.   (lines 14–16)

Fanshawe's poem, although it is only one of many which use the stage/scaffold analogy, seems to me a more likely inspiration for Marvell's

'Horatian Ode' than many which have been suggested. Charles's consent to Strafford's death was the one error for which he consistently blamed himself, even in his speech on the scaffold. It would be difficult for any writer to avoid thinking of the parallel between the two events.

Fanshawe's translation of *Il Pastor Fido* was originally presented to the Prince of Wales in 1646. Its first edition, in 1647, may not have been intended for public sale (Greg 1939–59, vol. II, p. 759). In 1648, however, its rights were sold to Humphrey Moseley, who characteristically brought it out in an edition emphasising the topical relevance of the work. The title page draws attention to the play's dedication to Prince Charles and to other works now included for the first time, particularly the 'short Discourse of the Long Civill Warres of Rome'. The reader is invited to expect parallels with contemporary events. These become immediately apparent in Fanshawe's dedication, with its description of the sick kingdom:

> a gasping *State* (once the most flourishing in the world): *A wild Boar (the Sword)* depopulating the *Country: the Pestilence* unpeopling the *Towns*; their gods themselves in the mercilesse *humane Sacrifices* exacting bloody contribution from *both*; and the *Priests* (a *third Estate of misery*) bearing the burden of *all* in the *Chorus*.
>
> (Fanshawe 1964a, p. 4)

Fanshawe suggested that the young man should see in the play 'a *Lantskip* of these Kingdoms, (your *Royall Patrimony*) as well in the former flourishing, as the present distractions thereof' (p. 5).

Guarini's play had a topical meaning: its allusion to the beneficent effects of a royal marriage had been a compliment to another Charles – Carlo Emmanuel, Duke of Savoy. Perhaps, Fanshawe suggests to the prince, the parallel between Britain and Arcadia might extend to a happy ending in the future:

> and also your self a great Instrument of it. Whether by some happy Royall Marriage (as in this *Pastorall*, and the case of *Savoy*, to which it alludes) thereby uniting a miserably divided people in a publick joy; or by such other wayes and means as it may have pleased *the Divine Providence* to ordain for an *end of our woe*; I leave to that Providence to determine. (p. 5)

If Fanshawe is deliberately vague in indicating the various ways in which Prince Charles might resemble Mirtillo, he makes up for it in his translation of the oracle, which is undoubtedly slanted towards the contemporary British predicament:

> Your woe shall end when two of Race Divine
> Love shall combine:
> And for a faithlesse Nymphs apostate state
> A faithfull Shepherd supererogate.
>
> (I.ii. 569–72)

As his editor points out in a note on the passage (p. 167), the precise translation of Guarini's 'di donna infedel l'antico errore' would be 'the ancient error of that unfaithful woman'. Fanshawe's 'apostate state', and his rendering of '*ammende*' (make amends) by the legal and religious term 'supererogate', must be intended to associate the faithless Lucrina with Britain herself, or that portion of it which had forsaken her king and church. His interpretation of the oracle naturally emphasised its more hopeful side – the averted tragedy, the reconciliation symbolised by marriage. In 1646 these hopes might not have seemed impossible. By 1648, they must have rung rather hollow. If either the king or the prince were to play the role of the Faithful Shepherd, he ran the risk of being a genuine sacrifice for the salvation of his country and experiencing not only the danger but also the death. Strafford's case was an obvious precedent.

Pamphlet tragicomedies

The publication of Fanshawe's translation coincided with the appearance of a number of short satiric pamphlets in dramatic form, many of which are called tragicomedies. Like Braithwait's *Mercurius Britannicus*, they are journalistic works, ascribed to the authors of the royalist mercuries; they differ from the numerous other dialogue pamphlets of the period in that they allude to and often parody the drama. Far from blending the tragic and comic elements, these plays juxtapose them with startling results. They are sometimes published as 'interludes' or 'comedies'. The best term for most of them would probably be 'mock-heroic'. Since they usually feature caricatures of parliamentarians, either generic types or historical characters, the dramatist tends to stress their 'lowness' (and, still more, that of their wives) through bombastic parodies of tragic style. Fanshawe's image of Strafford trying to untie the Gordian knot may be compared with the scene in which the eponymous hero of *Craftie Cromwell* (1648), 'the embleme of *Democracie*' (ii.i), announces his intention of making himself king and adds that he intends to satisfy the people's doubts 'As Alexander Gordius Knots untied'. The point is not simply that he is presented as a villain, but that, as a 'low' character, he has not even the right to aspire to tragic status. He is thus violating not only social but generic norms.

The various kinds of decorum go together. Simon Shepherd has suggested that, under Elizabeth I, the concept of linguistic decorum was an instrument of social control; Puritan preaching was condemned because 'it questioned rule of state and broke rules of form' (Shepherd 1986, p. 6), while 'a hierarchic perception is written into the reader's experience of the text' in its distinction between the 'high' style appropriate for the deeds of princes and the 'low' one used for common men (p. 8). Later writers deliberately link the breaking of decorum to the confusion of 'the times'. *Mercurius Melancholicus* both describes and, stylistically, embodies its horrified amazement at the imminent breakdown of the social hierarchy:

Ere long we shall have King James his reckoning on't, higly-pigly, all fellowes at football, hang this distance and this difference among men, Joan's as good as my lady, why should one be above another, one richer than another? Elder-brethren must have all, and the younger starve? No, no, wee'le have a Platonicall community, we will, aye marry will we.   (28 Oct.–4 Nov. 1647)

When such writers express this confusion in dramatic terms, they turn to an old-fashioned dramaturgy. Emphasis on the barbarity of the past may be a royalist reaction to parliamentary emphasis on getting back to older, purer times. A royalist news-sheet claimed that the arguments of its opponent, *Mercurius Britanicus*, 'would become the Tragedy of Doctor Faustus*, or rather a Puppet play farre better', while its attempts at verse and humour 'might have done well to make your great grandfather laugh in his Trunkes, or to be uttered in galloping rimes by a Vice in a Play, or the Clownes part' (*Britanicus Vapulans*, n.d. [Frank 1961 suggests Nov. 1648]). The devil, vice and clown were the symbols of a primitive, popular, naive drama which was supposed to have been reformed first by Shakespeare, and then, still more thoroughly, by Jonson and Fletcher. This view of the history of drama can be found in some of the commendatory verses to the Beaumont and Fletcher Folio of 1647, but it also recurs in the 1650s and after. Writers confidently describe the drama before 1600, most of which they had obviously never read, as a ludicrous mixture of styles and periods. There was supposed to have been a 'play of Adam and Eve' in which 'the good grandam is brought in with two or three waiting maides attending her, and in Paradise too, when there were but two in all the world' (Gayton 1654, p. 272). Even Marvell claims in *The Rehearsal Transprosed* (1672) to have heard of an Elizabethan touring company which put on a play in which Moses tried to persuade Julius Caesar not to cross the Rubicon (Marvell 1971, pp. 141–2). In keeping with this pseudo-history of drama, the quasi-dramatic satires on Puritans and Parliament mix real and allegorical characters and give their villains a language reminiscent of third-rate Marlowe.

The most interesting of the political 'tragicomedies' is probably *Craftie Cromwell* (1648), the two parts of which are attributed, respectively, to *Mercurius Melancholicus* and (probably falsely) *Mercurius Pragmaticus*; it belongs to the group of works associated with the Crouches (see chapter 1) and could have been written by any of the numerous authors involved in their pamphleteering factory. The prologue to part 1 explains why the plays are called tragicomic:

> Smooth *PLAUTUS, ARISTOPHANES* his veine
> We now affect, not SOPHOCLES high straine:
> Yet thus we differ, they for mirth were fixt,
> But we have *Joy* and *Dolor*, both commixt.

Tragicomedy, here, comes close to 'satura', the 'mixture' which is etymologically related to 'satire'. On this principle, apparently, each scene of part 1 of *Craftie Cromwell* has as little as possible to do with its predecessor. A serious discussion of contemporary politics by two merchants is followed by the appearance of the Ghost of Pym. The latter draws a curtain to reveal the sleeping Cromwell, who awakes and, inspired by his vision of the ghost, announces that he is determined to make himself ruler. The play also includes a conjuring scene, a soliloquy showing the irresolution of the King's jailer, Colonel Hammond, a drunken scene between two soldiers, and a final council scene where Cromwell and the other independents agree that the King must be destroyed. A Chorus attempts to put things in a wider perspective, lamenting the state of England and urging the common people to rise in support of the imprisoned Charles I.

The journalistic nature of *Craftie Cromwell*, like that of *Mercurius Britannicus*, made an ending hard to devise. Like other writers of pamphlet-plays, its author or authors therefore drew on the tragicomedy tradition of prophecies and oracles. These enabled the play to express royalist hopes without positively having to prove that they were justified. In part 1, two Jesuits conjure up the devil Behemoh (*sic*) and ask to know the future. He obliges with this:

> When the time comes that you shall see
> A headlesse Body Active be,
> And many horrid Deeds perform'd
> By a Trunk, without an Head adorn'd;
> If that same Body and the Head
> By Friendly Hands be soldered,
> Then happy Dayes may chance ensue,
> Or else for aye bid Peace adue.   (sig. B2ᵛ)

Though, with hindsight, this conditional prophecy sounds both ominous and true, it actually refers to the same outcome that Fanshawe believed to be symbolised by the averted execution and the marriage in *The Faithful*

Shepherd: reunion between king (head) and Parliament (body). The play's true ending, however, is left – literally – in the hands of its readers. Part I ends with a Chorus saying that Cromwell's ambition will be unstoppable unless

> some brave soule for vertue stand,
> And send his soule into Enio's hand. (sig. B4ᵛ)

In other words, the 'brave souls' among the readers of this play are being openly incited to assassinate Cromwell. In Part II the threat is somewhat less open: Cromwell is seen crowning himself king, but a song 'behind the arras' warns that the sword of Damocles hangs over unlawful rulers.

What is tragic and what is comic in such militant plays depends on where the reader stands. *The Scottish Politick Presbyter Slain by an English Independent* (1647), an allegory about the three-cornered struggle among royalists, presbyterians, and independents, ends when Anarchy, the independent, finds the presbyterian, Directory, in bed with his wife. He kills him, declaring, 'In thy death, *England* gathers Life, / Whose Happiness I wish' (v.i). So the 'tragic' ending is also a comic one – if the reader happens to share the author's political opinions.

Post-execution romance: Davenant's *Gondibert*

The Osborn collection at Yale contains a manuscript continuation of the *Arcadia*, thought to have been written by a member of the Digby family, which transforms the work into a *roman-à-clef*. In Book VI an oracle offers a glimpse of the future of Arcadia. It is evident that the author is writing with hindsight:

> And when that peace is by all good men sought,
> Then nought, but blood, is by these rebells thought;
> Who shall theire native country soe annoye,
> That they both King and kingdome will destroye:
> All this shall happen, that is toulde to thee;
> Before that twice sev'n ages passed bee.
> (*History of Arcadia*, p. 62)

The work ends with the beheading of the king, the execution of three royalist lords shortly after, and Parliament's edict against proclaiming a successor to him. Thus, the author concludes, 'they turned the fabrike of Monarchiale goverment [*sic*], into a confused chaos of Democracie and fulfilled the tenour of what the oracle to Basileus delivered in Delphos, by the end both of the King and Kingdome of Arcadia, wherewith this my history also, of Arcadia shall have an ende.' For this author at any rate, Arcadia's existence *as Arcadia* is totally dependent on its monarchical form of government. The 'confused chaos of Democracie' is simply not material from which to make romance or tragicomedy in the manner of Sidney. Not only the kingdom but the genre itself is thus destroyed by the king's execution.

What, then, does it mean when Sir William Davenant adopts the romance narrative mode in the period immediately following this event? Like Braithwait's tragicomedy, Davenant's *Gondibert* (1651) is incomplete. The reason for this is stated in the wry postscript which occurs halfway through Book III, and thus halfway through the projected poem:

> though I intended in this POEM to strip Nature naked, and clothe her again in the perfect shape of Vertue; yet even in so worthy a Designe I shall ask leave to desist, when I am interrupted by so great an experiment as Dying.
>
> (Davenant 1971, p. 250)

The author was in fact in prison and expecting execution at any moment. A poem written in such circumstances is bound to invite the reader to search for a political allegory. *Gondibert*'s editor, David Gladish, suggests that it is 'a veiled commentary on some of the spectacular events and personages of Davenant's lifetime', and offers a tentative key to it (pp. xxiii and xiv–xv). On the other hand, Earl Miner, though he recognises that Davenant's postscript licenses such speculation by mentioning his intention of presenting the reader with the 'Keys' to his building, nevertheless feels that '*Topical events illuminate the narrative, not the reverse*'; the italics are his (Miner 1974, p. 75). To take only one of many examples, the most obvious problem about identifying the exemplary Gondibert and the villainous Oswald with Charles I and Cromwell respectively is that the former kills the latter in the fourth canto of the first book. Moreover, royalists themselves were divided in their reception of *Gondibert*; Cowley, Waller, and Vaughan wrote in its praise, while Denham was one of those who in 1653 published verses ridiculing and parodying it. If Denham had regarded *Gondibert* as a straightforward example of royalist hagiography, it is unlikely that he would have considered it a suitable target for ridicule. Admittedly, there seems to have been an open season where Davenant was concerned, and there may have been other reasons, such as his conversion to Catholicism, to explain his apparent unpopularity with some of his own side. It may even be, given the fondness of the court circle for 'flytings' and private games, that the attacks are less vicious than they appear.

Another reason for the difficulty of interpretation is that Davenant seems to have wanted to make his poem as remote as possible from the present day. The epic poem usually draws on a shared world of memory and belief, reminding the listener/reader how the actions of its characters have influenced later history. The romance does the same thing more playfully. In *Gondibert* there is no such common ground. Its story, although supposedly historical, is far from being well known. The task of writing it is a race against time, 'ere my remnant of Life's Lamp be spent, / Whilst I in Lab'rinths stray amongst the Dead' (II.viii.84). Davenant repeatedly stresses the fact that his heroes need to be brought back from the darkness by the poet, himself envisaged as a man groping among labyrinths and tombs with a torch which may soon go out. His best-known innovation, the abandonment of the supernatural and of figures from pagan religions, removes the prophecies and oracles which normally show the relevance of the interests of the poem to those of its readers. The only obvious link between the two occurs through a prediction about the future development of science. Davenant accepts the view that many discoveries have been made in the past and then lost. Astragon's palace, an obviously Baconian establishment, has already found the loadstone and developed the heliocentric view of the universe. Yet these, we are told, will disappear from view and need to be rediscovered. One character, learning about the loadstone, predicts that the rediscovery will take place at a time when true religion needs to escape its enemies by sailing to 'Heav'n's reserv'd World'. in the West (II.vi.32). As he wrote this, Davenant was no doubt thinking already of his own forthcoming journey to America, which in the preface he calls 'another world'. He had originally been meant to act as secretary to Sir William Berkeley, the Governor of Virginia, another devoted royalist and fellow-playwright (author of *The Lost Lady*). Berkeley had been particularly assiduous in welcoming Church of England exiles and preventing Puritan settlement in his territory, which might thus have seemed like 'heav'n's reserv'd World'. Davenant's mission was later changed, and he was named governor of Maryland; on his way there, his ship was intercepted and he finished up under sentence of death. Thus, the one prediction that is confidently made in the poem turns out to be false as far as the poet himself is concerned.

Gondibert seems a strangely trivial story for a man of Davenant's experience to write at a time of personal and national crisis. Its chief concern is not whether the hero will defeat his rival Oswald (this happens early in the poem) but rather whether he will be able to avoid marrying Rhodalind, the princess of Lombardy, and becoming heir to the throne. This destiny, which might attract most romance heroes, has no appeal for

Gondibert, who has fallen in love with Birtha, the daughter of the magus Astragon. The absence of a clear political bias is one of the reasons why the reader is left in real suspense as to how Davenant proposed to extricate his characters from their difficulties. Which girl was Gondibert to marry? The answer would have implications for the poem's philosophy. Rhodalind stands for a life of public importance, Birtha for private life, though not for withdrawal from the world: her father's studies lead to discoveries of practical use, and she herself is a herbalist. Davenant seems more interested in Astragon and Birtha than in the world of the court. Yet the poem's stress on the importance of an active and responsible life seems to require Gondibert to accept Aribert's designation of him as his heir. At one point Gondibert gives Birtha a jewel which will change colour if he ever betrays her; narrative economy requires that he should eventually do just that. Moreover, she, unlike Rhodalind, has a waiting list of suitors ready to console her. It is possible, as Gladish suggests (p. xxii), that some way might have been found to give Gondibert both public and private fulfil-ment. What seems clear, however, is that, if any happiness is to be achieved in the poem, a large number of people are going to have to learn to love their second choice. The romantic notion of instant and eternal love is heavily qualified by the sense of the secret workings of time, which changes people's minds and enables them to accept what at first seemed unbearable. As *The Shepherds Paradise* had accommodated the romantic marriage of Charles and Henrietta to the brute facts of their history, perhaps *Gondi-bert* expresses Davenant's own reconciliation to the course of events, an attitude which might further explain why his poem aroused so much hostility in the early years of the Commonwealth.

In a poem so much based on intertwining love affairs, it is evident that all political and military action will be at the mercy of the private lives of the characters. Yet, curiously, this romantic emphasis can also be seen as a scientific one. Science for Davenant, as for other admirers of Bacon, means a deliberate attempt to correct what was seen as an imbalance between the study of the particular and the study of the general. Bacon, in fact, had already used the discovery of the loadstone as an example of what could result from the observation of small details:

So it cometh often to pass that mean and small things discover great better than great can discover the small; and therefore Aristotle noteth well, *that the nature of every thing is best seen in his smallest portions*, and for that cause he inquireth the nature of a commonwealth, first in a family, and the simple conjugations of man and wife, parent and child, master and servant, which are in every cottage: even so likewise the nature of this great city of the world and the policy thereof must be first sought in mean concordances and small portions. So we see how that secret of nature, of the turning of iron touched with the loadstone towards the north, was found out in needles of iron, not in bars of iron.

(*Advancement of Learning*, Book II, Bacon 1905, p. 81)

Davenant develops this view into a justification of his romantic plot when he argues, in the last lines of the last canto he wrote, that love intrigues, like Astragon's loadstone, are the apparently small causes of much greater events:

> They look but wrong on Courts who can derive
> No great Effects from outward Littleness;
> Thro Foolish Scorn they turn the Prospective,
> And so contract Courts little things to less.
>
> Man's little Heart in narrow space does hide
> Great Thoughts, such as have spacious Empire sway'd
> The little Needle does vast Carricks guide,
> And of small Atoms were the Mountains made.   (III.vii.106–7)

Because the causes of events are so often personal, the difficulty of arriving at the truth of courts and camps is constantly stressed. Davenant, as a courtier with inside personal knowledge of the people involved, is implicitly contrasting himself with mere historians such as those in Astragon's library.

> Who thought, swift Time they could in fetters binde;
> Till his Confessions they had ta'ne in Books:
>
> But Time oft scap'd them in the shades of Night;
> And was in Princes Closets oft conceal'd,
> And hid in Batails smoke; so what they write
> Of Courts and Camps, is oft by guess reveal'd.   (II.v.61–2)

Thus, if *Gondibert* is a coded narrative, the point of the code is not its precise equivalence between fictitious characters and events and those of Davenant's own time but rather its creation of a world where, as in royalist propaganda, private motives are privileged over public consequences. What count throughout the story are not actions but motives. As if to prove the point about the dependence of great events on trivial ones, it opens with a hunt which turns into an ambush. After this initial fight between the forces of Oswald and Gondibert, which leads to the deaths of a number of major characters, all the main events depend on secret motives, usually love. Thus, Gondibert's secret love for Birtha prevents him from taking advantage of the offer of Rhodalind's hand, while reasons of state prevent him from confessing that his affections are already engaged. He reveals his love to Goltho, who secretly loves Birtha himself; Goltho in turn reveals it to his sworn brother Ulfinore, who also secretly loves her. Another court lady, Laura, is mourning both the suitor she loved and his loyal rival, victims of the battle which opens the work, but another lover, still unknown to her, watches like a spy for the right moment to console her. Meanwhile, Gartha, Oswald's sister, is furthering her revenge on his killer by secretly contracting herself to Hermegild, a trusted adviser of Aribert's. As Hermegild says,

> If *Gartha* deignes to love, our love must grow
> Unseen, like *Mandrakes* wedded under ground. (ii.iv.48)

Hermegild's plots involve disguising Gartha as a man in order to cast doubt (through a variation of the trick best known from *Much Ado About Nothing*) on the chastity of another woman whose impending marriage means a potentially threatening alliance. He brings Gartha her male attire concealed in a 'fatal cabinet'; though she is depicted as a bold and energetic character – the poem's nearest equivalent to a female warrior – she reacts to the sight of it as to a snake (iii.i.55–6). The emotions here seem curiously out of keeping with the situation, and mention of the cabinet is accompanied by a comparison between the plotting of this pair and that of traitors engaged in the act of deciphering (iii.i.73). Gondibert also has a secret cabinet; it contains the emerald with secret powers (ii.iv.48–52). Although such cabinets played a genuine role both in the lives of princes and in the romance, it is possible that the apparently exaggerated emotion invested in these episodes has some relation to the fate of the king's cabinet and its letters.

The obsession with secrecy means that the ability to keep emotions to oneself is the chief sign of a truly heroic character. King Aribert's thoughts are prisoners in his breast (ii.ii.19) until he enlarges them by 'liberty of Tongue'. The superiority of Gondibert to Oswald is clarified at the start by the difference in their ways of dealing with love. Unlike Oswald, whose passion is a 'publick flame', Gondibert is discreet:

> Love's fire he carry'd, but no more in view
> Than vital heat which kept his heart still warm. (i.i.46)

Rhodalind feels the same as Gondibert about her 'Love's fire': 'She would not have it wast, nor publick grow' (ii.ii.87).

In bringing his torch to light up all these secret motives of long-dead characters, Davenant presents himself as the literary counterpart of Astragon, the scientist discovering the secrets of nature. His admirers also saw the poem as one which had dispelled the mists and darkness of superstition, as shown in the use of supernatural machinery. Vaughan, for instance, treats Homer's blindness as coextensive with his spiritual darkness and Davenant's poem as a rescue from superstition:

> And where before *heroic poems* were
> Made up of *spirits, prodigies*, and fear,
> And showed, (through all the *melancholy flight,*)
> Like some dark region overcast with night,
> As if the poet had been quite dismayed,
> While only *giants* and *enchantments* swayed,
> Thou like the Sun, whose eye brooks no disguise,
> Hast chased them hence.
>> (Vaughan 1976, 'To Sir William Davenant,
>> Upon His *Gondibert*', lines 13–20)

The most obvious evidence of the time in which *Gondibert* was written is its anti-clericalism, which is clearly related to Davenant's decision to abandon the usual supernatural epic machinery. Its absence curiously accentuates rather than diminishes the sense of mystery which hangs over the poem. No god is available to reassure the reader that there is an ultimate purpose behind events. An image which Davenant uses three times in the poem, that of 'Tullia's urn', perhaps indicates how he sees his role as a writer of 'heroic song' in a post-monarchical age. This legendary urn was supposed to have contained the body of a woman and a burning lamp, both dating from 1500 years ago (see Davenant 1971, p. 301n). On the opening of the container, the body disintegrated and the light went out. The fact that Rhodalind's love burns like the fire in Tullia's urn is thus an appropriate analogy for the general sense that revelation is dangerous. But it also has implications for Davenant's attitude to his own work. The seventh canto of the third book of *Gondibert* is dedicated to Charles Cotton (the poet's father) in lines, not published until after Davenant's death, which are more outspoken than the published poem. They suggest that he saw the act of writing heroic verse, from his prison, as an act of defiance against the new dark ages which were about to engulf his world, as they had swallowed up the heroes of his poem. He envisages his work surviving only in the peculiar sense that Tullia's body did: in total darkness and confinement, to be recovered in more enlightened times.

Unlucky Fire, which tho from Heaven deriv'd,
Is brought too late like Cordials to the Dead,
When all are of their Sovereign sence depriv'd,
And Honour which my rage should warm is fled.

Dead to Heroick Song this Isle appears,
The ancient Musick of Victorious Verse:
They tast no more, than he his Dirges hears,
Whose useless Mourners sing about his Herse.

Yet shall this Sacred Lamp in Prison burn,
And through the darksom Ages hence invade
The wondring World, like that in *Tullia*'s Urn,
Which tho by time conceal'd, was not decay'd.   (III.vii.1–12)

The king's death is mentioned only obliquely. Davenant seems to be
envisaging his reading public – or the nation – as metaphorically dead,
deprived of the reason and sense of honour which would enable them to
understand his work. The reason for this is made clear in the pun on
'Sovereign sence': 'heroic' values, inseparable from the king, have died
with him. Thus, despite the grandiose tone of some of his claims to future
fame, Davenant seems to expect to live only in the private world, in the
memories of lovers (young brides, he suggests, will bring flowers to his
tomb and thank him for teaching them how to love). His decision to leave
Gondibert unfinished seems an aesthetic necessity, in view of the suspense
about his own fate (the sentence was finally allowed to lapse and he was
released in 1652). The work and its context are inseparable, and require to
be completed by history.

Charles II and the mixed genre

One of Charles I's favourite pre-war plays had been Cartwright's *Royal
Slave*, in which divine thunder saves the hero from being executed. The
absence of such thunder at the king's own execution might be seen as the
definitive reply not only to the idea of the divine right of kings but also to
the literary genres associated with it. Like the continuation of the *Arcadia*
to which I have already referred, some plays of the period suggest that a
genre which depended for its effect on a special relation with reality had
become problematic now that the very nature of that reality had been called
into question. Thus, Cosmo Manuche wrote, in the dedication to his
unpublished play, *Love in Travel*:

> Few there be
> Is Crittick-prooffe, in Comick poetry.
> And for the buskin stage, that's quite lay'd by,
> Theres terror in't, where kings are forc'd to dye.

This barely coherent statement appears to be acknowledging that terror, the one element which Guarini found utterly incompatible with comedy, has also made all stage tragedies impossible. Certainly, the closet drama of the interregnum shows itself unable to deal directly with the act of regicide. Even *The Famous Tragedy of Charles I*, a short pamphlet-play dating from about May 1649, focuses largely on other events: the siege of Colchester, the murder of the leveller Rainsborough, Cromwell's relationship with Hugh Peter and his adultery with Lambert's wife. Charles never appears, and his execution is merely reported by letter in the final scene. Other responses to the event tend on the whole to avoid the tragic genre. An exception is Christopher Wase's translation of Sophocles' *Electra* (see above, pp. 53–4), where a prince and princess avenge their father's death. As one of the translator's friends wrote, in his commendatory verses,

> Our *Agamemnon's* dead, *Electra* grieves,
> The onely hope is that *Orestes* lives.

But fantasies of revenge are rare. Much commoner is the transformation of the unbearable experience through the kind of tragicomic plot in which characters are saved from death at the last minute or reunited with those whom they had believed dead. The element of wish-fulfilment is not surprising in the works of impecunious and exiled writers. Cosmo Manuche was a soldier in the royalist army whose plays may have been performed in the house of his commanding officer, the Earl of Northampton. He published only two of them: both are called tragicomedies, and both involve a last-minute rescue from the scaffold. The play in which Dorothy Osborne and other amateur actors participated in 1654, William Berkeley's *The Lost Lady*, may have been chosen simply as a nostalgic relic of court drama, but its central situation – a grief-stricken hero discovers that his mistress is not dead after all – would have taken on greater meaning since the first production in 1638. Typically, the compensatory fantasies of drama take the form of the reunion of lovers rather than that of father and children. This is in keeping with the most popular kind of plot, but it also reflects the way in which Charles I had been seen by writers for most of his life, and in which he perhaps saw himself, judging from his decision to be crowned dressed in white like a bridegroom. Even the language of politics reflects this romantic view. The Long Parliament complained in its early years of its 'jealousies and fears' in relation to the king; 'Jealousie in State, like that of Love,' wrote *The Kingdomes Weekly Intelligencer* in 1646, 'hath a double passion, of feare and hate' (4–11 July).

It is not so much that all tragicomedies were read as royalist allegories; rather, the language of politics under the Stuarts, with its emphasis on the family and the succession, makes the domestic and the political interchangeable. James I's contention that the kingdom was his wife, Charles I's marriage to a Roman Catholic queen, their idealisation as the perfect romantic pair, and the large family which made Charles a father figure in more senses than one, provided a never-failing source of imagery. The parting of lovers, and false accusations against one or the other of the pair, were the most obvious analogy between Charles's situation and that of a tragicomedy hero. Milton's divorce pamphlets were shocking, in part, because they propose legalising divorce on grounds which, if rigidly applied, would have affected the king and queen themselves. Royalists accuse Parliament of attempting to divorce king and kingdom, just as they had effectively divorced king and queen (who never met again after Henrietta Maria's departure in 1644). There had been other attempts on the Parliamentary side to disrupt the continuity of the royal family, with proposals to put Charles I on trial for the murder of his father (an old accusation which had been around since 1626) and to depose him in favour of the Prince of Wales, if the latter had been willing to cooperate (McCormack 1973, pp. 103–4, 161–9).

One of Charles II's first appearances in popular art is in an anti-royalist caricature dating from some time between 1649 and 1651. It depicts 'The Scots Holding their young Kinges Nose to the Grindstone' – an allusion to their insistence that he take the Covenant as the price of their support – while he indignantly asks,

> You Covinant Pretenders must I bee
> The subject of your Tradgie-Comedie?   ('Old Sayings' 1651)

What makes the scene a tragicomedy is the fact that the prince is being made a subject. In Charles I's case, the inversion of 'natural' hierarchy had sometimes inspired a grotesque kind of comedy, such as Cleveland had stressed in 'The King's Disguise', but the comic/cosmic absurdity of his situation was also felt as painful. By contrast, Charles II is generally portrayed as taking a jaunty sort of pleasure in his experience. The adventures following his escape from Worcester, which became well known in

England almost as soon as he had arrived in France, were at once seen (admiringly or disparagingly) as the stuff of romance. A good indication of the kind of myth-making that he attracted is the fact that his escape was soon attributed to the assistance of James Hind, 'the famous Robber whom they call his scout-master Generall' (*The Weekly Intelligencer*, 17 Oct.–3 Nov., 1651). It is difficult to imagine anyone wanting to link Charles I's name with that of a convicted highwayman. The story was disproved when Hind was finally captured and executed, but there are some accounts of his last days in which he is quoted uttering impeccably royalist sentiments. *The Prince of Prig's Revels* (1651), a short pamphlet play about Hind's career, even shows him promising to assist 'the Scots king' and be true to him. Like some of the other tragicomedies already noted, the play then breaks off and re-enters 'real life'; the author ('J.S.') says that he has heard a rumour of Hind's capture and is going out to see whether it is true. As the play's very title indicates, the Highwayman has become a Lord of Misrule, and some of his speeches ('I feel a kind of Civil War within me') also imply that England's disorder is merely a punishment for her crime.

It is Charles II himself who seems to be a Lord of Misrule in cavalier literature of the 1650s, a period of frustration and financial insecurity. It was also a period when ballads appeared in surprisingly large numbers despite press restrictions (Rollins 1923, pp. 51–8); the year 1656–7 saw the registration of ten on the subject of Robin Hood (p. 70). His popularity is hardly surprising. The mingling of nobly-born characters with criminal types is of course a very old theme, reflecting a sense that the two groups – one above the law and one outside it – have more in common with each other than either does with the middle class. It can be found, for example, in Jonson's very successful masque of *The Gypsies Metamorphosed*, in which Buckingham and his family actually played the parts of gypsies (Randall 1975). Further back still is the 'disguised ruler' plot, which Anne Barton has traced in the Robin Hood plays and 'comical histories' of the 1590s and which is most memorably treated in the Prince Hal / Henry V plays (Barton 1975). When the *Henry IV* plays were published in Betterton's adaptation of 1700, they were in fact called a tragicomedy (Ristine 1910, p. 216).

In earlier literature, however, the disguised aristocrat usually represents a standard of honour. In the 1650s the difficulties of maintaining that standard often seem insuperable. Dorothy Osborne commented in 1654 on the effect on young people of 'the want of a court to govern themselv's bv'. 'Though that was noe perfect scoole of Vertue,' she adds, 'yet Vice there wore her maske, and apeard soe unlike her selfe that she gave noe scandall'

(Osborne 1928, p. 143). The association of virtue with Puritan hypocrisy naturally seemed an inducement for vice to display itself openly. The new models for the impoverished cavalier include other *déclassé* figures from Caroline comedy like the family of Lord Frampul in Jonson's *New Inn* and the young gentlefolk of Brome's *Jovial Crew* (acted 1642), who wander off with a troop of singing beggars. In Manuche's unpublished *Love in Travel,* a cavalier's daughter runs away to live with the gypsies and is reunited with her family only at the end. The Marquis of Newcastle, a former patron of Brome's, left England in 1644 after he had been defeated at Marston Moor; he seems to enter into the spirit of Brome's play when, shortly after, he writes love verses to his future wife:

> Sweet Harte, we are beggars; our Comfort's t'is seene,
> That we are undone for the Kinge and the Queene;
> Which doth make us rejoyce, with Royall braggs,
> That now we doe foote it with Royall raggs.   (Cavendish 1956, p. 75)

All these authors enjoy depicting scenes of swindling. Like Buckingham's willingness to play the part of the gypsy, which in a sense he *was,* Newcastle's rather amusing scenes of picaresque swindling, sketched out under the title of *Pleasant and Merry Humour of a Rogue,* show how far this aristocrat (whose difficulties with his creditors were freely admitted in his wife's memoirs) felt himself from the criminal type which he created with such affection. His wife, who shared his admiration for the older drama and constantly insisted that she had no time for romances, appears to have been parodying the form in her play *Bell in Campo.* It depicts a war between the kingdoms of Reformation and Faction. Lord General wants to leave his young wife Victoria behind, but she persuades him to let her accompany him along with an army of 'Heroickesses' which she single-handedly raises, ordering it to march to the sound of flutes rather than drums and trumpets. The soldiers wonder why her husband wants to be so encumbered, since, as they point out, war is 'the only time a married man hath to enjoy a Mistress without jealousy.' However, Lady Victoria's army ends up being more successful than the men's. She is given a triumphal entry into her city, and the King, to reward her, allows various privileges to women, including the permission to 'wear what fashioned clothes they will' (Cavendish 1662, p. 625). The works of the Duchess of Newcastle may sound scatty at times, but somewhere behind them is a basically realistic view of her life.

Just as the marriage of King to Kingdom requires a Mirtillo, the two worlds of court and tavern need a Prince Hal figure to reconcile them. The desire to turn Charles II into such a figure has already been noted. Where a play fails to establish this kind of contact between ruler and subject, its tragicomic structure accentuates rather than reconciles social divisions. The separation of the two worlds is particularly conspicuous in an untitled and unpublished play by Manuche's patron, James Compton, Earl of Northampton (BL Add MS 60279). Though both the beginning and end of the manuscript are missing, it is clearly a tragicomedy about a rebellion against one King Leontius of Sardinia, in which the rebels claim to be fighting for freedom and for the removal of the king's evil counsellors. One of the rebel generals, Melantius, lives in constant torment because on the one hand he believes in supporting monarchy and on the other he is obliged to act on the orders of his own king, the ruler of neighbouring Sicily. Northampton was obviously acquainted with the *Henry IV* plays, the sources of his scenes of drunkenness and malpractice in the rebel army: one soldier says during a battle, 'My tatterdemalions are pepperd, I have not halfe left that I led on' (p. 22ᵛ). One rebel captain asks another what they are fighting about; the reply is, 'Let them that imploy us tell that when they are asked, we fight for pay' (p. 22ᵛ). There are many examples of shifting loyalties on both sides, but only Melantius's dilemma is taken seriously. It is finally resolved when a messenger brings him word that the old king of Sicily is dead. The new king, a young man, knows that he will need allies and feels that

> Kings with Kings far better will agree
> then Kings with those that quite have cast away
> the ties of lawfull Sovraignity.   (p. 27)

On hearing this news, Melantius promptly changes sides, thus ensuring the victory of Leontius. 'I always thought,' one of the King's advisers declares, 'Kings did imitate ye sun that sometimes is darken'd by contagious clouds, but with his beames att last disperses those vapours, and shows in greater brightnesse' (p. 30). The Shakespearean echo is remarkably inept: old Leontius bears little resemblance to any Shakespearean sun-king, and it is Melantius's change of heart rather than any action on the king's part which brings about the happy ending. Unless Northampton was gifted with prophetic power it is likely that he wrote this play after the Restoration, which, similarly, was brought about by disunity in the army and the support given by General Monk. The distinction between disloyal and loyal vacillation is as unclear in the play as it was in 1660.

Manuche's *Banished Shepherdess* also deals with the Restoration, attempting to fuse the romantic and comic aspects of Charles II's cause. The action moves between tavern and forest. The forest is really a court of royalty in exile, rather as in *As You Like It*, but, like Northampton's play, keeps the truly noble characters carefully separate from the rest. Each act ends with songs and dances by the courtiers, and in Act II they have a 'vision' of the hero's coronation, another variation, obviously dependent on hindsight, on the prophecy/oracle of earlier tragicomedies. Corilliana (Henrietta Maria) and Charilaus (Charles II) have a relatively small role in the play, which is just as well, as Manuche feels obliged to make their behaviour completely exemplary: Charilaus, beginning a toast to the 'ffayre and vertuous Mistresses' of his followers, points out that he hates 'immoderate drinking' (Manuche p. 33). He and the rest of the royal family enjoy their idyllic shepherds' lives and express nothing but merciful and charitable sentiments towards their enemies. It is only in a separate part of the plot that their courtiers curse the roundheads, mostly comic rascals, and play practical jokes on them. Even these courtiers appear to be free from the vices usually associated with cavaliers, though one of them has to fend off the advances of a lecherous landlady. A vaguely Shakespearean influence makes itself felt chiefly in echoes (again) of the history plays: 'discresion / Is the greatest part of vallor' (p. 16); 'trailed the puissant pike' (p. 54).

Another banished ruler in a pastoral setting is the hero of *Alfred, or Right Reinthron'd*, which exists in a manuscript copy dedicated by one R. K. (Kirkham, apparently) to his sister, Lady Blount. This is a historical romance, but the initial situation is so strikingly like Charles's that there is no doubt as to how it would have been read in 1659/60. Alfred and his men have been defeated by the Danes. The king's mother laments his fate: 'death would be lesse painfull to me then a life, which hath seene my son disthron'd, and fertile Britain groaning under th' oppression of a cruel tyrant' ([Kirkham], Act I). A hermit advises Alfred not to be ashamed of his poor disguise, since Christ himself 'chose to live obscurely in a Cottage' (Act IV). Prophecies and dreams of Alfred's restoration are finally fulfilled, and the poor peasants who have helped him and his family are duly rewarded. This is an extremely enjoyable play; Alfred Harbage, the only critic to my knowledge who has taken notice of it, comments that it 'returns to an older, fresher day' (Harbage 1936, p. 225). This is truer than he realised, for *Alfred* is actually a translation from William Drury's *Alfredus, sive Aluredus* (1619), and its appropriateness to the circumstances of the late 1650s is accidental. But it could never have been published under a Protestant ruler. It was written for the English Seminary at Douai and its secret meaning is made clear in the Epilogue by St Cuthbert:

O wretched England! would thou still did'st know
That ancient happy state; thou wouldst not now
As from ye world thou separated art,
So from the world's true faith be kept apart.   (Act v, Epilogue)

What concerned Drury was that England had banished not the true king but the true faith. R. Kirkham may have hoped that the restoration of Charles II would also mean the restoration of Catholicism in England.

The tragicomic ending and the Restoration

The two Charleses acted out virtually every role available to a ruler in romance or drama: the disguised lover, the husband parted from his wife/kingdom, the loving father of his country, the sacrificial victim, the wandering prince. The domination of this period by tragicomedies, both high and low in style, can thus be seen not as an escape from reality but as a reflection of it. For royalists, the world after 1642 *was* an appalling confusion of classes, creeds, and genres, and the only acceptable model for events was one in which a divine purpose could be seen fulfilling itself slowly but surely. Marvell's distinction, in 'The First Anniversary', between the painfully slow and circular workings of kings and the speed with which a divinely inspired hero like Cromwell can move is simply a reversal of this model. Marvell's poem (perhaps recalling Fanshawe's poem on Strafford) depicts a representative of kingship lamenting that Cromwell's approach to intrigue was like Alexander's: 'And still his Falchion all our knots unties' (Marvell 1972, p. 136, line 384). The elaborate tying and untying of knots, so crucial to the art of tragicomedy, is too slow and devious for an age which needs rapid and constructive action. Yet it is the model which every party always had ready for consolation when its affairs were not going well: similar warnings of impatience can be found in parliamentary sermons and journals during the war, with a reminder that all good things come slowly. The last sermon Charles I heard, preached to him by Henry Ferne at Newport in November 1648, was on the text 'though it tarry, wait for it: because it will surely come, it will not tarry' (Habakkuk 2:3).

The assimilation of contemporary history to literary models was a way of making sense of the disturbing and unprecedented nature of much that was happening in 1640–60. I argued earlier that the formulae of romance and tragicomedy actually helped the pre-war court to come to terms with real events. Their effect may have been more purely escapist in the 1650s, when those who argued for the reopening of the playhouses generally claimed that drama would act as the opium of the people. Edmund Gayton's entertaining *Pleasant Notes on Don Quixote* (1654) reflects an awareness of the dual aspect of the romantic imagination – absurd yet somehow necessary as a harmless escape outlet. As he pointed out, despite the popularity of romances 'no man dare say, but here is a well-governed Commonwealth,' and he suggested that stage-plays should be permitted because, like romances, they diverted those who otherwise might become 'troublesome Judges of the State and Church wherein they live'.

> For want of these chimera's (which had no more harm in them, than their impossibility) reall phantasmes, and strong delusions have succeeded and possessed not a few, who transported with their own imaginations, doe not write Romances, but act them, and fill the world with substantial Tragedies.   (p. 270)

Secrecy, mystification, and equivocation – qualities of the romance plot – were frequent accusations against the real-life plots of royalists, and these are justified to some extent by their own words. Deception, particularly of those they consider beneath them, is in any case a common practice among romance heroes, from Sidney's Pyrocles onward. The heroine of *The Lost Lady* argues that

> The Gods give us permission to be false,
> when they exclude us from all other wayes
> wch may preserue our faith.   (lines 1036–8)

Anne Murray, later Lady Halkett, tells in her autobiography how, having promised her mother never to see a particular young man again, 'itt presently came in my mind that if I blindfolded my eyes that would secure mee from seeing him' (Loftis 1979, p. 18). Perhaps she knew Cowley's *The Guardian* (1641), where this stratagem is actually used. In *Alfred*, the deposed king and his followers resort to disguise and deception in order to win back the kingdom: demonstrating the qualities often associated with Catholic conspiracy, they argue that ' 'Tis fit sometimes by such deceits to temporize' (Kirkham, p. 5). A ballad of 1649 takes for granted that 'When Caveliers are poor, they by their wits must double' ('The Credit of Yorkshire', Rollins 1923, p. 272). In Margaret Cavendish's *The Sociable Wits* (1668), a sergeant comments on how well the cavaliers have deceived him. The reply is, 'They have been so often deceived themselves, that they have learned by their misfortunes' (p. 82).

It is possible that the tragicomedy model, with its stress on the almost exclusive importance of the ruler's actions, or those of Providence on his behalf, made it easier for even the most loyal followers of the two Charleses to abdicate responsibility and leave matters in the hands of fate. The typical romance plot, in which elaborately intertwining intrigues are resolved by quasi-miraculous means, corresponds to a view of life which, of necessity, became that of many royalists after 1651. A letter written to Sir Edward Nicholas by the Marquis of Ormond sums it up. The failure of all attempts on the royalist party seemed to him a message from God:

And His not blessing all our endeavours in so just a cause, I would fain understand to be a command to stand still and see the salvation He will work for us. He hath raised the Rebels to the top of success; if that produce pride and oppression in them it will not be madness to expect their sudden fall.   (Nicholas 1955, pp. 256–7)

This, as B. H. G. Wormald has argued, was also the view of Edward Hyde, later Earl of Clarendon, who advocated a waiting policy, believing that the nation was being punished for 'individual wickedness and error' and must wait until the 'gigantic necessities' of divine will had played themselves out (Wormald 1951, p. 237).

The Restoration was to vindicate that policy, and reactions to it therefore show a determination to emphasise the divine pattern behind events. Robert Wild's *Iter Boreale* (1660), the most popular of the many poems on the subject, celebrates Monk's march from Scotland, the decisive step in making the Restoration possible. Wild seems an odd writer to become the unofficial laureate of such an occasion: though he had been a royalist since 1649, he was also a Presbyterian clergyman (and friend of George Thomason) who wrote elegies on a number of fellow-Presbyterian ministers and who, only two years later, was to be expelled from his living as a nonconformist. But the success of his poem is due precisely to the fact that he was not a cavalier in the usual sense. Rather, he represents that large part of the population which had been initially hostile to the king and which now required to be consoled and justified through participation in the collective national rejoicing. Wild's poems are generally extravagant in style and disarmingly frank in their admission of the author's inadequacy. His deliberate exaggeration and fantasy have been compared to Cleveland's. In this poem he puts them at the service of a view of history as a wonderful series of incongruous surprises.

Iter Boreale thus begins by making a calculated leap from the tragic world of Melpomene, banished in the opening lines, to one which is mock-heroic rather than heroic in tone and presided over by 'the merriest of the nine'. The poem proceeds to undo the history of the past twenty years, deliberately turning back the clock to find parallels with the romantic past. In particular, Wild recalls the days when the royal martyr had

himself been a romantic traveller. History is now repeating itself: Charles
II had just made a journey to Spain, in the company of Lord George Digby,
with a view to pressing for some recognition of his claims as part of the
treaty being negotiated between France and Spain at Fuenterrabia. Perhaps, indeed, he had been influenced by a desire to repeat his father's
adventures of some thirty-five years before. However much George Digby
might resemble George Villiers, it was hardly in anyone's interest to draw
that particular parallel. Wild instead transforms a more congenial hero, the
Presbyterian George Monk, into a reincarnation both of St George and of
George Villiers (Buckingham), who was now remote enough in time to be
romanticised:

> We have another Charles to fetch from Spain;
> Be thou the George to bring him back again,   (Wild 1963, lines 350–1)

Probably recalling Waller's poem on the return of the Prince and Duke,
Wild contrasts the storm of 1624 with the calm sea which he envisages
wafting them home in 1660:

> There is no danger of the winds at all,
> Unless together by the ears they fall
> Who shall the honour have to waft a king:
> And they who gain it while they work shall sing.
> Methinks I see how those triumphant gales,
> Proud of the great employment, swell the sails:
> The joyful ship shall dance, the sea shall laugh,
> And loyal fish their master's health shall quaff.
> See how the dolphins croud and thrust their large
> And scaly shoulders, to assist the barge;
> The peaceful kingfishers are met together
> About the decks, and prophesy calm weather;
> Poor crabs and lobsters have gone down to creep,
> And search for pearls and jewels in the deep;
> And when they have the booty, crawl before,
> And leave them for his welcome to the shore.   (lines 354–69)

This is Wild's way of acknowledging the quality in the Restoration which
most struck contemporaries, its rapid and almost miraculous nature. Waller's poem on the same event uses the familiar analogy of the dénouement:

> If then such praise the Macedonian got
> For having rudely cut the Gordian knot,
> What glory's due to him that could divide
> Such ravelled interests; has the knot untied,
> And without stroke so smooth a passage made,
> Where craft and malice such impeachments laid?
> ('To the King, upon His Majesty's Happy Return',
>   Waller 1901, lines 77–82)

It is as if the tragicomic ending unsuccessfully attempted by Strafford is at
last to be completed.

Other writers attempted to lift Charles's return to the dignity of a
different literary mode: one declared that the heroes of Homer and Virgil
were themselves mere romance figures by comparison with the epic of
Charles II's life:

> *Old Poets*, hush, be still; your Pages swell
> With weak and poor Romances, when ye tell
> Your storys of the Grecian Traveller,
> Or Him, that wandred from the Trojan warre.
> They never prov'd such angry fates as he,
> Nor such Encounters met by Land or Sea.
>   (Mayhew 1660, *Upon the Joyful and Welcome Return*)

It may even be significant that the Restoration was to take particular pride
in the genre of the 'heroic play', and that 'heroick' should be used (e.g. in
Aphra Behn's *The Roundheads*) as virtually synonymous with Cavalier.
The psychological need to interpret the Restoration as the comic ending to
a tragic sequence might even be one of the factors in the period's notorious
inability to write tragedy. It was tragicomedy that remained associated
with Charles II, and the interpretation of tragicomedy found in the royalist
political satires paved the way for the mock-heroic of *Absalom and
Achitophel*.

The most striking example of the interrelation of literature and life is the
extraordinary two-part pamphlet play, *Newmarket Fair* (1649), by 'the
Man in the Moon' (John Crouch). Written shortly after the king's execution, it represents the tragicomic mode at its wildest extreme of fantasy.
Both the action and the prophecies seem completely out of control, corresponding with the events that have taken place. Part I opens with a Crier
selling the king's regalia in the streets, a deliberately outrageous depiction
of an event (the disposing of the king's property) which had been received
with outrage in the royalist press:

> O yes, O yes, O yes, Here is a Golden Crowne Worth many a hundred Pound; 'twill
> fit the head of a Fool, Knave, or Clowne; 'twas lately tane from the Royall Head, of
> a King *martyred*; who bids most?   (sig. A2)

The ending of this part is equally sensational: Fairfax and Cromwell,
hearing the news of a popular uprising, die in the high Roman fashion by
falling on their swords. Part II begins with the casual explanation that they
have been revived by necromancy. A ghost – that of the murdered
Commonwealth envoy Dorislaus – is raised up to prophesy. He reveals

that hell is full of dead roundheads, that Charles I is in heaven, and that, 'Though the first be gone, the second shall reigne' (p. 9). The play ends with a second rebellion, the murder of Mrs Cromwell by Lady Fairfax, and the crowd's decision to petition Charles II to return. The wishful thinking has been carried so far as to become – intentionally – comic. The play seems to have been popular. At the Restoration it became still more so. In 1661 Part I was reprinted, according to the publisher, Edward Crouch, 'at the request of some young Gentlemen, to *Act* in *Christmas Holy-dayes*' (Greg 1939–59, vol. II, p. 808). Events had transformed the fantastic prophecies into reality, and the mock tragedy into true tragicomedy.

4

Intertextuality and identity: literary codes

No Man in his time did surpass him for his ready and dextrous interlarding his common discourses among them with Verses from the Poets or Sentences from classical Authors. Which being then all the fashion in the University, made his Company more acceptable.

(Anthony à Wood on Robert Burton; quoted in Bush 1945, p. 286)

Literary self-consciousness

The emphasis of the previous chapters has been on the way in which the royalist literary community coped with defeat by adopting what might be called a philosophy of secrecy. Whether through surreptitious distribution, through the use of various kinds of private language, or through literary forms which emphasised the ultimate mysteriousness of human and divine purposes, royalist literature fulfilled the functions most necessary for the culture of a repressed group: enabling communication and consolidating its sense of itself as an elite. In this chapter, I shall turn from communication to expression, from the way in which codes work on their readers to the purposes they serve for the writers themselves. As the previous chapter examined the transformation of experience by genre and of genre by experience, this one will be concerned with the two-way encoding of words and images. I shall be concerned primarily with the widespread phenomenon of literary borrowing – borrowing, that is, not merely of the language of other writers but also of the persona which is created by that language.

In the previous chapter, where I suggested a possible influence of Fanshawe's Strafford on Marvell's image of Charles I as tragic actor, I added one more name to the list of contemporary authors from whom Marvell is said to have 'borrowed': 'Cleveland, Waller, Jonson, Donne, Thomas May, Mildmay Fane, St Amant, Hermann Hugo, Henry Hawkins, Crashaw, Cowley, and a host of less convincing likenesses' (Patterson 1978, p. 13). And this leaves out the perhaps still more numerous classical sources. Elizabeth Story Donno stresses the difficulty of knowing 'whether an appropriation served to indicate a knowing reference to a current literary piece, a reflection of *imitatio* directed to a purposed end, an overt tribute to a contemporary – rival or friend – or, simply, a bold filching' (Donno 1978, p. 25). But, as she recognises, none of these possibilities can explain the motives of a writer like Marvell, whose most elaborately derivative poems were apparently written only for himself and close acquaintances. 'Borrowing' is obviously a misleading term, since it implies that a word or image belongs to its first identifiable user. The names given to seventeenth-century anthologies – 'treasuries', 'commonplaces' – suggest that language was seen as the property of the community not the individual. This is why the compilers of such books often quote passages out of context and without mention of their authors. The practice can be seen as an example of what Walter J. Ong (1971) has called the 'residual oralism' (p. 34) of pre-romantic culture, still concerned to 'hand on' rather than to innovate (p. 21). But Jonson's satires on plagiarists, the doubts being expressed as early as the 1630s about Jonson's own heavy indebtedness to classical sources, and Milton's gleeful pouncing on the prayer from Sidney's *Arcadia* in some editions of the *Eikon Basilike*, are all sufficient evidence that writers did have a concept of plagiarism and took it seriously.

Most published Renaissance works are scrupulous in the acknowledgement of classical and biblical sources, because it was in their interest to be so: controversial literature relied on the citing of authorities, and both sides were eager to stake their claim to the possession of crucial texts. By the early seventeenth century, however, some works of English literature had acquired a sufficiently classic status to become part of the world of literary discourse. Burton's *Anatomy* (first published 1621) draws with equal enthusiasm on the historical and the fictitious, on the Bible, Greek romance, and such figures as 'Benedick and Beatrice in the Comedy' (Burton 1955, p. 696). The effect of this expansion of the literary field has not been sufficiently recognised.

The existence of a common area of reference creates the possibility for dialogic writing, for effects of what is now known as intertextuality. The most obvious examples probably occurred in the drama; the various Allusion books and G. E. Bentley's *Shakespeare and Jonson* show just how widespread the practice was. Richard Brome, for example, openly sets his plays in the tradition of his 'master' Ben Jonson: three of his characters unite in an 'Indenture Tripartite ... like Subtle, Doll, and Face'; another compares himself to justice Overdo (Bentley 1945, pp. 84, 105–6). But self-consciousness informs all areas of writing, and writers can hand on a

tradition while situating themselves in opposition to it. Just as the persona
of Donne's love poetry sometimes portrays himself in opposition to a
Petrarchan straw man, so the Marquis of Newcastle, writing his own love
verses in the 1640s, uses Donne himself as a straw man:

> Love, forty years agoe, serv'd Doctor Dunn,
> But wee'r beyond it far.   (Cavendish 1956, p. 63)

Even formal Characters become self-conscious about their relation to
literary models, which are mentioned not only as guarantees of a Character's realism but also as the causes of his behaviour. In Wye Saltonstall's
Picturae Loquentes (1631 and 1635), we are told that the 'honest rudeness'
of the Forest Keeper has been formed by his reading about himself in
fiction, where he learns that his destiny is to play a small but sympathetic
role in other people's lives: 'in the fictions of Duells & ravishments, who
come in still to rescue, but a Keeper?' (1946, p. 54). This figure sounds a
little like a humbler version of Don Quixote, who is mentioned in a
number of the Character-books of the civil war period (Boyce 1955,
pp. 121–2). But the keeper's use of literature as a model for life is treated
sympathetically in this pre-war work, whereas, as we have seen, civil war
writers on both sides see such behaviour in their opponents in a more
sinister light.

Literary allusion is a special kind of communication. Whereas quotations in foreign languages draw attention to themselves as a code by the
use of italics and marginal references, those in English can easily be
confused with the author's own words. This means that the identification
of an author may serve a purpose separate from that of the quotation itself.
Thomas Blount's *Academie of Eloquence*, published by Moseley in 1654,
offers, under the guise of a handbook of rhetoric and commonplaces, what
is virtually an anthology of royalist writers. Such figures as Davenant,
Walter Montague and Kenelm Digby get a surprising amount of space; one
of the book's examples of elegant formulae is taken from the *Eikon
Basilike*; and there is a section of commonplaces on the subject 'Of the K:
and his letters intercepted 1645'. In the anthology of verse which forms one
section of *Wit's Interpreter* (Cotgrave, 1655b), the only poems ascribed to
specific authors are those by men of rank, Sir Walter Ralegh and Sir
Kenelm Digby. Cotgrave's collection was supposedly aimed at fashionable
readers, and this was one way of showing that he shared their sense of
priorities. On the other hand, some of the writers most frequently quoted
after 1642, like Donne and Herbert, may be named for the sake of their
association with the Church of England. In the funeral sermon on the

Countess of Suffolk, who died in 1649, her chaplain declared that she had been able to complete almost any poem by George Herbert after hearing the opening lines (Rainbowe 1649, p. 13). In such a context, it is difficult to separate admiration for the author and what he stood for. Cleveland was probably quoted as much for his well-known royalism as for his words: many of them, like 'ring the bells backward', recur throughout the royalist pamphlet literature. *Cooper's Hill* seems to have had a similar status, though Brendan O Hehir, Denham's biographer, has found some of its lines, adapted by an Oxford poet, in a panegyric to Cromwell published in 1653 (O Hehir 1969, p. 293). It is possible that the publication of the revised edition of Denham's poem in 1655 (see above, pp. 21) was intended not only to stress but to *reclaim* its royalist significance.

One reason for the prevalence of allusion and quotation in this period is the stress laid on memory in early education and all aspects of later life. A book published in 1653 refers to a blind man 'who can repeat the first four Books of *Homers Illiades*, the first six of *Virgil Eneids*, all *Ovids Epistles*, *Johnsons Cataline* and *Alchemist*, Shakespears *Othello*' ('S. S.' 1653, p. 18). It is significant that all the English examples in this list are plays. Like Ancient Pistol, writers of all parties seem to remember drama better than anything else. This is not necessarily a compliment to the theatre. Jonas Barish (1981) has compiled massive evidence that English phrases with theatrical connotations usually have a pejorative sense. Theatrical language as used by parliamentarians is often a parody of the supposed theatricality of the cavaliers. (An example is the adaptation in 1643 of part of the text of Shirley's pre-war masque, *The Triumph of Peace*, as an anti-cavalier tract called *The Cruel War*.) To judge from their choice of quotations and allusions, even the royalist writers seem to have remembered plays primarily as sources of bad examples: comic characters, villains, and rebels. Allusions to specific plays are sometimes deceptive, however, as it is evident that many of them are named simply for the sake of their titles: *A King and No King*, so relevant to Charles I's situation in the 1640s and Charles II's in the 1650s, is an obvious case. An anonymous answer to Waller's panegyric on Cromwell says that the exiled king may yet make the usurper 'act *The Tamer Tamed*' (*The Anti-Panegyrike*, p. 11). In the pre-war period, and again with the approach of the Restoration, pamphleteers frequently played the game of applying well-known play titles to contemporary characters and events: in 1642 it was *The Valiant Scot* and *The Cardinal's Conspiracy* (*A Second Discovery of the Northern Scout*, p. 8); in 1660 *The Changeling* was Marchamont Nedham, who had written on both sides (*Mercurius Phanaticus*, 14–20 March, 1660); *The Costly Whore* was suggested as suitable for Henry Marten, whose private life was notorious (*Free-parliament Queries*, 1660, p. 4).

Interesting evidence of one man's preferences in drama can be found in John Cotgrave's *English Treasury of Wit* (1655a), the only collection of the period to consist entirely of extracts from plays. Like other compilers of anthologies, Cotgrave removes his extracts from their context, omits their sources, and groups them under thematic headings. Dialogue is turned into monologue, names of characters are removed. What he admired most in these playwrights, according to his preface, was their own treatment of their sources: 'they have culled the choicest Flowers out of the greater number of Greeke, Latin, Italian, Spanish, and French Authors, (Poets especially) to embellish and enrich the English Scene withall, besides, almost a prodigious accrewment of their own luxuriant fancies.' The careful work of G. E. Bentley (1943), much assisted by several unknown annotators of the British Library copy, has identified Cotgrave's extracts and thus established the ranking order of the dramatists in his collection. At first sight, it seems fairly predictable. Cotgrave included 154 passages from Shakespeare; 111 or 112 from each of the acknowledged giants: Chapman, Jonson, and the 'Beaumont and Fletcher' group; 110 from Fulke Greville; and 104 from Webster, who stands well above Shirley (85) and Middleton (78). But, as Bentley pointed out (p. 202), Shakespeare's apparent preeminence is due to the large number of plays from which the editor quoted, which may be due to the convenience of having them all collected in the Folio. When Cotgrave's selections are used as a guide to the quotability of individual plays, *The Duchess of Malfi* (40) and *The White Devil* (36) are second only to Fulke Greville's *Alaham* and *Mustapha*, the two most frequently quoted plays in the book. *Catiline*, with 33 quotations, comes next. The most popular of Shakespeare's plays is *Hamlet*, with 18 extracts. It is surprising, however, to find that those next in popularity are *The Merchant of Venice* and *Timon of Athens* with 11 quotations each, and *Measure for Measure* with 10. The two *Henry IV* plays between them total 8, the same number as from *Troilus and Cressida*; *Julius Caesar* and an apocryphal comedy, *The Puritan*, have 7 each. As Bentley points out (pp. 197–8), the compiler obviously preferred the generalised and sententious. This accounts for the predominance of lines from plays which discuss justice, mercy, the evils of money, and so on; *The Puritan*, I suspect, figures so largely because of its title and its satirical treatment of the title character. Political bias may also have influenced Cotgrave in the section headed 'The People', where he includes a number of Coriolanus's most hostile speeches about mob behaviour, with no indication of the way in which they are qualified by their context.

Cotgrave's anthology is probably not entirely typical of mid-seventeenth-century taste; his fondness for Greville's closet drama, for instance, seems to have been a personal one. Like other commonplace-books and anthologies, it shows what was thought quotable, but not necessarily what was most read or what had been most theatrically successful. Cotgrave does not quote at all from the immensely popular acting play *Richard III*, and only twice from *Richard II*, four times from *Macbeth*. Bentley points out (p. 199) that nearly all the works quoted were printed after 1600. This 'modern' emphasis may reflect the compiler's personal taste, the availability of texts, or general acceptance of the view that earlier English drama had lacked 'refinement' (see above, pp. 90–1). In fact, a reading of the more popular literature of the period shows that the earlier drama had not been so completely forgotten. I have found a number of quotations from Marlowe in works of the 1640s (Potter 1988), and a verse pamphlet of 1659 (or 1649?), *Duke Hamilton's Ghost*, contains a reference to *The Spanish Tragedy* which would be meaningless without some knowledge of the plot:

> So dealt they with me in hopes of Reprieve
> I spent my last minute, like to *Pedringane* ...

In the case of Shakespeare, the fact that pamphleteers often refer to characters rather than quoting from the plays might suggest that they are recalling the experience of performance rather than that of reading. As other allusion collectors have already noted, the most striking fact is the immense popularity of Falstaff, as an archetype both for the drinker and the bad soldier. Other characters from the histories are also mentioned, but it is not always clear whether references to Richard III, for instance, are to the historical or the dramatic character. *The Famous Tragedy of Charles I* (1649) draws on the relationship of Richard and Buckingham for the dialogue of Cromwell and Hugh Peters which opens the play. Cromwell refers to Peters as 'my better *Genius*' whom he trusts more than the Delphian oracle (p. 3), and Peters soliloquises that 'This fellow (sure) was born (as the Third *Richard*, who once rul'd this Land) with his mouth full of teeth' (p. 7). Cromwell's title of Lord Protector made him, after 1653, look still more like Richard on his way to the throne. When Oliver was succeeded by his son Richard, also Protector, the parallels became even more tempting. At least one royalist satirist must have been reading the play in search of lines to quote or parody, since two exchanges from the scene between Richard and Lady Anne (one of them transformed into something of a Punch and Judy routine) occur in pamphlets of 1660, *The Black Book* and *The Life and Death of Mrs Rump*. On the other hand, the two other plays most obviously relevant to contemporary events barely appear at all. Although the historical Richard II is often mentioned, the play itself is not. Nor is *Macbeth*. I shall return to this interesting gap – or repression? – in my final chapter.

   Cotgrave is probably most typical of seventeenth-century attitudes in his representation of Jonson and Webster. Jonson's *Catiline*, whose title and subject are obviously relevant to the 1640s, is one of the most frequently mentioned plays of the period. But it is not one of the most frequently quoted (Bentley 1945), and most writers who do quote from it tend to choose the same lines. An exception is the parliamentarian Thomas May, a playwright himself, whose *History of Parliament* refers to the women taking notes at Strafford's trial as 'so many Sempronias' (the comic female intellectual in *Catiline*). Few other writers give this impression of personal response to the play. Just as *Tamburlaine* (perhaps because mediated through Ancient Pistol) is always represented by 'Holla, ye pampered jades of Asia!' (e.g. in *Mercurius Melancholicus*, 12–19 Feb. 1648), so *Catiline* nearly always means Sylla's ghost, the drawing of a curtain to reveal the eponymous hero-villain, and his opening line, 'It is decreed'. Even those who had not read the play could quote and recognise this much of it. 'It is decreed' recurs as the opening line of Cromwell's soliloquy in the 'tragicomedy' *Crafty Cromwell* (1648), in an elegy on Lord Hastings in 1649 by 'M. N.' (possibly Marchamont Nedham), and in Robert Wild's poem about the 'tragedy' of the Presbyterian royalist conspirator Christopher Love (1651). In so far as the rest of the play was remembered, it was probably for the horrific image of rebel behaviour in the opening scene, where Catiline and his followers drink the blood of a newly killed slave as they swear destruction to their country, and Cethegus expresses his insane desire for universal slaughter. In *The Levellers Levelled* (Dec. 1647), a pamphlet-play which caricatures Lilburne and the levellers, the rebel leaders lay their hands on a picture of Catiline as they swear Charles's death and the abrogation of all laws and property. Jonson's tragedy was an important point of reference in royalist culture, but only partly because it depicted a conspiracy against the state. That it had initially been unsuccessful on the stage proved the foolishness of 'vulgar' judgements, while its elaborate scholarly apparatus proved that the writing of plays could require as much research as a theological tract.

Unlike Jonson, Webster is remembered for his works rather than as a public figure, which is why he is much less frequently mentioned by name. If the preface to *The White Devil* is telling the truth when it says that the play had been unsuccessful in the theatre, Webster may have shared with Jonson a tendency to write above the heads of his audience. Like Jonson, he worked from a commonplace book; some of his dramatic speeches are little more than a carefully wrought tissue of quotations. As these make him a very quotable writer, he has a surprisingly pervasive effect on the language of the period (see Forker 1986, pp. 458–64, 493–531). That his borrowing was by no means unconscious or lazy can be seen in his highly symbolic use of the echo in the ruined cloister of *The Duchess of Malfi* (v.iii). In Act I, Antonio had responded to the Duchess's courtship with 'These words should be mine'; in Act v, his voice is echoed by that of the dead Duchess, dramatising the idea that husband and wife are one. Webster's echoes of earlier authors are a similar act of homage. When he echoes voices which had not yet died away, it is harder to be sure of the intended effect. Bosola, in *The Duchess of Malfi*, murmurs, 'Break, heart,' over the dying Antonio (v.iv.72); the actor who played the part may well have been the same one who, as Kent, had murmured, 'Break, heart, I prithee break,' over the dying Lear. In *The White Devil* an old woman whose son has been murdered goes mad and offers flowers to a group of bystanders: 'Here's rosemary for you, and rue for you' (v.iv.77). Webster must surely have expected his sources to be recognised by at least part of his audience. Yet the pleasure of recognising them clashes with the emotional response which the two scenes appear to demand.

The same clash of responses is written into the plays themselves. The stage malcontents Flamineo and Bosola respond to the tragedies in which they figure with a mixture of involvement and detachment, the result of the same literary self-consciousness which at least part of their audience would have experienced. A few minutes after observing his mother's mad scene, Flamineo sees a ghost. Just as Hamlet's reaction to his father's ghost is set against that of a hypothetical tragic revenger, so Flamineo's is in turn set against Hamlet's. Each character is placed simultaneously in an emotionally harrowing situation and in a dramatic tradition against which, even as he participates in it, he is also fighting. When, in his next scene, Flamineo announces his intention of committing suicide, he speculates whether the afterlife will resemble Lucian's 'ridiculous purgatory' (v.vi.107–8). The reference to Lucian opens another hall of mirrors, for

Lucian frequently quoted and parodied earlier writers. Webster's most striking characters thus create their sense of identity through the literary self-consciousness which makes them both absorb and attack their own fictions.

So far, I have been discussing the self-dramatising of seventeenth-century authors in terms of the dramatists who most influenced them. But there are other important influences which are only semi-dramatic. One is that of Nashe and the Marprelate writers, whose role as prototypes for the pamphlet wars of the 1640s is frequently acknowledged: John Taylor's *Differing Worships* (1640) is attributed to 'Tom Nash's Ghost', his *Aqua-Muse* (1645a) acknowledges *Pierce Penniless* as a model, and *Crop-Eare Curried* (1645b) describes Nashe's ghost appearing to him. Another is Burton's *Anatomy of Melancholy*. Part of the popularity of this work was due to the fact that Burton not only analysed but imitated the manner of the stage malcontent whose jesting is obviously only a disguise for 'that within that passeth show'. Marie Gimmelfarb-Brack (1979) is probably right in suggesting that the Burtonian source for the names of the journals *Mercurius Melancholicus*, *Mercurius Democritus*, and *The Man in the Moon* was evidence of a common author or publisher (pp. 437–50). But it is also true that borrowings from *The Anatomy*, and imitations of its style, are extremely common in the mid-century. Simply to say that melancholy was fashionable does not go far enough in attempting to explain this vogue. I think that it can be related to the same elitism that contributed to the popularity of Jonson and Webster. In their plays, the sense of melancholy often seems to be purely economic in origin, related to the problem of the poor scholar and the intellectual's sense of isolation in a money-conscious society. In the mid-century, this personal isolation is subsumed in political and social isolation. What Nashe, Burton and the stage melancholic have in common is their learning, their wit, and a style which justifies its own self-indulgence on the grounds that it is either expressing or concealing mental disturbance, and is in any case a reflection of the madness of the times. As Taylor put it, in his attack on Wither, 'Nonsense is Rebellion' (*Aqua-Muse* 1645a, p. 11). It is a style which creates a strong sense of personality, despite the fact that much of it is made up of other people's words. Chapter 1 has already shown the effect which underground journalism and the sense of decorum in debate had on the creation of a composite royalist personality. The emergencies where one writer took over from another must have been an added incentive to the development of a style striking enough to conceal both the identity and the quality of a number of different authors.

The plural 'I' and Samuel Sheppard

The distinction between allusion and plagiarism depends on how well an author expects his readers to know his source. In drama, of necessity, literary borrowings cannot easily be acknowledged without holding up the action. When Jonson's characters quote or steal lines from well-known writers, the fact is frequently signalled by comment within the play, but when it is the author rather than the character who borrows, he must rely on the discrimination of the audience to distinguish skill from theft, or to understand how far Truewit's paradoxical speeches in *Epicoene* express the views of Ovid and Juvenal, those of the character, or those of the author himself. Jonson's commonplace book, published after his death as *Timber, or Discoveries*, was read for many years as a collection of original critical essays, aphorisms, and personal comments. Scholarship has made it increasingly clear that Jonson was in fact drawing on classical sources even in those passages which, on the face of it, seem the most personal. As Ian Donaldson (1985) remarks, this means that the pronoun 'I' often has a plural sense; the writer cannot honestly separate his individual voice from those of the authors who, inevitably, have become part of him (pp. xii–xvi). The very fact that an author is writing for himself makes the acknowledgement of sources unnecessary; *he* knows where the words come from. This may explain why Marvell, most of whose works seem to have been written for a very small circle of acquaintances, is such a highly literary writer. We have learned to accept, even admire, the way in which an individual voice rises from the chorus of tradition, as Nicéron's composite pictures create one face out of many. But there are writers whose use of the plural 'I' raises questions about their own sense of identity. One of these is Samuel Sheppard.

Sheppard has already been mentioned in chapter 1 as a prolific contributor to royalist propaganda in the late 1640s. What little is known of his life (mostly from Rollins 1927) suggests an ideological movement typical of the period. He was apparently a clergyman. In 1646 he was a Presbyterian pamphleteer, a supporter of the parliamentary cause, and an admirer of Fairfax; within two years he had turned against Parliament and was writing fervently royalist propaganda for the news-sheets, some of it in the form of miniature plays. In February 1648 he published an anonymous 'seditious and blasphemous' piece of writing, *Ecce The New Testament of our Lords and Saviours, the House of Commons at Westminster*, which offended the House so much that a reward was offered for the apprehension of its author.[1] He was finally imprisoned in May of that year, but not for long; he was back to journalism almost at once. In 1649 he was taken again for helping to write the illegal *Mercurius Elencticus* and suffered his longest period of imprisonment, fourteen months. He spent most of this time writing. *The Loves of Amandus and Sophronia*, a prose romance, was published in 1650; some of it takes place in prison. He also began his chief project, which he hoped would be his masterpiece, an epic poem in *ottava rima* called *The Faerie King*. After his release he published a collection of *Epigrams* (1651); he also continued to write pamphlets, including pseudonymous mock almanacs for 1653 and 1654. Davenant's publication of *Gondibert* (1651), in an unfinished state, may have inspired Sheppard to start preparing the still unfinished *Faerie King* for publication though, for some reason, it remained in manuscript until 1984.

That Sheppard was a particularly wide-ranging plagiarist has been known at least since 1691, when Gerard Langbaine's *Account of the English Dramatic Poets* identified the most obvious sources of his miniature two-part comedy, *The Committee-Man Curried* (1647). Its subtitle, *a Comedy presented to the view of all men*, draws attention to the fact that Sheppard was not afraid to publish it under his own name. It contains no serious political or religious comment, merely satire on a number of types who would probably have been generally recognised as the unacceptable face of post-war England. Moreover, Sheppard's apparently open acknowledgement of his authorship is only partly true. The play is heavily indebted to other authors, especially Stapylton, Suckling and Webster. Since part of Sheppard's purpose in writing it was to comment on the renewal of the ordinance against stage-plays in July 1647, the inclusion of two drinking songs from Suckling's plays and some of Webster's easily detachable sententious couplets might have been a way of reminding theatre-starved readers of what they had been missing. Elsewhere, it is less easy to justify his borrowings. His romance, *The Loves of Amandus and Sophronia* (1650), contains a truly appalling imitation of one of Suckling's most famous lyrics:

> Why so coy and nice dear Lady,
> Pray you, why so nice?
> You long to make your Lord a Daddy,
> Is kissing then a vice,
>   pray you, why so nice.   (p. 37)

Homage or parody? His prologue to part II of *The Committee-man Curried* offers a rather attractive evocation of the pre-war theatre,

> Which once a hackney Coach convey'd you to,
> Where you sate scorning all the raine could doe.

The only trouble is that the lines are adapted from Suckling, who used the present tense because the pleasures he describes were still available to him at the time of writing (Suckling 1971, p. 70). So Sheppard is appropriating not only the words but the experience of his predecessor.

Personal and confessional passages like this are among the most attractive in Sheppard's work, so it is disconcerting to find that they are neither personal nor confessional. An early pamphlet expresses his sense of the topsy-turvy world which the levellers' proposals would create. It enrages him, he declares,

to see a Faulkner or Huntsman get better wages then a Student, a spruce Lawyer get more in an houre then a plaine Philosopher in a moneth.

> (*The False Alarm*, 1646, preface)

In a late pamphlet, *The Weepers* (1652), he is disarmingly apologetic: 'Thou canst not think worse of me (Reader) than I doe of my selfe' (p. 12). Both passages are taken, almost unaltered, from *The Anatomy of Melancholy* (Burton 1955, pp. 55, 20). Sheppard's Epigram, 'On My Self', contains what appears to be a lively self-portrait:

> Just in the Planetary houre
> Of *Satturne* (who doth ever lowre)
> I viewd the light; it much doth winne mee,
> I have part of that Plannet in me.
> No way facetious am I
> To toyish mirth or Jollitie,
> Yet in one dreame I can compose
> A *Comedy*, in Verse or Prose,
> Behold the Action, apprehend
> The Jest, and the quaint plot commend,
> And so much of the sence partake,
> As serv's to laugh my selfe awake.   (1651, *Epigrams*, p. 12)

This, for all its ingenuous appearance, is simply a versification of a passage on dreams from Browne's *Religio Medici* (1643):

I was borne in the Planetary houre of *Saturne*, and I think I have a peece of that Leaden Planet in me. I am no way facetious, nor disposed for the mirth and galliardize of company, yet in one dreame I can compose a whole Comedy, behold the action, apprehend the jests, and laugh my selfe awake at the conceits thereof.

> (Browne 1964, p. 71)

Because of his penchant for experiencing life in the words of other people, and the confusion over the authorship of the royalist journals in 1647–51, it is difficult to trace the development of Sheppard's political views. However, his enthusiasm for Webster's *White Devil* may provide a clue to some of his activities between the autumn of 1647 and the spring of 1648. *Mercurius Anti-Pragmaticus* quotes from the play in each of its first three numbers: the author paraphrases Vittoria's comparison of her detractors to men who 'go pistol flies' (12–19 Oct. 1647) and Montecelso's comparison of her to the counterfeit coin 'which whosoever stamps, brings in trouble all that receive it' (21–8 Oct. 1647). One allusion in particular – when the writer suggests that his rival *Pragmaticus* is in danger of being 'tripped up in the rushes like another *Camillo*' (28 Oct.–4 Nov. 1647) – would have been meaningless to a reader who did not know Webster's play well. *Mercurius Pragmaticus* has picked up the same habit by January 1648, when it borrows Flamineo's description of a Machiavellian as one who tickles his enemies to death and Vittoria's reference to poison hidden in gilded pills (11–18 Jan. 1648). A few weeks later, *Mercurius Dogmaticus* (27 Jan. – 7 Feb. 1648) adapts, with reference to Parliament and its supporters, a couplet about Webster's sinful lovers Bracciano and Vittoria. In July 1648 another pamphlet echoes Flamineo's reference to Lucian's 'ridiculous purgatory' (*The Last Will and Testament of Tom Fairfax and the Army under his Command* [9 July] 1648). The sheer number of these quotations, and the fact that they reflect such close knowledge of the play, make it likely that one person was responsible for them all, and Sheppard, who had already echoed Webster in an acknowledged work and was to publish an Epigram 'On Mr Webster's most excellent Tragedy, called the White Devill' (*Epigrams*, v, 27), is the most obvious candidate. If this is true, then the Websterian echoes convict him of having written, in quick succession, for two rival journals, *Mercurius Anti-Pragmaticus* and *Mercurius Pragmaticus*. Probably the rivalry was factitious, an attempt to boost circulation. He may have played this trick more than once. When his most scandalous pamphlet, *Ecce the New Testament* (1648), was publicly condemned for its blasphemous language ('Now the birth, or beginning of this Parliament, was on this wise'), the author of *Mercurius Elencticus*, despite his royalism, dissociated himself from it (23 Feb.–1 March 1648). Sheppard was one of the writers of *Elencticus* at this period; it is possible that he himself wrote the denunciation, trying simultaneously to give his work some extra publicity and to conceal his involvement in both the journal and the pamphlet.

The recent edition of *The Faerie King* by P. J. Klemp has finally made it possible to see with what sort of work Sheppard hoped to leave his name to posterity. Its interest, such as it is, does not lie in its qualities as a poetic *roman-à-clef*. When the author wishes to discuss historical characters, he uses their real names: he lists Richard III and Richelieu among the inhabitants of hell (II.v.9, 13), and names both James I and Charles I in his list of great British writers (v.vi.59, 74). He also attacks presbytery and the Scots by name. There is, of course, an obvious resemblance between pre-war England and the situation of the fictitious Ruina, which 'had long surfeited on peace' at the point when the poem begins. But if Sheppard is writing a coded history, he has succeeded in making it largely impenetrable.

As it stands – unfinished, in six books of six cantos each – *The Faerie King* tells two stories. One is that of Ariodant, who succeeds to the throne at the beginning of the poem and immediately resolves on war with his uncle, the murderer of his father. When a wise old counsellor points out that his uncle's army is superior to his in numbers, Ariodant throws him in prison. He further complicates his political situation by antagonising his father-in-law and sends his queen, Olympia, to make peace with him. This embassy serves the further purpose of removing her from the court at a time when he has begun to lust after a newly arrived female warrior, Olivia. However, his lecherous designs come to nothing. He and his uncle Sansonet meet in battle and, although the latter's forces are victorious, Ariodant succeeds in killing him. The sight of his slaughtered troops awakens a much needed sense of responsibility in the young king; at this point, however, he meets the figure of Despair on whose persuasion he commits suicide.

The interest of the action then shifts to Olivia and her true lover, Byanor, survivors of the fight but separated by it. They undergo a series of mainly allegorical ordeals before they meet again, engage in a duel to the death, and are saved by an old hermit who converts them to Christianity. During this, the most Spenserian part of the poem, they visit the House of Eloquence, where Sheppard gives one of those lists of Great Writers so popular in this period. The final book returns to non-allegorical romance. Olivia and Byanor are shipwrecked on the coast of Ruina, where they find Olympia, Ariodant's widowed queen, just in time to see her murdered. The poem breaks off as a new intrigue seems to be developing: we are told that Sansonet's widow has conquered all of Ruina, partly by the treachery of Ariodant's viceroy and partly by killing Ariodant's father-in-law in battle. Presumably Byanor and Olivia (whose name means the olive of peace) were intended to defeat her at last, thus fulfilling a mysterious prophecy (v.v.34) which indicates that a ruler who unites three crowns will be the ultimate victor.

As is evident from the title, the poem offers itself as a homage to Spenser.

Sheppard may also be thinking of James Howell's allegory *Dodona's Grove*, in which the kingdom of Druina stands for England. His other literary borrowings include (at IV.i.17) a passage from *The Faerie Queene* which had already been plagiarised in *Crafty Cromwell* (1648), and he quotes yet again the much-quoted 'ring the bells backward', from Cleveland's 'Rebel Scot' and Webster's fable of Reputation, Love and Death, from *The Duchess of Malfi*. Insofar as any aspect of the poem can be called peculiar to Sheppard, it is, unfortunately, his social snobbery. He appears to have no doubt as to the right of his heroes to dispose of the lives of their followers as they see fit. At sea in a storm, Byanor and Olivia astutely get into the cockboat of their ship before their sailors think of it, and when the latter start struggling to join them Byanor is 'forc'd to Massacre them all' (VI.iv.29), so that only he and his bride come safely to land. But Sheppard's plot is sufficiently original, and sufficiently confused, to leave one in genuine suspense as to how it would have ended. Byanor, the converted Christian, may be the true Fairy King of the title. Or perhaps Olivia's name is an allusion to Cromwell's, which, by 1654, had often been associated with the olives of peace (see below, p. 195). In that case, the poem might reflect Sheppard's willingness to compromise with the Protectorate. But it is not even clear whether his intentions are tragicomic or tragic. The multiplicity of influences on his writing extends even to his view of life. He seems to be equally divided between the Spenserian model in which good triumphs over evil and the Websterian one in which virtue is almost inevitably doomed to be a victim. Suckling's double ending for *Aglaura* – played as a comedy one night and a tragedy the next – might have suited this poem very well.

Sheppard's ambivalence about acknowledging other people's authorship is part of an equal ambivalence about his own. At one point, he claims that his choice of the genre of heroic romance is an act of defiance to his age:

> while Wrath, & Malice, Envie, Discord, Rage
> fell Furie, and all hells black broode are come
> to Act their parts upon our English stage
> setting on fire, the face of Christendome,
> I, in this cursed, cruell, monstrous Age
> doe chaunt it, to the musick of the Drum
> to let men know, Mars, his stentorian tone
> can mix with the soft Aires of Helicon.   (IV.v.2)

But this heroic declaration is somewhat undermined by the fact that Sheppard never published the poem. His *Epigrams* (1651) include two poems on *The Faerie King*, so he obviously had no hesitation in advertising its existence. Yet its editor has noted the 'tantalizing contradiction in Sheppard's willingness to admit his responsibility for the poem', as indicated by the state of the manuscript, where he cuts his name off the page in one place, writes it in at another, then crosses it out again, 'but so half-heartedly that it is still visible' (x). It is possible that the work would have gone to press if Sheppard had lived longer (nothing is heard of him after 1655), but it is equally possible that his nerve would have failed him.

Like *The Faerie King*, his most interesting works, the mock almanacs of 1653 and 1654, reflect the mixture of self-advertisement and timidity with which Sheppard approached his literary career. Although he did not publish them under his own name, the one he used, Raphael Desmus, was an anagram of it (Rollins 1927, 535–8). Almanacs, based on the reading of the stars and containing predictions for each day the following year, as well as useful general information, were a politically sensitive kind of publication as well as a lucrative one. During the civil war the almanacs of the astrologer William Lilly, mostly predicting Parliamentary successes, had been countered by those of George Wharton, Sheppard's colleague on *Mercurius Elencticus*, which, with less and less success, had predicted victories for the royal party. Sheppard thus knew something about the genre. His own almanacs, however, are a parody of it, with obviously comic predictions and lists of saints including Catiline, Sejanus, the Earl of Gowrie and Messalina. It is not surprising that he felt he needed to publish under a pseudonym. He had presumably been pardoned and released from prison on the understanding that he would avoid writing against the government. His 1651 *Epigrams* include verses addressed to Cromwell (p. 170) as well as advice to 'the Pamphleteers of the times' to stop vexing the state (p. 148). But he does not seem to have been comfortable in his conformity. He wrote a commendatory poem to Thomas Manley's *Veni, Vidi, Vici, the Triumphs of the Most Excellent and Industrious Oliver Cromwell* (1651), but in it refers to the hero as 'our famous Nol'. Is this an affectionate assimilation of Cromwell to the popular mode, or an attempt to sabotage Manley's poem?

The mock almanacs embody his political uncertainty by employing quotations in a dialogic relationship. In the 1653 almanac there are, for instance, a number of echoes of Donne's poems, which he appears to have been reading around this time: he quotes, among others, Satire IV, the famous passages from the 'First Anniversary' about 'new philosophy' and loss of coherence, and the opening of 'The Calm':

> Our storm is past, and that storms tyrannous rage
> A stupid calme, but nothing it, doth swage.

It is evident from the context that the stupid calm is the state of post-war England. As if to counteract the effect of this comment, he also asserts, 'People of *England* you can never be happy, till you adhere to the lawfull power, linger as long as ye list, PLENARY POSSESSION MAKES A LAWFUL POWER ... there's Divinity for you' (sig B1). But which is the lawful power? What makes his attitude uncertain is that he is almost certainly echoing Ferdinand's sarcastic ranting in the last scene of *The Duchess of Malfi*: 'pain many times is taken away with the apprehension of greater, as the tooth-ache with the sight of a barber that comes to pull it out – there's philosophy for you' (v.v.59–62). Yet his views are not always hidden even as carefully as his name. The verses preceding his table of English kings, a standard feature of almanacs, end thus:

> Yet be it known, that once we had a King.
> Take caution CAVIE ['little Cavalier'], for there stands one near,
> Will take thy eyes out, if thou shed a tear.   (sig. A6)

To be afraid of censorship, and yet to say *openly* that one is afraid of it, is utterly consistent with the whole of Sheppard's pattern of behaviour. Apparently, he cannot decide whether he does or does not accept the end of monarchy; he can neither speak his mind openly nor remain silent.

The most charitable thing Langbaine could think of to say about Sheppard was that his loyalty was 'far better than his Poetry' (1691, p. 471). Rollins, the only other person to pay any attention to him, was intrigued by the fact that he openly praised the writers whom he secretly pilfered. The two comments are interrelated, and can be explained, on my theory, by the game of hide-and-seek that Sheppard was playing. This game had an ironic effect on his reputation. Until Rollins did the research on which his article is based, Sheppard's one claim to fame (preserved in the *DNB* account of him) was that he was supposed to have been Jonson's amanuensis in the first decade of the seventeenth century. This would have made him rather elderly for a career of underground journalism in 1646–54. Rollins pointed out that this assumption was based on a misreading of some lines in Sheppard's early poem, *The Times Displayed* (1646): it is Apollo, not Sheppard himself, who, in the course of a lament for the state of poetry, claims to have held the pen for Ben Jonson (Rollins 1927, pp. 511–12). It is characteristic of Sheppard that, despite his eagerness for fame and his constant name-dropping, he could not manage even to convey a clear account of the basic facts about himself. But the verses which he wrote to accompany the decorated title page of his *Epigrams* make me wonder whether this confusion was, after all, just what he intended. He describes himself as

> one
> Whose *Language* and *Invention*
> Whether Legitimate or no,
> He knowes, but few will care to know.[2]

A small picture at the bottom of the page shows the plainly dressed author handing his book to Mercury, who is famous as a notorious liar and patron of journalists.

Metaphor and reality

Sheppard is a particularly extreme example of a phenomenon which also occurs in the work of better-known writers. It can be argued that what bewilders one in Sheppard is simply the result of incompetent writing on his part. But what happens when we compare him with Marvell? The latter describes experiences which may or may not be real; he frequently uses the persona of someone else; his 'echoing song' echoes many other voices; and his attitudes, in precisely the period covered by Sheppard's writing, are notoriously hard to pin down. The usual reaction is either to praise his detachment or claim that he was really a fully committed writer from the outset. Occasionally, however, someone expresses doubts about Marvell which are very like those to which Sheppard's work gives rise: 'I don't think it's impossible for a man to explore his private thoughts by meditating on or even imitating the work of another . . . but it is also possible for a man to use another's thought and manner to evade his own' (Shrapnel 1971, pp. 172–3). Is it possible that the mystifications of Sheppard and Marvell might be the ultimate secret code, one intended to keep them from understanding themselves?

I shall come back to this question at the end of this chapter. Meanwhile, I should like to examine the extent of this subordination of life to literature in other writers. Sheppard's habit of appropriating other people's experiences may not have seemed as odd to his contemporaries as it does to us. The claim to have been an eye-witness of events must have been made by the authors of many narratives purely to increase their saleability. When publishing his *Historical Memoirs* of the reigns of Elizabeth and James, which are based largely on gossip and hearsay, the amateur historian Francis Osborne (1658) admitted that 'It is ordinarily affirmed, *I have seen this or that*, when the most of it hath arrived at us from Report. And in this sense, I may be said to have seen *these*' (preface). The practice of historians who make up a speech for a character where they feel one is needed, and the dramatic accounts of battles by messengers who apparently have total recall of everything said and done by the major combatants in different parts of the field, are examples of generally accepted conventions which Osborne may be using to justify his own unreliable memoirs. What happens in the mid-century is that the line between literal and metaphorical or analogical truth becomes increasingly hard to draw.

Josephine Miles (1948), in a study of the words most commonly used in poetry of the 1640s, found that a vocabulary dominated by 'heaven', 'earth', 'eye', 'heart', 'make', and 'see' was common to both the verse and the prose of writers otherwise totally different in political and religious allegiance (pp. 120–1). The distinguishing feature of this vocabulary, she argues, is 'its sense of relationship between two worlds, in place, time, and feeling, and moral responsibility' (p. 110). It was this shared concern which united writers imaginatively even as it divided them in practice. Man himself was the link between these two worlds, able to 'see' their relation through the 'eye' and 'heart', or to 'make' it visible to others. This view, as Browne among others expressed it, makes the whole visible world a code devised by God (Browne 1964, pp. 15, 33–4).

Since Miles's work focused on common rather than rare vocabulary it did not touch on the personal and peculiar kinds of language which tend to be best remembered, precisely because they occur so rarely. But the emphasis on majority vocabulary is helpful in reminding us that language in itself does not necessarily identify a particular political party. One reason for this, which Miles does not go into, is the fact that writers on both sides not only rely on, but seek to appropriate, the same biblical images such as the sun, the eagle, the Woman in the Wilderness, King David, and so on. Bunyan's image of his spiritual struggle in *Grace Abounding* – literally 'tugging' against the devil for the possession of a particular text (Bunyan 1966, p. 70) – is not unlike the struggle that went on between royalists and parliamentarians. Either literally or metaphorically (and the controversy over Scripture interpretation hinged on just this point), both sides were able to see themselves as reliving biblical episodes. The troubles of Israel under a succession of idolatrous tyrants, as recounted in the two books of Kings, were applied by one side to Charles I's Laudian reforms and by the other to the state of the country under, successively, Pym, Fairfax, and Cromwell. The outrageous accusations which each party makes against its opponents are not simply mud-slinging; they derive from such biblical verses as 'What peace, so long as the whoredoms of thy mother Jezebel and her witchcrafts are so many?' (2 Kings 9:22), 'the land hath committed great whoredom, departing from the Lord' (Hosea 1:2), and another text, very popular with royalists, 'rebellion is as the sin of witchcraft' (1 Samuel 25:23). These key texts naturally took on a new meaning in this period. Hosea's vision of Israel as a cesspool of evil, doomed to divine wrath, was of burning relevance for the preachers to Parliament in the early 1640s, when the idols of Charles's Catholic queen were being set up in the high places and the land was in danger of departing from the Lord if it did not make a covenant with Him. It seemed equally relevant to royalist sympathisers in the last half of the decade, who quoted the verse about 'swearing falsely in making a covenant' (Hosea 10:4) and observed that 'Mistress' Parliament, by tolerating competing religious sects, had become more of a prostitute than her old enemy, the Whore of Babylon, 'drunken with the blood of the saints' (Revelation 17:6; see Potter 1987, p. 112). It is only a step from this to accusing the leading parliamentarians of being cuckolds and adulterers. Feelings about the Catholic Henrietta Maria became inseparable from feelings about the Whore of Babylon.

The meaning of biblical references depends on the recognition that they *are* biblical. Not to recognise them is to exclude oneself, either deliberately (e.g. villains) or unconsciously (e.g. fools), from the interpretative community. In the anonymous late fifteenth-century play *Mankind*, Mercy's sermon, with its warning about the imminent separation of the grain from the chaff, is interrupted by the vice Mischief who claims to be worried about this news because he is trying to get a job as a thresher. Mischief's refusal to understand the language of metaphor and parable is a wilful rejection of the idea that language has any non-material reference; literary competence – in this case, a capacity to understand figurative language – is equivalent to a capacity for religious experience. The reading public is thus divided, not into those who do or don't understand the code, but into those who do or don't recognise that a code is being used. But the habit of seeing real events in biblical terms, and vice versa, makes it hard to tell whether biblical analogies are expressive or performative utterances. When Bishop Duppa's correspondence was seized in 1659, special attention was paid to a letter in which he referred to the Israelites crossing the Red Sea (Bosher 1951, pp. 96–7). Those who read it thought it was a coded reference to the return of the royalists and the Church of England; for Duppa, it may have been only a consoling analogy.

In May 1641 a panic about a fire in the House of Commons was inadvertently started by someone who said, on leaving a debate, that there was 'hot work and a great fire within' (R. Baillie, *Letters* 1841, vol I, p. 352; quoted Fletcher 1981, p. 15). This confusion is an example of what has been called 'the destabilising of metaphor' (Wilcox 1990), the use of images in a relation to the real world so close as to suggest identity rather than merely likeness. The idea of an image is itself problematic in the context of a period which saw so many attacks on idolatry. Ernest Gilman (1986) has suggested that this sin was sometimes given an extreme interpretation: 'anyone who carnally conceives in himself a false image is no less guilty of idolatry than if he had bowed down before a block of wood' (p. 45). This fear of the power of the verbal image, paradoxically, makes it all the more vivid. Even to mention a contemptible object, even to use it metaphorically in a context of disapprobation, was still to lend ammunition to an opponent eager to argue that the words themselves had some sort of real status in the life of the person who used them. This is why writers of controversial literature harp so irritatingly on one another's choice of imagery, as when Joseph Hall and Milton pretend that references to 'old cloaks, false beards, night-walkers, and salt lotion' prove familiarity with 'playhouses and bordellos' (Milton 1953, *An Apology*, p. 886). When a writer speaks of members of one's own family betraying one, or of the penitence which may be a cordial for a king, it may be a general point, a biblical reference, or an allusion to contemporary events. The contemporary associations are sometimes so strong as to overpower the image itself, as when Davenant writes of two conspirators

> wilde with hast,
> As Traytors are whom Visitants surprise;
> Decyph'ring that which fearfully they cast
> In some dark place, where viler Treason lies.
>
> (*Gondibert*, III. i.73)

The common theme of withdrawal from an uncongenial world into solitude and darkness – for instance, in Henry Vaughan's poetry – is equally ambiguous: is the world a hostile place simply because it *is* the world, or because its dominant political or religious trends are uncongenial to the writer? Vaughan's parables, unlike Herbert's, do not always make clear which is the plain text and which the coded one. Is the exile of earthly life a purely metaphysical concept in an age when so many royalists were living in exile or had lost part of their estates? The standard metaphors for human existence are almost indistinguishable from the conditions in which writers actually felt themselves to be living: an atmosphere of darkness, imprisonment, isolation, drunkenness, and possession. This atmosphere in turn affects their ability to speak 'as themselves'.

Divine rites: the prison and the tavern

The peculiarity of what Joan Webber (1968) calls the royalist-anglican literary persona is that it is at once extremely vivid and extremely generalised: a 'cosmic personality' which is at the same time self-conscious, 'obscure, ambiguous, many-sided' (pp. 7–8). If Sheppard's literary personality has these qualities, it is partly because he is modelling himself on some of the same prose writers that Webber discusses, notably Burton and Browne, and on poems and plays by others with similar personae like Donne, Webster, and Suckling. These writers are linked by two common factors: they are themselves highly 'literary'; and they or their characters are also self-confessed melancholics. Their mental world is painted in chiaroscuro; their characteristic imagery is that of confinement. The royalist mode in the mid-century is increasingly characterised by this sense of darkness and confined spaces.

Many poems of the period could be described as nocturnals. Lovelace, whose names for his mistresses (Lucasta/light, Althea/truth) are obviously significant, ends 'To Lucasta from Prison' with a vision of the king as the only source of light and truth in a world of darkness and error:

> And now an univerall mist
>   Of Error is spread or'e each breast,
> With such a fury edg'd, as is
>   Not found in th'inwards of th'Abysse.
>
> Oh from thy glorious Starry Waine
>   Dispense on me one sacred Beame
> To light me where I soone may see
>   How to serve you, and you trust me.

It is in many ways a Websterian vision: life is seen as 'a general mist of error' (*Duchess*, iv.ii.188) irradiated only by an occasional bright glimpse of human integrity emerging from the darkness.

It is often difficult to separate literal from metaphorical darkness. In 1647, the seventh number of *Mercurius Melancholicus* opened with the announcement that the author had just come

> Forth from my sad and loansome Cell,
>   and from a place as dark as Hell.   (9–16 Oct. 1647)

James Howell's *New Volume of Letters* had appeared shortly before *Melancholicus* (the dedication is signed 1 May; the book probably came out a month or two later). Howell, dedicating his collection to the Duke of York, described it as having been 'born a captive, and bred up in the dark shades of melancholy'. The result of this phrasing was that he was then suspected, briefly, of being the author of *Melancholicus* (Potter 1987, p. 104). What Howell was actually referring to was the Fleet Prison, where he had already been confined for four years. The shades of melancholy and those of prison are indeed hardly distinguishable in the language of the period.

The centrality of prison in the lives of the reading public can be seen from the fact that even *Wit's Interpreter* (1655b), John Cotgrave's collection of literature and pastimes for the fashionable and would-be fashionable, includes a dialogue for a lover and his mistress who is visiting him in prison (p. 55). Douglas Bush, in his history of pre-Restoration literature, draws attention to the number of 'writers who suffered imprisonment, civil or political' (Bush 1945, p. 29). It is a long one and includes representatives of both sides in the civil war. Not only did writers become prisoners, prisoners also became writers. They seem to have had access to unlimited supplies of pens and paper, and to have been so successful in conveying their work to the outside world that at one point there were rumours of a secret press in the Tower (Cotton 1971, p. 27). The stream of pamphlets from the imprisoned levellers, Lilburne and Overton, can be paralleled on the royalist side by the voluminous correspondence of Lilburne's fellow-prisoner, Sir Lewis Dyve, who wrote secretly to the king every few days (Dyve 1958, p. 50). Charles I was probably the most prolific correspondent of all. According to the calculations of a recent biographer (Carlton 1983), he may have written over a thousand letters in 1648 alone (p. 330).

Prison literature was already a genre in its own right for the Eliza-bethans, but the mid-century prisoner differed from most of his prede-cessors in that he could present himself as a guiltless sufferer for reasons of conscience: a 'loyal traitor', to use Sir Francis Wortley's phrase. The role must have had a certain glamour, since a large number of writers adopt it. As we have already seen, Davenant told his readers that the last completed book of *Gondibert* was written in prison, and Samuel Sheppard describes his *Fairie King* as having been 'pen'd for the most part in severall Prisons' (1984 p, 23). One of the most popular poems of the period was 'The Liberty of the Imprisoned Royalist' (1647), somewhat doubtfully at-tributed to Sir Roger L'Estrange. The authorship of prison poems is not always easy to determine; like the 'last Goodnight', they were likely to be attributed to any prisoner known to have been poetically inclined – Sir Walter Ralegh, for example. Even people not previously thought of as poets had verses ascribed to them, as when a ballad, supposedly by Straf-ford, was published immediately after his execution:

> Go empty joys wth all your noise
> And leave me here alone
> In sweet sad silence to bemoan,
> Poor fickle worldly wight,
> Whose danger none can see alone
> Whilst your false splendour dims the light[3]

The verses clearly belong to a *contemptus mundi* tradition which owes nothing to Strafford's own life and character. But even if they had been his, they might well have been written in equally general terms. It is often hard to tell whether poems of imprisonment derive from real experience or merely from, say, the idea of the body as the prison of the soul. Henry King's verse 'Essay on Death and a Prison' is basically a statement of the commonplace that thought is free even when the thinker is imprisoned. The author writes as if from personal experience:

> Whilst I in Prison ly, nothing is free,
> Nothing enlarg'd, but Thought and Misery.   (1965, pp. 139–40)

But the 'I' of this poem, which dates from King's youth, is purely hypothetical. It reflects nothing of his later experience when the Parliamentary army plundered the Episcopal palace at Chichester and came close to arresting him. Likewise, when Henry Vaughan addresses the first poem in *Thalia Rediviva* (1658) to 'His Learned Friend and Loyal Fellow-Prisoner', Thomas Powell, 'imprisonment' appears to mean something more like exile or a sense of restraint (Powell had been sequestered from his living). The same appears to be true for Robert Wild, who describes himself in *Iter Boreale* (1660) as one 'who whilom sat and sung in cage / My King's and country's ruin' (Wild 1963, p. 4, lines 23–4), though as deForest Lord points out in his note to these lines he seems never in fact to have been imprisoned. These writers may indeed have *felt* themselves confined by an uncongenial society.

Even the genuine prisoner may find it easier to apprehend his experience through literature. The compilation of a commonplace-book, into which lengthy texts were laboriously copied, is not only a way of passing the time but a source of consolation, because it shows the prisoner that he is not alone in his suffering. John Gibson, imprisoned for five years in Durham Castle, seems to have begun his commonplace-book with a transcription of some works by St John Chrysostom, 'to passe away my melancholy' (p. 5ᵛ). The book may have begun as a totally private work. Some of its contents are addressed to himself as a reproof against impatience: 'St Paul was far a more considerable person than thou canst be, and yet it pleased

God to shut him in prison for two yeeres' (p. 113ᵛ). This theme becomes
something of an obsession: there are lists of worthy figures of the past who
have suffered unjustly, and of bad men who have prospered. Gibson
worked out a coat of arms for himself, and a motto, 'In Infaelicitate Faelix'
(p. 162); he drew 'the house of my pilgrimage'; a prison below and a palace
above (p. 161); and pasted in pictures from other sources, including a
number of emblems and an engraved portrait of Charles I. He also included
a number of poems and meditations of his own, some of them rather
attractive laments for a grove on his estate of which he was particularly
fond. He shares with other 'prison' writers the ability to move effortlessly
between his own thoughts and words and those of others. Those represented in the book include royalist favourites: George Herbert, the sermon
which Laud preached on the scaffold, Jeremy Taylor, and Cleveland.
Gibson's royalism seems, if anything, to have grown with his imprisonment. He includes large numbers of poems on the king's death and gives a
list of Scripture passages which fit the heading 'Royall and Loyall'. His
sense of his intended audience grew. In 1656 he wrote a dedication to his
son, and after his release in 1660 he thought of publishing his reflections
under the title *Amara Dulcis, or, the bitter-sweet sufferings of the Saints
and Servants of God in all ages of the World*, and of bringing out a separate
volume of his own meditations called *Immured Phansyes*. He got as far as
writing an address to its hypothetical reader; after signing his name, he
crossed it out, replacing it with 'Carolophylos' (p. 213). Like Sheppard, he
seems to have taken the project no further.

Gibson's commonplace-book is a much more personal work than much
prison writing that I have examined, partly because he seems to have had
very little company in Durham Castle and partly because he refers to his
home more frequently than most: because his wife's name was Penelope,
he calls it his Ithaca. Solitude and isolation create a desire for pattern: he
fills pages with anagrams on his and his wife's names, lists of significant
dates, and parallels between the lives of Thomas Cromwell and Oliver
Cromwell. For other writers, like those in the overcrowded London
prisons, it was possible to create collective rituals which satisfied the same
desire for pattern and meaning. This is part of the point of their constant
references to drinking, probably the best-known feature of 'cavalier' verse.
The dominance of this theme has been seen by critics, much as it was seen
by contemporary satirists, as a sign of the increasing degeneracy and
demoralisation of the king's cause in the period of defeat. Wedgwood
(1960), for instance, sees a steady decline from the spirit of Lovelace's 'To
Althea from Prison': 'In the imitations written on the same theme this

noble element is gradually weakened; there is a good deal about loyalty, more about mistresses, still more about drink' (p. 107). If she had extended her survey from poems to plays she would have found even more about drink, since one feature rarely missing from comedies, even the miniature comedies and tragicomedies of the 1640s, is the tavern scene complete with drinking song. Idealisation of the rituals of getting drunk was the kind of thing that gave the cavaliers a bad name (some called them 'cabs', short for caballeros). Charles I was never, in this sense, the 'brave Prince of Cavaliers' that Herrick called him ('To the King, upon his comming with his Army into the West'); his own lack of sympathy with heavy drinking is well known, and it was to him that Prynne had dedicated his pamphlet against the practice of drinking healths (*Health's Sickness*) in 1628. Some drinking songs of the mid-century are no more than a restatement of themes developed before the war (for instance, in Cartwright's *Royal Slave*, which condemns elaborate drinking rituals but also includes a lively song in which the prisoners praise the 'liberty' which drinking gives them). Some writers, however, go beyond this vulgar cavalierism to a philosophy which deserves closer attention.

A characteristic often noticed in cavalier writing is its endowing of private settings and rituals with a transcendental meaning. Earl Miner's study of *The Cavalier Mode* (1971) traces the theme of the cavalier 'winter' and its relation to the themes of retirement and friendship, whose existence is consciously celebrated and preserved. Leah Marcus (1986) suggests that these private rituals were a reaction against the transformation of old holiday pastimes into sources of genuinely popular rebellion: royalists, alarmed by this growing anarchy, were seeking shelter in 'protective enclosures: estates, gardens, mystical groves' (p. 214). The prison and the tavern are other such enclosures, in which, with the help of alcohol, the cavalier can carry on rituals of loyalty. The parliamentary satirist, John Hall, recognised the importance of this element when he advised royalist writers to 'contain your selves at your Clubs, and there under the *Rose* vent all your set forms of execrations against the Parliament' (*Mercurius Britanicus*, 11 July 1648). 'Set forms' was the term commonly used for the words of the Church of England liturgy and Book of Common Prayer, and the link between these and tavern society is not the joke which Hall's remark might suggest. The fact was that drinking rituals, once a private *macho* routine, had become both a secular liturgy and a way of parodying the authority of a government they refused to recognise.

Probably the greatest failure of the Parliamentary and Commonwealth leaders was their inability to find a satisfactory replacement for those aspects of popular culture which were linked with Church of England practice. Despite the general dislike of the increasing political power of some bishops and of Laudian innovations in worship, radical reformers were mistaken in thinking that they had been given a brief to alter all aspects of the Church. John Morrill has shown that, whereas parishes readily discarded practices recently introduced by Laud, orders to replace other traditional aspects of Anglicanism were widely ignored (Morrill 1982, pp. 94–5). There was, he argues, genuine popular enthusiasm for the 'rhythm of worship, piety, practice, that had earthed itself into the Englishman's consciousness and had sunk deep roots into popular culture' (p. 113).

Parliament attempted to channel popular celebrations in a more militantly Protestant direction (Underdown 1987, p. 70) with such symbolic spectacles as the mock battle between Cavaliers and Roundheads staged in 1645 at Blackheath, Kent, by the local Parliamentary commander (p. 258) and the Guy Fawkes' Night display of 1647, which featured 'Fire-Bals burning in the water, and rising out of the water burning, shewing the Papists conjunction and consultation with infernall Spirits' (*Modell of the Fire-Workes*). However, the chief means by which it sought to achieve a sense of communal unity was the proclamation of public fasts and thanksgivings. These had always been associated with the Puritan element in Parliament, which no doubt is why Elizabeth I indignantly rejected the first request for a public fast, in 1580 (Wilson 1969, pp. 22–3). Charles I had been equally unenthusiastic about those initiated by Parliament, as opposed to those which he himself proposed. In 1628, though he granted a petition from both houses for a public fast in commemoration of the sufferings of Protestant churches on the continent, he added that he hoped it would not become a precedent (*Bibliotheca Regia* 1659, p. 233). He may have suspected the true intention of the proposers: to set up a godly alternative to the traditional public holidays. Both the Short and the Long Parliament proposed public fasts as soon as they had assembled, and, after December 1641, there was a regular monthly fast, while other fasts or thanksgivings were proclaimed in response to events in the war (Wilson 1969, p. 57). Eventually, the second Tuesday of each month was set aside for a thanksgiving.

Royalists responded with parodies of every aspect of each occasion, from the form of its proclamation to the speeches and sermons which were its centrepiece. In 1643 a royalist company deliberately spent the day after a parliamentary fast in riotous drinking and singing, while another town got into a fight over the celebration of a thanksgiving (Underdown 1987,

P. 257). A fast-sermon of 1644 shows how each side celebrated in defiance of the other: the dedication reminds members of Parliament that 'when perhaps some elsewhere Nobles [he is probably thinking of the court at Oxford], may be solemnizing these approaching Idolized Festivals, with Playes and Interludes … Your Honours, I hope, will be fasting, praying, hearing, and receiving the word with all readines of mind' (Staunton 1644). But the appeal of the communal fasts did not survive the end of the war. The regular monthly fast was finally discontinued on 23 April 1649, because the regular occasion had been found, 'by sad experience', to have 'declined by degrees from that solemnity and due Reverence wherewith the same was at the first Institution thereof entertained' (*Act for Setting Apart* 1649). The decline may to some extent be due to the consistent sniping of the royalist pamphleteers.

Thanksgivings were a still better satiric target than fasts, since comic feasts (as I showed in chapter 1) are a traditional satiric topos. The parodies inspired by these occasions may have been intended for reading aloud or singing in private homes. In the summer of 1649 Parliament proclaimed a thanksgiving for victories in Ireland. The royalist response, a short play called *A Bartholomew Fairing* (1649), was sent, its title page explains, as 'a preparatory present to the great Thanksgiving day'. The title refers to the fact that it came out near the time of Bartholomew Fair, when people were expected to give each other souvenirs, or 'fairings', of a visit. The prologue, spoken by a pedlar with fairings for sale, ends with the suggestion that 'honest Citizens' should buy the book,

> and on the day of joy
> Laugh at old *Nol*, and drink to the *black Boy*.

Royalists, in other words, could spend the thanksgiving day in reading the play aloud among themselves. One of its scenes depicts hypocritical and probably lecherous Puritan preachers feasting with the wives of Commonwealth leaders. The long grace pronounced at their thanksgiving, full of 'O Lards', could have been performed as a parody of the 'true' thanksgiving going on in godly houses elsewhere in the kingdom.

The cult of irrationality

A short-lived publication of 1648, *Mercurius Insanus Insanissimus*, printed a song which represents drunkenness as the only rational reaction to the irrationality of Parliamentary rule:

Harke boys harke, where doe you thinke boyes,
Shall we go drinke boyes,
 For the worlds turn'd topsi turvi,
The Gentry's orethrowne,
And none knowes his owne,
 For which we may thanke a scurvy

Parliament I meane,
Who have banished cleane
 All Honesty, Right, and reason;
And now rule the Roast,
Like Knights of the Post,
 By their base and damnable Treason.   (28 March 1648)

Drunkenness, as well as being a hostile gesture toward the sectarians, could parody the 'inspiration' on which they claimed to act. It could also be taken more seriously as an example of the release from the prison of the body into a world of quasi-mystical experience. The language of Vaughan's religious writing, invoking the 'deep and dazzling darkness' of mystical experience and the longing to dissolve into unity with God ('The Night'), is a transformation of the images which haunt his secular poetry. 'The Rhapsody', published in his first collection of 1646, was inspired, its title says, by a room in the Globe Tavern 'painted over head with a cloudy sky and some few dispersed stars and on the sides with land-scapes, hills, shepherds, and sheep'. Part of the effect of the poem comes from the writer's alternation between apparent belief in the reality of these images and awareness that they are only painted (and badly painted at that):

Darkness, & stars i' the mid day! they invite
Our active fancies to believe it night:
For taverns need no sun, but for a sign,
Where rich tobacco and quick tapers shine;
And royal witty sack, the poets' soul,
With brighter suns than he doth gild the bowl;
As though the pot and poet did agree
Sack should to both illuminator be.   (1976, lines 1–8)

At this stage, the poem is aware of the difference between reality (noon, in a painted tavern room representing night) and metaphor (the 'illuminating' effects of drink and smoking on a dark room). It then proceeds to blur the two, as the darkening of the room and the sight of the painted shepherd going home with his flock make the poet think that it is night; as his eyes travel to the painted moon he sees it rise. Has he indeed spent all afternoon drinking, or is it only the painting that has distorted his sense of time? He imagines the world outside the tavern as it would be if it really were night:

> Should we go now a wandering, we should meet
> With catchpoles, whores, & carts in every street:
> Now when each narrow lane, each nook & cave,
> Sign-posts, & shop-doors, pimp for every knave. (lines 35–8)

Rather than go out into an uncongenial world, the poet proposes two toasts, first to Caligula, then to Caesar and Sylla. These unlikely heroes are clearly celebrated in an ironic spirit. Caligula is praised for making his horse a Senator; with a gesture at the parliamentarians, Vaughan remarks,

> the gallant, jolly beast
> Of all the herd (you'll say) was not the least. (lines 49–50)

Caesar and Sylla are probably, as has been suggested, Charles I and Strafford in disguise (note on lines 47–57, pp. 451–2). The external and internal become still more confused when Vaughan conflates Caesar's invasion of the Senate with the rush of blood to the face:

> Now crown the second bowl, rich as his worth,
> I'll drink it to; he! that like fire broke forth
> Into the Senate's face, crossed Rubicon,
> And the State's pillars, with the laws thereon:
> And made the dull grey beards, & furred gowns fly
> Into *Brundusium* to consult and lie: (lines 51–6)

Is it the drunkard's face that flushes with blood and excitement, or is the poet describing the red-faced and cowardly senators, as they realise the threat to their power?

Vaughan ends by envisaging a state in which the drinkers become 'divine', 'Possessors of more souls, and nobler fire'. Like Falstaff and Ben Jonson, whose enormous pot-bellies are sometimes compared to a 'womb', the poets imagine themselves 'pregnant' from the effects of the wine, 'big with sack and mirth'. Looking at the painted sky, they are inspired to carry on drinking until they fall asleep,

> And in our merry mad mirth run
> Faster, and further than the Sun. (lines 73–4)

Marvell's speaker, in 'To His Coy Mistress', outruns the sun through the intensity of sexual experience; Vaughan's removes the need for sexual experience by making drunkenness the source both of pleasure and of creation.

The drinking song is often indistinguishable from that other kind of 'rhapsody', the Pindaric Ode, which also abdicates responsibility for both form and content. Annabel Patterson (1984) has commented illuminatingly on Cowley's adoption of the stance of the 'transported' writer to justify deliberate ambiguity and obscurity (pp. 146–7). The prophet and the drunk are variations on the royalist type I have already discussed: the melancholy man with his surprising bursts of wild laughter. The deliberate incoherence of the poem allows the author to interpolate his political views, as Vaughan does, in the manner of a drunken joker, stage malcontent, or all-licensed fool. It was in this spirit that Sir Francis Wortley wrote a poem under the persona of 'Mad Tom of Bedlam' (see above, p. 28). *Mercurius Mercuriorum, Stultissimus* (1647) explains in its first sentence that, 'Though this Pamphlet hath a foolish Title, yet in many places it plaies the foole wittily, as blind men catch Hares by chance' (sig. A2).

The female counterpart of the 'wild' cavalier is the careless, even eccentric, lady described in Herrick's 'Delight in Disorder':

> A sweet disorder in the dresse
> Kindles in cloathes a wantonnesse;
> A Lawne about the shoulders thrown
> Into a fine distraction:
> An erring Lace, which here and there
> Enthralls the Crimson Stomacher:
> A Cuffe neglectfull, and thereby
> Ribbands to flow confusedly:
> A winning wave (deserving Note)
> In the tempestuous petticote:
> A careless shooe-string, in whose tye
> I see a wilde civility:
> Doe more bewitch me, then when Art
> Is too precise in every part.   (Herrick 1965, p. 28)

The attraction of the woman whose clothes show this degree of carelessness is only partly that they make her look sexually available; the opposite of her behaviour, 'when Art/Is too precise in every part', is Puritan hypocrisy. In fact, as Herrick's phrase 'wild civility' suggests, sexy dressing in the cavalier lady is the counterpart of the drinking which 'made us nobly wild, not mad' ('An Ode for him [Ben Jonson]', p. 289). Just as the cavalier can drink heavily without getting drunk, the lady can be chaste despite her provocative dress – provocative only in the eyes of the hypocritical Puritan whose outrage results from his own lustful response. The assumption behind the wildness of the cavaliers, male and female, is that only they themselves have the right to make the rules by which they live. The fact that the lady's clothes are in rebellion against her can be seen as a humorous, unthreatening parody of real rebellion. Hers is a '*sweet* disorder', a 'fine distraction' in the midst of the distracted times.

Both these cavalier types of the irrational, however, have their dark side. In Herrick's poems it is a joke and a compliment when he says that his disordered mistress can 'bewitch' him with her wildness, or when, in one of the poems addressed 'To His Mistresses', he calls on 'my pretty Witch-crafts all' to restore his youth and potency as Medea restored Aeson's (p. 10). The image, however, corresponds to a real phenomenon of the period. The peak for witch trials, in English history, was 1645–7 (Thomas 1978, p. 537). This was partly because of the energetic 'witch-finding' of Matthew Hopkins, which ended when he himself was hanged as a witch in 1647, but it can also be explained, as it is by Keith Thomas, in terms of the increased encouragement to spy on one's neighbours in wartime and the number of unsettling events for which a scapegoat was needed. There was no ideological split between the two sides on this subject of witchcraft. Each blamed the other for the apparent epidemic. *The Parliaments Post* claimed that 'the spirit of the Cavaliers because it could not prevail with our men, hath met with some of our women, and it hath turned them into Witches' (27 July–5 Aug. 1645). Drawing on the standard biblical text (1 Samuel 15:23), *Mercurius Aulicus* observed, predictably, that witchcraft is 'an usuall Attendant on former Rebellions' (10–17 Aug. 1645). Cleveland's 'Rebel Scot' identified the Scots with witches and suggested the folk remedy of 'scratching':

> *Scots* are like Witches; do but whet your pen,
> Scratch til the blood come; they'l not hurt you then.   (lines 31–2)

Whereas drunkenness was a voluntary 'possession', witchcraft was not. Nor was the other sinister idea associated with it, the birth of monsters. The double meaning built into the word 'conception' makes it inevitable that creativity should be (as at the end of Vaughan's 'Rhapsody') associated with childbirth. It is remarkable, however, that writers on both sides rarely seem to see it as a natural process. From the time of the first meeting of the Long Parliament, the language of its preachers was full of the idea of Reformation as a 'Babe of Grace', a child about to bring joy to the whole kingdom. Just as a woman rejoices when a man-child is born, so, Jeremiah Burroughs argued in a thanksgiving sermon of September 1641, the nation should rejoice at the birth of a tough, male child of Reformation, who, going even beyond Hercules, 'presently crusheth those *Babylonish* Brats of innovations, lately hatched' (p. 43). The metaphor was still very much alive in the period between Naseby and the execution, as the Westminster Assembly, in its last, exhausted years, attempted to perform its appointed task of bringing forth a new state church and form of worship. The royalist-anglican party parodied its ambitions: 'And they shall bring forth a sonne, and shall call his name *Reformation*, and he shall save his people from their sinnes' ([Sheppard] 1648). The Presbyterian ministers who signed the *Testimony to the Truth of Jesus Christ, and to Our Solemn League and Covenant* (January 1648) lamented that the Reformation was turning out to be a deformation, and that England 'after so long travail' had 'brought forth an hideous Monster of *Toleration!*' (p. 33).

Monstrous births, of course, were, like witchcraft, the staple news of ballads and broadsheets. Some of those narrated in popular literature seem meant to be taken literally; others are clearly allegorical, like that of the monstrous child, born in Scotland and thus symbolising presbytery, who precociously announces, 'I am thus deformed for the sinnes of my parents' (*Strange Newes from Scotland* 1647). A series of pamphlets written between late April and late June of 1648 developed a series of anti-feminist images in semi-dramatic form. Supposedly the work of *Mercurius Melancholicus*, they begin with *Mistress Parliament Brought to Bed of a Monstrous Child Reformation*. The monstrous child is clearly the new religion – deformed rather than reformed, headless because it denied the king's authority, and monstrous because in its toleration of the sects it was combining a number of different beasts into one. But Mistress Parliament is also the Whore of Babylon; in another pamphlet of the same series, *Mrs Parliament her Gossipping*, she enters like the scarlet woman of Revelation, and the pamphlet ends with a jury of women discovering 'witches' marks' on her. The equation between rebellion and witchcraft was psychologically useful in allowing the observable fact of popular support for Parliament in the early 1640s to be explained as collective possession.

The common factor in all these images – drunkenness, inspiration, witchcraft, monstrous pregnancy – is that they portray the subject as the victim of some external invader, welcome in some cases, feared in others, to the point where he or she virtually loses the capacity for responsible thought or action. This brings us back to the melancholy figure. As with Hamlet's melancholy persona and the behaviour of the Jacobean malcontents, it is difficult to distinguish between those who feign and those who feel serious mental disturbance. In Burton's conception, the melancholic himself cooperates with his own condition, drifting from a state in which it is self-indulgently enjoyed to one in which it cannot be shaken off. But cavalier melancholy usually presents itself as a response to external events. A full study of the subject would need to develop the element already discussed in that other poem of enclosed spaces, Davenant's *Gondibert*: the resignation to darkness and oblivion which follows the execution of the king. Charles Cotton (to whose father Davenant dedicated part of *Gondibert*) explores the experience of melancholy in a number of his early poems. He can be compared to the 'prison writers' already discussed in that his poems were private, more consistently and genuinely private than Sheppard's: they circulated among a small circle of royalist friends and were not published until after his death. They may represent his attitude in the 1650s, or they may show how that attitude looked with post-Restoration hindsight. His Pindaric Ode on 'Melancholy', obviously written after the death of Cromwell, conceives of melancholy as an externally induced condition. The poet refuses to believe that his own feelings of aggression and depression *are* his. Bewildered as to their origin, he decides that

> 'Tis not then I, but something in my breast,
> With which unwittingly I am possest,

and, via the key words 'sovereign' and 'reason', envisages himself as a country invaded by a usurper:

> Alas! my reason's overcast,
> That sovereign guide is quite displac't,
> Clearly dismounted from his throne,
> Banished his empire, fled and gone,
>   And in his room
>   An infamous usurper's come,
> Whose name is sounding in mine ear
> Like that, methinks of *Oliver*.
>   Nay, I remember in his life,
> Such a disease as mine was mighty rife,
>   And yet, methinks, it cannot be,
>   That he
>   Should be crept into me,
> My skin could ne'er contain sure so much evil,
> Nor any place but Hell can hold so great a Devil.
>   (Cotton 1923, pp. 207–8)

The image of invasion is made doubly appropriate, since the poet's mental state corresponds to what he depicts as the state of the country under Cromwellian rule. The idea that he might be possessed by the Cromwell bogey-man is perhaps half a joke, but not one with which he feels comfortable. Backing off from this explanation, the poet concludes, rather unconvincingly, that his melancholy must result from a sense of guilt over the wrongs committed by others:

> Thus man, who of this world a member is,
>   Is by good nature subject made
> To smart for what his fellows do amiss,
>   As he were guilty, when he is betray'd,
> And mourning for the vices of the time,
> Suffers unjustly for another's crime.   (p. 210)

The same confusion between personal grievance and political hostility, subject and object, action and reaction, the same suggestion of outside invasion, enables Cotton, in another poem, to treat Waller's poem to Cromwell as an inversion of itself: an elegy on the writer rather than a panegyric on its subject; a gesture of courage rather than cowardice, since 'He's stout that dares flatter a tyrant thus'. This means that Cotton can both blame and excuse him:

> Where was thy reason then, when thou began
> To write against the sense of God, and man?
> Within thy guilty breast despair took place,
> Thou would'st despairing die in spite of Grace.
> At once th'art Judge, and Malefactor shown,
> Each sentence in thy poem is thine own.   ('To Poet E. W.', p. 277)

Again, subject and object are interchangeable: for Waller to praise Cromwell is to damn himself, but his poem sentences him with his own sentences, as if he were not really their author. If melancholy has invaded Cotton 'like' Oliver, Oliver himself has invaded Waller, who is possessed with his subject to the point of sharing and celebrating his reckless despair.

The reason for this confusion between active and passive complicity is not hard to find. The royalist's sense of guilt and shame about crimes committed by others conceals a fear that these crimes may also be his own. Royalists in the late 1650s and after the Restoration had to ask themselves whether they had all been collaborators, guilty of failure to resist the government strongly enough, guilty even of beginning to feel comfortable under it. It is understandable that they should resort to language which implies that something or someone else – whether drink, imprisonment, madness, or an evil spirit in the person of Oliver – is responsible for their actions. The writer represents himself as a helpless figure – a defeated cavalier, often a prisoner – who achieves a sense of freedom by voluntarily submitting himself to other kinds of passive experience: drunkenness, 'inspiration', and complete, unquestioning loyalty to his kind. As the church-like settings suggest, this submissive attitude is a religious one. In a poem published in the *Rump Songs* of 1661, a royalist collection, the speaker, supposedly writing at a time when the Restoration is imminent, says farewell to the time of secret rituals:

> Wee'l drink and pray no longer
> For the King in mystical fashions:
>   But with Trumpets sound
>   His Health shall go round,
> And our Prayers be Proclamations.
>
> ('The Cock Crowing at the Approach of a Free Parliament',
> *Rump* 1662, vol. II, p. 176)

Drinking and praying are inseparable kinds of secret rite.

But it is surprising how quickly celebration gives way to nostalgia. The two drinking songs with which Cotton appears to be greeting the Restoration recall a time when drinking healths to the king was still forbidden. Night is at first a time of security, offering a hiding place for the loyal drinkers:

> Then let us drink, Time to improve,
>   Secure of Cromwell and his spies,
> Night will conceal our healths, and Love
>   For all her thousand thousand eyes.

By the end of the poem, day has dawned, and night has become a time fit only for the king's enemies or lukewarm friends:

> Then let us quaff it, whilst the night
>   Serves but to hide such guilty souls,
> As fly the beauty of the light;
>   Or dare not pledge our loyal bowls.   (Cotton 1923, pp. 360–1)

In fact, however, light is less congenial to these drinkers than the familiar enclosed spaces. The sense of a hostile world outside turns out to be essential to the atmosphere of loyal camaraderie. Cotton's 'Epode' to Alexander Brome, though it is an open celebration of the Restoration, shows them deliberately seeking out darkness:

> Light up the silent tapers, let them shine,
>   To give complexion to our wine;
> Fill each a pipe of the rich Indian fume,
>   To vapour incense in the room,
> That we may in that artificial shade
>   Drink all a night our selves have made.   (p. 362)

The tapers and the incense-like tobacco suggest, if not exactly the newly restored Church of England ritual, some kind of religious setting. Free to drink and worship in public, the speaker prefers to return to the voluntary darkness of the tavern, 'a night our selves have made'. The phrase is disturbingly ambiguous.

Quotation and the psychology of writing

It will be apparent that the images I have been discussing share a common factor: the image of the private self as a dark, enclosed space which the poet becomes increasingly reluctant to leave. The outdoor world is rarely seen in these poems, and when it is, as in Cotton, the emphasis is on its potential for concealment: the caves of Derbyshire, the underground cellars in which he suggests hiding from the heat of the sun ('Noon Quatrains') or from the approach of 'General Winter' ('Winter Quatrains'), the rivers and valleys where the angler vanishes from sight into a classless but obviously royalist society. Danger comes from the outside. It may be presented as invasion or unnatural pregnancy, or as one of the experiences – inspiration, possession, or madness – for which these are metaphors. Drunkenness is a parody of the kinds of irrationality which the drinker really fears. What lies behind this language, I think, is the writer's desire to escape responsibility for his own state. By depicting himself as 'irrational', in fact, he doubly escapes, because the irrationality itself is blamed on 'the times'. His participation in a common world of images makes him typically rather than individually guilty. The literary 'borrowing' with which this chapter began, and its creation of the 'composite personality', are ways of hiding oneself in a crowd. Francis Meres saw Shakespeare as the reincarnation of the soul of honey-tongued Ovid; Shakespeare's Holofernes had a different image for the effect of immersion in literature – to eat paper or drink ink. To quote a writer extensively is to be possessed by him, to have deliberately internalised him, as if by a process of cannibalism.

La Bruyère, who analysed a compulsive quoter in his *Caractères* under the name of Hérille, reached the conclusion that the real motive of such a character was neither to give his words more authority, nor to show off his knowledge, but simply the fact that 'il veut citer' (1962, p. 371). In other words, there is a pleasure in the mere act of quoting which is quite separate from the belief in the truth embodied in the quotation or the desire to let everyone know that one knows it. I would suggest that literary quotation has something of the same magic effect as the oracles and prophecies in romance literature. Indeed, earlier literature was sometimes thought to have had the force of prophecy; Sheppard, echoing the language of some of the commendatory verses to the Cartwright volume, calls his *Royal Slave* a 'Prophetic Play' (1984, p. 73). This kind of prophecy differs from the overt prophecies of political tragicomedies like *Newmarket Fair*, in that it is recognisable as prophecy only with hindsight. This is equally true of many of the so-called 'ancient prophecies' published in the seventeenth century;

they attracted attention only *after* events had seemed to prove them right. Keith Thomas (1978) suggests an explanation of their function:

> The truth seems to be that at the heart of the belief in prophecies there lay an urge to believe that even the most revolutionary doings of contemporaries had been foreseen by the sages of the past. For what these predictions did was to demonstrate that there was a link between contemporary aspirations and those of remote antiquity. Their function was to persuade men that some proposed change was not so radical that it had not been foreseen by their ancestors ... They justified wars and rebellions and they made periods of unprecedented change emotionally acceptable to those who lived in them.
> (pp. 502–3)

But while this treatment of the past can work, as Thomas suggests, to support political radicalism, it seems to me that it can also have precisely the opposite effect. This is because anything that can be made to fit a pattern can be accepted, and anything that can be accepted can also be assimilated into a dominant ideology. An obvious example is the way in which (as I showed in the last chapter) a whole genre, romance, created the royalist *plot* in two senses of the word. Its strength is that it takes the very fact that most disturbs people – the unpredictable and confused nature of events – and subordinates it to an overall design which is coherent and ultimately beneficent. One might add to this project of assimilation the popularity of the formal Character, which tames the threateningly wide variety of religious and political views by treating each of them as the property of a recognisable type ('the Anabaptist', 'the Presbyter', and so on). The neat epigrams with which the author pins them down make their behaviour more predictable and thus more controllable. Websterian *sententiae*, like proverbs in general, provide an almost tangible verbal reminder of their own contention: that tragic experience is not unique but part of human destiny. To quote another author in a context which makes his words look prophetic is always, therefore, a faint source of comfort, even when, as with La Bruyère's Hérille, one is only uttering banalities.

The indecision whether or not to publish, already noted in Sheppard and Gibson, reflects doubt as to whether the act of writing can ever be a completely private gesture. This is not a feeling unique to this period. In *The Anatomy of Melancholy* Burton insists on his desire for anonymity: 'Seek not after that which is hid; if the contents please thee, and be for thy use, suppose the Man in the Moon, or whom thou wilt to be the Author; I would not willingly be known' (p. 11). In fact, he gave his name in the first edition, removing it only in the second and later ones. Confinement and enforced leisure may have provided not only the opportunity but the excuse for something which many of these authors would otherwise have found difficult to justify. They learned much from Burton's rambling and self-mocking way of pre-empting criticism by first turning it on himself. *Mercurius Elencticus* (in a number which was probably Sheppard's) describes himself as a compulsive writer: 'I must confesse *I* have *Gravidum Cor, fetum Caput,* a kind of *Impostume* in my head, which *I* would be delivered of, and know no other way of *Evacuation,* that can please me like this' (23 Feb.–1 March 1648). Is he borrowing from Burton (p. 16) merely to cover up the fact that he is short of news to report? Or is he trying, with some embarrassment, to explain the almost inexplicable: why engage in illegal journalism, given the small remuneration and the high risks about which he so frequently complains? In fact, why write at all? Burton's famous claim, in the same passage, that he wrote of melancholy in order to avoid melancholy provided an answer to such questions. It is an answer frequently given by others too: they claim to write 'to divert my minde from the serious thoughts of publick and private calamities' (Rivers 1647, sig A2) or 'to take my mind off from poring upon my misfortunes' (Osborne 1983, p. 5). Mildmay Fane, Earl of Westmorland, called his privately printed collection *Otia Sacra* (1648) and wrote, in the last lines of the book, that

> whoever shall peruse these Rimes,
> Must know, they were beguilers of spare times.

A particularly transparent example of defensiveness is the Beinecke Library's manuscript commonplace-book of 'W. S.', a prisoner in Exeter jail, who, in the midst of all his verbal doodling, added stern notes: 'A foule & first draught not to be read by any' and 'This is the rude Coppye as sudden invention writt it, wch therefore is noe measure of the abilitys or of the designe of the Authour' (p. 115).

There are of course reasons why writers of the 1650s might have felt inhibited about publishing. Some of them probably did take the Treason Act seriously. Robert Wild, who wrote an elegy on the Presbyterian minister Christopher Love, executed in 1651, did not publish it until after the Restoration, and his last lines indicate that he felt the poem a dangerous one to have written:

> Shelter, bless'd *Love,* this verse within thy Shroud,
> For none but Heav'n dares take thy part aloud.
> The Author begs this, lest, if it be known,
> Whilst he bewails thy Head, he lose his own.   (Wild 1671, p. 28)

Even if these lines themselves (and indeed the whole elegy) are post-

Restoration, they probably reflect a real feeling among writers, and one which was not wholly unjustified. While the government was much more concerned with religious radicalism than with mere poets, it did, according to Anthony à Wood, imprison and try the clergyman Thomas Weaver for his *Songs and Poems of Love and Drollery* (1654), a strongly royalist collection including a number of anti-Puritan verses. The book appeared without the names of printer or publisher, but the author had made the mistake of putting his initials on the title page. However, if we can believe Wood, the judge instructed the jury that the defendant was 'a scholar and a man of wit'; they duly acquitted him, and Weaver was henceforth 'highly valued by the boon and generous royalist' (*DNB*, 'Weaver'; Wood 1813, vol. III, pp. 622–3). Whether true or not, the story confirms the sense of possible danger conveyed in many cavalier poems. This possibility certainly affects the language in which writers describe their own activity. Marvell, for instance, pictures himself in the wood at Appleton House as a sort of literary guerrilla, launching poems from a safe hiding place:

> How safe, methinks, and strong behind
> These trees have I encamped my mind:
> Where beauty, aiming at the heart,
> Bends in some tree its useless dart;
> And where the world no certain shot
> Can make, or me it toucheth not.
> But I on it securely play,
> And gall its horsemen all the day.
>
> ('Upon Appleton House', Stanza 76)

Yet, on second view, this image turns out to be deceptive. As so often, Marvell has reversed tenor and vehicle: hiding from military danger is a metaphor for withdrawal from worldly temptation, particularly sex. There is a similar confusion, to which Barbara Everett has drawn attention, at the opening of the 'Horatian Ode':

> The forward youth who would appear
> Must now forsake his muses dear.

Here, 'would appear' combines the idea of achieving fame with that of 'uncertainty, reservation, perhaps illusion' (Everett 1979, p. 75), creating an ambiguity further clouded by the 'grammatical uncertainty' between transitive and intransitive, active and passive verbs (pp. 76–7). Since the youth has been singing 'languishing' numbers in the shadows, the passage further suggests that his relation with the muses has been only a kind of sporting with Amaryllis in the shade. The possible allusion to *Lycidas* only

emphasises the contrast between the two poems. Milton also begins diffi-
dently, apparently seeing himself as too 'forward' in writing on his subject.
Just as Milton's too-early plucking of the laurels matches the too-early
death of Lycidas, so Marvell's 'forward youth' abandons the muses for the
world of political verse to match Cromwell's abandonment of his private
garden for the public world. But in *Lycidas* the diffidence about writing is
openly expressed, as is the desire for fame, and there is no embarrassment
about offering a 'melodious tear' to the dead poet; the tear is a synonym for
the poem itself. For Marvell, all these things seem to have become problematic, and the presence of the erotic as a temptation or danger in the
background is much stronger than in Milton.

Some indication of the reason for his diffidence may be found in his
poem to Lovelace's *Lucasta*. *Lucasta* appeared in May 1649; but it had been
held up in the press for an unusually long time, and Marvell's poem must
certainly have been written in 1648, well before the king's execution. His
sense of the difference between the present age and the past one is expressed
in terms of their different attitudes not to political issues but to literary
aspiration:

> That candid age no other way could tell
> To be ingenious, but by speaking well.
> Who best could praise had then the greatest praise,
> 'Twas more esteemed to give than wear the bays.
> ('To His Noble Friend Mr Richard Lovelace', lines 5–8)

The main effect of the civil war, as far as poets are concerned, has been
simply to increase the number and power of the 'word-peckers, paper-rats,
book-scorpions' (line 19), the 'barbed censurers' (line 21) who will fall
upon a new book as soon as it appears. The light tone of the last part of the
poem introduces a surprising erotic element and makes the author's situation look mock-heroic. Having heard 'that their deare *Lovelace* was
endanger'd', the fair ladies

> all in mutiny though yet undressed
> Sallied, and would in his defence contest. (lines 39–40)

The poet then describes himself as suffering the metaphorical assaults of
one of these ladies (who 'mine eyes invaded') and having to assure her that
he is on their side. The cavalier hero is of course supposed to be both fighter
and lover, but there is something slightly ludicrous in the stress on the
enthusiasm of his female fan club, typically 'cavalier' themselves in their
dishabille. The much more openly royalist 'Elegy on the Lord Francis
Villiers', probably written about the same time, may or may not be by

Marvell, but it is strikingly similar in its stress on the dead man's popularity with 'the ladies'. He is a romance hero single-handedly carrying all the heroines with him into battle:

> How comely and how terrible he sits
> At once, and war as well as love befits!
> Ride where thou wilt and bold adventures find:
> But all the ladies are got up behind.
> Guard them, though not thyself: for in thy death
> Th' eleven thousand virgins lose their breath.
>
> (Marvell 1972, lines 91–6)

The resemblance can be explained if, as I think, the Lovelace poem is influenced by the one on Villiers. Lovelace had been in danger before, but at present, unlike Villiers, he is threatened by nothing more than the prospect of hostile criticism. Like the opening of the 'Horatian Ode', then, the poem suggests a parallel between the danger of the soldier going to the war and that of the writer about to 'appear' in print. Although offered in a tone of humorous self-deprecation, it is a valid comparison. Before 1642, the most dangerous occasion for a writer must have been the opening night of a play. To be 'brought on a stage' had been a synonym for embarrassing exposure. Now, to be 'published' had the same sense. The author coming into print is in competition with cheap, lightweight, often scurrilous pamphlet literature, the product of the press explosion, which makes readers intolerant towards more serious work. All these complaints are echoed in Cotton's lines to his friend, the translator Edmund Prestwich, in 1651:

> Hard is thy fate (great Wit) thus to advance
> Thy poem in this age of ignorance,
> To send it forth in such a time as this,
> Where none must judge, but such as judge amiss;
> Coarse, sordid censurers, that think their eyes
> Abus'd, if fix'd, on aught but Mercuries.
>
> (Cotton 1923, p. 402)

Cotton politicises the writer's situation more openly than Marvell (the reference to judging amiss refers to courts of law as well as to the critical tribunal, and the ignorance and coarseness he mentions are surely related to class as much as to intellect). But he shows how closely interwoven were the ideas of political and critical hostility. Time and again in this period, the language of political threat – imprisonment or death – merges with that which anticipates hostile criticism. Controversial writers needed an elaborate system of defences against both. Prison-writers, writers beguiling a time of enforced leisure, writers whose works were confined to commonplace-books and yet contained elaborate prefaces and dedications, or disclaimers of any intention of publication, all show the curious uneasiness about their own intentions and abilities which one might expect in people who did and yet didn't want to be taken seriously as writers. The various personae which the royalist writers assumed – the drunkard, the melancholy man with his forced gaiety, the prisoner writing in difficult circumstances, perhaps even under sentence of death – were certainly protective devices, but what they protected was not the author's life, nor even his liberty, but what matters still more for a writer, the sense of identity which enables him to go on writing.

5

The royal image: Charles I as text

Unvalued CHARLS: Thou art so hard a Text,
Writ in one Age, not understood i' th' next.

(Anonymous verse on the king's death, first published in
Vaticinium Votivum: or, Palaemon's Prophetick Prayer, c. 11 March 1649)

Royal images

This book has so far been concerned with tracing the royalist transformation of public events through an increasingly 'literary' series of codes. In
this chapter I hope finally to come to terms with the factor that makes
royalists what they were, their devotion to Charles I and the kinds of
imaginative effort that maintained it. As has already become apparent, the
king himself represents the most conspicuous combination of the secret
and the public; his reputation for secretiveness resulted from the fact that
his secrets had an unfortunate tendency to be revealed. The problem for his
followers was to defend his conduct, not only to others but also to
themselves. While the concept of *arcana imperii* justifies royal secrecy on
an analogy with the mysteriousness of the divine purpose, it is too authori-
tarian and symbolic a theory for propaganda purposes. As John M. Wallace
(1968) has shown, Parliament's success in forcing concessions from the
king in 1640–1, combined with the need to present a broadly acceptable
case for the royalist cause, had undermined the argument not only for
absolute monarchy but also for hereditary monarchy. To insist on the
divine origin only of power itself, rather than the power of a particular
king, made it impossible to deny the legitimacy of any successful usurper
(pp. 11–27), and thus opened the way to the 'loyalist' position which makes
it possible for Marvell and Waller to support Cromwell. One reason why
royalists cannot accept this position is that the disruption of hereditary
monarchy is also the disruption of other kinds of hereditary privilege (see
the lines quoted above, pp. 28–9). The conjunction of this self-interest with
the personal devotion which many of them probably did feel towards the

king himself made the analysis of Charles's character, in the period 1646–51, a matter of urgency. As I suggested in chapter 2, writers attempted to go behind his apparently reprehensible actions to a secret meaning which made such actions not only forgivable but laudable. They treated him, essentially, like a literary character whose motives can be explained by the author like those of any other character. Just as the jesting melancholy of the cavalier hero depends for its effect on the spectator's belief in an inner life which is more important – more 'real' – than mere outward behaviour, so the apparent deceptiveness of Charles's behaviour had to be reconciled through emphasis on the deceptiveness of *all* appearances in the case of this particular monarch. This chapter will therefore deal with the effect of Charles I himself on royalist writers, and, in particular, on the special importance of the *Eikon Basilike*, whose title means 'the king's image', and which purported also to give readers the king's own words.

It is important to realise how completely, until his death, Charles I was a king of images rather than words. He was known as a dancer, not a speaker or singer. Perhaps his speech impediment contributed to his preference for self-presentation through visual rather than aural means, but he made it a matter of choice as well as necessity. In his opening speech to his first Parliament he informed them that his 'natural disability to speak', combined with the need for urgent action, was going to make him brief; as Sir John Eliot wrote in his diary, this 'brevity and plainness, more like to truth than art', was such a welcome contrast with James I's longwinded orations that it drew long applause (Jansson and Bidwell 1987, pp. 492–3). One of the reasons why spectacle is so much a part of monarchy is that the visual without the verbal always retains a sense of mystery: hence, as I indicated in chapter 2, its inadequacy as a code. In masques and triumphs, for instance, the figure of supreme authority is never the one who speaks; the audience hears only personifications of his or her attributes. When, in addition, the machinery of the spectacle is hidden, the various miracles involved in the change of scene can be attributed to the presence of the silent, wonder-working monarch. The masques were moving pictures, showing both a real monarch and an allegorical *alter ego*.

As an art-collector, Charles was skilled at the analysis of paintings like those of Titian, which presented the human face as a book where men might read strange matters. The kind of royal portraiture which he patronised, by contrast with the emblematic, iconic paintings of Elizabeth I, *internalised* the symbols of royalty. Thus, the king never wears a crown in

Van Dyck's portraits, though there may be one on a nearby table. In what seems to have been one of his favourite compositions – it was first painted by Mytens, then by Van Dyck – Henrietta Maria, holding an olive branch in one hand, offers him with the other a wreath of myrtle and laurel. This, the painting implies, is the sort of glory which he most admires. The couple were also painted in the costumes of shepherd and shepherdess in 1628, though the paintings have not survived (Kettering 1983, p. 177). Like the disguised rulers of pastoral tragicomedy, they are shown to need no royal trappings to convey their innate regality. The paintings encourage speculation as to the feelings of the royal sitters. It may be a fashion for melancholy, as Roy Strong (1972) suggests, that influences the expression depicted so often on the king's face (pp. 95–6), but there are other possible explanations. Charles I had grown up in a world of secret diplomacy where it was taken for granted that secrecy was an important part of the art of government. What we are probably meant to see in his portraits is a figure on whom this burden weighs heavily, though it is of course borne with dignity. It was not only hindsight, as Strong insists, that turned him into a King of Sorrows.

It is also possible that Charles's own reserved manner made it necessary for the secretive temperament to be elevated into a virtue. Poems about the king dwell on his external aspect to such an extent that they almost seem to anticipate the later genre of 'Advice to a Painter'. Unlike the latter, however, they dwell on the extent to which painting may conceal as well as reveal. Waller's 'Of His Majesties receiving the newes of the Duke of Buckinghams death' deals with a historical fact, Charles's public impassivity when the news of his friend's murder was brought him while he was at prayers. His facade had been so convincing that, Warren Chernaik suggests, the poem had to be written partly to counteract rumours that the king had already ceased to care for Buckingham. With some delicacy, Waller attributes Charles's behaviour both to the extent of his devotion and to his possession of a truly royal self-control. By comparing the act of praying to Jacob's wrestling with the angel, Waller not only stresses the heroism involved in apparently passive behaviour but also hints at the 'constant strain' involved in the dual roles of man and king (Chernaik 1968, pp. 137–43). As in his poem on Charles's behaviour in the storm on his way back from Spain (see above, p. 78), Waller sets him in a classical context in order to show the superiority of the Christian to the pagan. Comparing the pious dignity of Charles's refusal to break off his devotions with the violent grief of Homer's Achilles on hearing of the death of Patroclus, the poet goes on to remember another classical precedent, probably the well-known story in Pliny of the painting of Iphigenia's sacrifice in which the

face of Agamemnon is hidden because the painter would not presume to
intrude on his feelings:

> The famous painter could allow no place
> For private sorrow in a prince's face;
> Yet, that his piece might not exceed belief,
> He cast a veil upon supposed grief.
>
> (Waller 1902, vol. I, p. 11, lines 18–21)

This early Caroline poem already foreshadows the emphasis in later
writers on the king's dignified response to suffering, a response which in
itself has the force of action.

Almost as if responding to Waller's description, Laud, in a sermon given
in 1631, praises the effect of the image of a praying king:

And it is an excellent thing to see a King at his prayers: for then you see two things at
once; a greater, and a lesser King, *God and the King*. And though we cannot see
God, as we see the King; yet when we see Majesty humbled, and in the posture of a
Supplicant, we cannot in a sort but see that infinite, unspeakable Majesty of that
God, whom even Kings adore. (1651, p. 313)

But to see God in the king is to see the king as an infinitely mysterious
being. It is evident that this is what is implicit in the conventions of royal
portraiture and the favourite royal devices illustrated in Frances Yates's
Astraea (1975). The temerity of the artist, who must gaze on majesty in
order to paint it, is symbolised by the use of symbols which show how the
sun becomes visible to mortal eyes: through the clouds, in a rainbow, as
reflected light. As we saw in chapter 2, poetry of the civil war period
depicts Charles himself as a sun hidden in a cloud. A parliamentary
pamphlet called *The Great Eclipse* (1644) claims that the queen is coming
between him and his people. 'The General Eclipse', a poem attributed to
Cleveland but perhaps the work of several writers (Cleveland 1967,
p. xxxviii), sees the king and the queen as having 'lost their Beams' and the
aristocracy only as 'glimmering Peers' (p. 69). The Lovelace poem already
quoted and the Lely painting to which it refers are the most successful
embodiments of this image. The poem's publication in *Lucasta*, which
appeared in May 1649, probably influenced two short anonymous poems,
based on Edward Bower's portrait of the king during his trial, which
eventually found their way into *Reliquiae Sacrae Carolinae*, a collection of
the king's writings published by Royston. 'Upon the Picture of His
Majesty, sitting in His Chair before the High Court of Injustice', sees the
king, in adversity, as a representative of the same kind of clouded majesty
that fascinated Lovelace. The reference to 'oil' may be a punning reference
to the anointing at the coronation:

Not so majestick in thy Chair of State!
On that but Men, Here God and Angels wait:
Expecting whether hopes of Life, or fear
Of death, can move thee from thy Kingly sphear.
Constant and fixt, whom no black storms can foyl,
Thy Colours, Head, and Soul, are all in oyl.

Another, 'Upon the Picture of His *Majesty* in His blew Wastcoat', compares him to Moses, and treats the star he wears as a symbol for his own
radiance:

Here shines in a Feild *Azure* such a Star,
As at whose Fall Kingdoms amazed are,
Fixt by his fall Chief of the sparkling train,
'Bove *Ariadnes* Crown, or his own Wayn.
   Look! what a ray he darts! So *Moses* shone
   While stupid *Israel* 'fore a Calf was thrown.
   Onely the difference make, you must account
   Him coming from, this going to the Mount.

Both poems stress the 'fixt' nature of the king's character, as unchanging
as the colours on the canvas. He expresses no emotions of 'hope or fear',
but his face is said to shine like that of Moses when he returned from
Mount Sinai. This iconic quality is particularly important in a memorial
image.

Marshall's extraordinary engraving for *Eikon Basilike* (plate 2, repro-
duced above, p. 69) exists in a number of versions (this one is the earliest)
but they all share the same emphasis on constancy. Charles is portrayed
kneeling, apparently in a chapel at the edge of the sea, oblivious of any
spectators but with his eyes firmly fixed on the heavenly crown that awaits
him. In the third edition of the *Eikon* (probably mid-March), and in many
after that, a portrait of the prince, now Charles II, is also included. As one
writer noted, in *The Frontispiece of the King's Book Opened* (1649), the
prince was another *eikon*, or image, of his father. The Latin and Greek tags
left further space for interpretation. The Greek message following the
explanatory verses means 'neither χι nor καππα have harmed the
state'. Only a select few would have understood the meaning of this
reference to the letters which, in Greek, begin the names of Christos and
Carolus.

Twentieth-century readers of the book usually associate the frontispiece
with traditional depictions of Christ's agony in the Garden of Gethsemane
(see, e.g., Strong 1972, p. 30). But even Milton does not accuse the *Eikon*
of blasphemy on that scale. Like many of the book's first readers, he

5 William Marshall, frontispiece to Virgilio Malvezzi, *Il Davide Perseguitato*,
translated by Robert Ashley (1647)

recognised in it a reworking of the psalms of David, modelled 'into the
form of a private psalter' (*Eikonoklastes* 1962, p. 360). The model was
clearly indicated by the supposed author himself in his chapter of 'Peneten-
tial Meditations': 'I come far short of David's piety; yet since I may equal
David's afflictions, give me also the comforts and the sure mercies of
David' (*Eikon* 1966, p. 149). For a book published by Moseley in 1647–8,
and typical of that publisher's devious cultural subversion, Marshall had
already engraved a frontispiece (plate 5) which, by giving David the face of
Charles I, transformed the neutral-sounding translation, *David Persecuted*, into an obvious contemporary analogy. At the Restoration, a
number of paintings based on the *Eikon* frontispiece were sent to local
authorities for display in prominent places. The inscription under the one
at Cambridge was 'Lord, remember David and all his troubles' (Gray 1935,

pp. 101–7). Charles is thus seen as a type of David, as all good kings were supposed to be.

If we can believe the book's probable ghost-writer, John Gauden, and its publisher, Richard Royston, the king's original suggestion for the frontis-piece was a design of three crowns. Gauden claimed that he himself worked out the elaborate emblematic imagery eventually engraved by William Marshall, but Marshall's signature, in the unusual form *delinea: et sculpsit*, suggests that he felt himself at least partly responsible for the design and had no hesitation about acknowledging it (Corbett and Norton 1964, p. 151). He was well known as an illustrator of emblem books, including those of the two most popular writers of emblem verse, Wither and Quarles (who was a personal friend). The emblems he used in his compos-ite picture have been traced to several sources (Corbett and Norton, pp. 149–53; Gilman 1986, pp. 154–6). Both La Perrière's *Morosophie* (1553) and Don Diego Saavedra Fajardo's *Idea de Un Principe Politico Christianeo Rapresentada en cien Empresas* (1640) had included the image of a royal crown intertwined with a crown of thorns. Perhaps a more likely source was a book which had belonged successively to Henry and Charles as Prince of Wales, Henry Peacham's hand-drawn and coloured book of emblems based on James I's *Basilikon Doron*. Peacham's devices, many of which eventually found their way into his published *Minerva Britanna* (1612), included several based on crowns. The image may also, as has been suggested, derive directly from James's own reference to 'the thorny cares' of a king (quoted in Gilbert 1939–40, p. 157).

The picture aroused almost as many comments as the text to which it was prefixed. Milton's sarcastic comments on it ('conceited portraiture … drawn out to the full measure of a Masking Scene, and sett there to catch fools and silly gazers') were predictable (*Eikonoklastes*, p. 342). Ironically, Marshall's other claim to fame, the frontispiece to Milton's *Poems* (1645), had already inspired the poet to write a rude Greek verse about the incompetence of the engraver. It was long ago suggested that Marshall's portrait of Milton was so bad as almost to suggest 'deliberate sabotage' (Martz 1965, pp. 5–7) and that Moseley's presentation of the volume was designed to turn his author, against his will, into a crypto-royalist. Martz thinks that Milton was deliberately presenting himself in this book as a man of letters, rising serenely above his recent involvement in politics. More recently, Michael Wilding has argued that Milton fought back against Moseley's presentation through such additions as the headnote to *Lycidas* drawing attention to the prophetic force of the St Peter passage: 'Moseley may have endured Milton's radicalism as Milton may have endured Moseley's conservatism' (Wilding 1987, p. 9). It remains true that Milton never used Moseley as his publisher again, and it is likely that some of his harshness toward the *Eikon* frontispiece is based on memories of the earlier episode. Despite his preference for seeing himself as an inspired singer in the manner of a classical bard, Milton had always been strongly aware of the physical properties of the published book. For instance, in his attack on Hall's *Modest Confutation* (1642), he objects to the author's incorporating part of his argument into the title itself, whereas 'a modest title should only informe the buyer what the book contains without furder insinuation'; he attacks him for dedicating a sermon to Christ in large letters, as if equating the Saviour with an ordinary patron, and complains that Hall cannot even find enough room in his margin for all his references, but 'must cut out large docks and creeks into his text, to unlade the foolish frigate of his unseasonable autorities' (*An Apology against a Pamphlet* 1953, pp. 876, 877, 922). That meaning could be found in every aspect of a book's presentation, not merely in its content, was something of which he would show himself still more aware when he came to analyse the *Eikon Basilike.*

Even some of the king's admirers found the frontispiece an embarrassment. In the two French translations it is replaced by engravings considered more suitable to a sophisticated public, and one of the translators in his preface comments harshly on the pedantry of 'ce chaos de lumière, de ténèbres, de mers, de roches, de jardins, de poids d'horloge, & tout ce fatras qu'ils ont mis dans la Taille-douce' (de Marsys, sig. IV. See also Madan 1949, pp. 64–5). But however much the frontispiece may have been ridiculed, it was evidently considered effective; indeed, the very extent of the ridicule indicates as much. Royston continued to use Marshall as his illustrator. His next commission was for the illustration to a book which appeared at the end of May 1649: *The Papers Which Passed at Newcastle Betwixt His Sacred Majestie and Mr Al: Henderson, Concerning the Change of Church-Government.* The exchange of letters had taken place in 1646. The most obvious reason for publishing it at this point, apart from the fact that the public seemed to have an insatiable appetite for books about Charles, was to leave readers in no doubt as to the king's stance on religion. For this volume, Royston commissioned a new frontispiece from Marshall (plate 6). Labelled 'Fidei Defensor', it shows the king sitting behind a large globe on which a disproportionately large Britain takes up the whole of one hemisphere. Its two parts are labelled 'Anglicana Ecclesia' and 'Scotica Ecclesia'. Charles is holding his pen poised over the final 'a' of 'Scotica'. As a depiction of a man in the act of writing, the picture leaves something to be desired, but the absurdity was forced on the engraver by

6   William Marshall, frontispiece to *The Papers which Passed at Newcastle Betwixt His sacred Majestie and Mr. Alexander Henderson*

the allegory: Charles's pen is the weapon of the champion of the English church, and it is being used, like a sword, to prick the arguments of one of the Scots' ablest ministers. So it attacks not 'ecclesia' (the church) but 'ecclesia Scotica' (the Scottish church). The mottos which decorate the picture (characteristic overkill on the artist's part) further emphasise the king's status as a spokesman for the national religion. This frontispiece was obviously considered quite effective, as it was used (sometimes, as here, with the top portion cut off) in a number of other books published up to and beyond the Restoration. One reason for its popularity may be that any illustration of Charles in the act of writing reinforced his claim to the authorship of the *Eikon Basilike*.

In 1651, the year of Charles II's attempted invasion, Royston published a translation of Hobbes's *De Cive*, under the title *Philosophical Rudiments*. He was not one of Hobbes's usual publishers, and the work was a strange choice for so straight-laced an Anglican. But the secret of Royston's edition, anonymously translated, lies in its illustrations, which are not the ones originally published with the book. M. M. Goldsmith has traced them to the classical emblems of Otto van Veen, first published in 1607 as *Q. Horati Flacci Emblemata*. Two of them copy the original van Veen illustrations. The third (plate 7), while clearly based on van Veen's illustrations for the motto 'Innocentia Ubique Tuta', has had its meaning dramatically altered by its new context. Not only has it become an illustration to the section on Religion, but the figure representing Religion has been given the features of Charles I (Goldsmith 1981, pp. 232–7). A further irony, not noted by Goldsmith, is that the original van Veen illustration had already been used in an equally distorted form in a broadside of 1646, *The Watchman's Warning-Piece*, where it was used to argue, not that innocence is safe anywhere, but that the Army had better not drop its weapons until it has destroyed all its enemies. (The ubiquitous Samuel Sheppard, in *The False Alarm*, 1646, recommends that the broadside be suppressed.) The anonymous artist of this little piece of covert hagiography was probably not Marshall, who seems to have died at about this time, and I suspect that the idea for the picture came from Royston himself.

The royal actor

As Charles's portraits show, he was constantly perceived to be acting a series of emblematic roles. Sometimes, as in Waller's poems, he is praised for the self-control which enables him to do so in a specific historical

Integer vitæ scelerifque purus
Non eget Mauri jaculis nec arcu,
Nec venenatis gravida fagittis
    Fufce pharetra.
Sive per Syrtes iter æftuofas,
Sive facturus per inhofpitalem
Caucafum, vel quæ loca fabulofus
    Lambit Hidafpis.

7   Anon., 'Religion', illustration to part three of *Philosophical Rudiments*, the
      English translation of Hobbes's *De Cive* (1651)

context. This is 'acting' in the sense of suppressing rather than feigning emotion, and it is done, supposedly, in the interest of a higher purpose. When the king appears in an engraving as King David or a personification of Religion, the acting is of a different kind: he simply reveals an aspect of his symbolic character. The distinction between these two kinds of role-playing is obviously crucial for an understanding of the actor image so frequently used in this period.

It was not Marvell alone who commended the performance given by Charles I on the scaffold. According to Gilbert Burnet, the king's 'serious and Christian deportment in it made all his former errors be quite forgot, and raised a compassionate regard to him, that drew a lasting hatred on the actors, and was the true cause of the great turn of the nation in the year 1660' (Burnet 1897, vol. I, pp. 86–7). Burnet's awareness of the element of performance in the occasion does not prevent him from drawing a contrast between Charles's 'deportment' and the Commonwealth 'actors'. He wishes to see the king not as acting but as revealing his true self, a self from which he could now be seen as having 'erred' or wandered in his past actions. As this passage shows, the image of the execution as a stage-play is so common in this period as to be a cliché, a fact already apparent in Fanshawe's poem on the trial and execution of the Earl of Strafford (see above, pp. 87–9). The comparison may perhaps have acquired extra topicality because of the banning of real stage-plays in the public theatres. But it was in any case accurate. The words 'stage' and 'scaffold' were interchangeable; the word 'actor' is inherently ambiguous. But there were particular reasons why the notion of acting should be relevant to the king's trial and execution.

The reason why most speeches at the scaffold sound so much like speeches in a play is that they were normally written out – either before the execution, by the victim, or afterwards, by someone who wished to make the whole thing as exemplary as possible. The presence of a team of shorthand writers, not only at the king's trial but at his execution, was apparently a new practice, and it indicates Parliament's concern to have an accurate record of both events. As C. V. Wedgwood (1964) has shown, considerable trouble was taken to compare the shorthand record with Charles's own notes, which he gave to Bishop Juxon; these were confiscated immediately after the event and carefully examined to make sure that they were authentic (pp. 195–6). The shorthand writers were brought in again for the beheading of three royalist lords – Holland, Hamilton, and Capel – in March of the same year, and their presence seems to have come as a surprise. According to the reporter, Hamilton said, 'had I thought my speech would have been thus taken, I would have digested it into some better method than now I can, and shall desire these Gentlemen that does write it, that they will not wrong me in it, and that it may not in this manner be published to my disadvantage' (Hamilton 1649, p. 9). It sounds as if Hamilton had been counting on someone else to write up, or even make up, his lines for him. On the other hand, the government's intention was to ensure that the public knew what the victims really had said, not what they, or some royalist speech-writer, thought they should have said.

It has been shown that scaffold speeches were a form with their own rules and conventions (Sharpe 1985). But there is a sense in which both the shorthand writer and the person who wrote a fictitious speech for publication could have seen themselves as truthful. If a speaker, or his representative, sees himself as standing outside history, like Jonson in his *Discoveries*, then his words need not be true, in the sense of being his, so long as they are 'true' in a general sense. The distinction is like that between 'set forms' and improvisation which dominated so many discussions of church worship. One should not exaggerate the difference between Webber's 'conservative Anglican' and 'radical Puritan' (Webber 1968, p. 255), when it came to public speaking. Both types cultivated a 'spoken' rather than a written style and relied on an impression of spontaneity which was probably achieved in many cases by careful learning of a written text. Nevertheless, the dispute between those who defended 'set forms' and those who believed in improvisation was an explicitly stated one.

Both the trial and the execution of the king were dominated by a disagreement as to what constituted authentic speech. It was the intransigence of both sides on this point which made the king's trial disappointingly unlike the great rhetorical contest that might have been expected. Charles refused to answer the charges against him, because he refused to acknowledge the authority of the court. His refusal meant that the Attorney General, John Cook, was likewise unable to make his speech for the prosecution. Both the king and his chaplain, Bishop Juxon, stuck rigidly to the words of the Book of Common Prayer in the period before the execution; use of this book had been banned, but an exception was made for this occasion. It meant that Charles's audience was deprived of the opportunity to hear spontaneous expressions of feeling from him. *The Moderate Intelligencer* (25 Jan.–1 Feb. 1649) sneers at this 'speaking by the book':

It was to be wish'd that there had been Prayers in it more pertinent, it's the great wonder that men of most excellent parts, able to speake largely (without premeditation, not having writing or print before them) to men, yet in prayer not ten words.

Since Parliament refused to make any further exception in favour of the Prayer Book, the king's funeral was the source of another controversy. It was decreed, as another journal, *The Moderate*, put it, 'if the Dr. [Juxon] had any exhortation to say without book, he should have leave, but he could say nothing without book' (6–13 Feb. 1649). The result was that the funeral took place in complete silence. The parliamentary journal writers present both the king and the bishop as actors who, like Viola, can 'say little more than they have studied'. It was not, of course, that Juxon would necessarily have been incapable of extemporal prayer on either occasion; his refusal was a matter of principle, corresponding to the king's. For the anti-ritualist, the written word, like the shorthand transcripts, could be authenticated only by the fact that it had previously been spoken, whereas in the tradition represented by Charles the written word is prior to the spoken one; it is permanent, reproducible, independent of the historical occasion, like the script of a play.

Barbara Everett (1979) has noted that Marvell's 'Horatian Ode' presents 'a masque, almost a ballet, of pure action – of the appearance of events' (p. 83). The event did almost happen in mime. Frustration and silence surround the whole of the trial and execution, from the king's first refusal to recognise the court to his scaffold speech which begins, truthfully, 'I shall be very little heard by anybody here' (*King Charles His Speech Made upon the Scaffold* 1649). An unprecedented and, for many people, cataclysmic event had taken place without the element of ceremony which might have helped to make it emotionally bearable. Shortly after the execution, a number of publications came on the market, in an attempt to fill this enormous vacuum. *His Majesties Reasons*, the arguments Charles had tried unsuccessfully to present in court, appeared on February 5. But the *Eikon* itself spoke for him more effectively still. Though it may have been sold on the streets as early as the day of the execution (Madan 1949, p. 165), it seems to have reached the bookstalls on February 9, the same day as John Cook's *Case of King Charles*, which included not only what the Attorney General had actually said at the trial but also what he had intended to say. So the two men who had been unable fully to speak at the trial now faced each other in print. Charles had succeeded, posthumously, in making himself heard on his own terms, in what Milton called the 'op'n and monumental Court of his own erecting' (*Eikonoklastes*, p. 341).

The royal author

Of all the images of the king, it was the one he was supposed to have drawn himself which had the most pervasive influence. The admiration for the *Eikon Basilike*, which resulted in thirty-five English editions and twenty-five foreign ones in the year 1649 (Madan 1949, p. 1), is one of the most important facts of the period. Bishop Burnet later summed up the general view:

> There was in it a nobleness and a justness of thought, with a greatness of style, that made it to be looked on as the best writ book in the English language: and the piety of the prayers made all people cry out against the murder of a prince, who thought so seriously of all his affairs in his secret meditations before God. I was bred up with a high veneration of this book.   (Burnet 1897, vol. 1, p. 87)

The reaction described here is riddled with contradictions of a familiar kind. On the one hand, the king's book is a literary masterpiece; on the other, it is a totally private – 'secret' – work. Like the king's disguise as seen by Cleveland and the Lely picture as interpreted by Lovelace, it reveals while seeming to conceal. If the thought and style are noble, it must be because these qualities are inherent in its author. Charles is a transparent figure, making an impression without seeking to make one.

The *Eikon* posed problems for which seventeenth-century readers, both royalist and parliamentarian, were mostly unprepared. One was a problem of genre. How was the book to be read? Was it a literary work, a series of religious meditations, or a political tract? In many ways, it was closest to the 'prison writing' already discussed, though of course it lacked the 'cavalier' dimension. The manner in which it was presented suggested that it was meant to be seen as transcending, not influencing, history. The Greek title refers to an 'image' (Eikon) of the king. From the point of view of many Protestants this is a rather ill-chosen word; most early editions print it in small type, using a larger type-face for the subtitle, 'A Portraiture of His Sacred Majesty in His Solitudes and Sufferings'. The one title suggests a symbolic figure, the other a historical one. The question of reconciling the two Charleses was to preoccupy many writers.

It was not only the frontispiece that hovered ambiguously between symbol and portrait. Though the book itself is written in the first person, the chapter headings are in the third person. (The French translation by De Marsys, noting this awkwardness, puts them into the first person.) There is no preface or introduction, no explanation as to how the papers have come into the hands of the printer or who has undertaken the editorial work of obtaining the frontispiece and writing the chapter headings. Instead, the reader is plunged into a series of chapters on different events of the war and its aftermath. These are not always in strict chronological order. Sometimes they appear to be written *in medias res*, sometimes with hindsight. Each chapter ends with a prayer or psalm, except that one chapter consists entirely of prayers and meditations and one takes the form of a letter to the Prince of Wales. In its earliest edition the book ends with the king's meditations on death, supposedly written on the Isle of Wight, and with a Latin motto which might have been his or the editor's: *Vota dabunt, quae bella negarunt.* This last ambiguity was potentially dangerous. If the king is hoping that prayers will do what war could not, what is the actual object of his prayers? Is it inner peace for himself, or the love of his subjects, or is it victory for his cause – a propaganda victory, or perhaps even a more tangible one, if only through the succession of his son? Charles had told Alexander Henderson in 1646 that '*Preces & lacrymae sunt Arma Ecclesiae*' (*Reliquiae* 1650, p. 200). At that time he was arguing against the militancy of the Scots. But tears, as the language of royalist elegy shows, can also be the motive for vengeance. This familiar confusion between the language of active purpose and that of passive suffering is something which Milton, for one, easily recognised: 'though the Picture sett in Front would Martyr him and Saint him to befool the people, yet the Latin Motto in the end, which they understand not, leaves him as it were a politic contriver' (*Eikonoklastes*, p. 343). At several points in *Eikonoklastes* he tries to turn inside out both the king's supposedly passive resignation and the supposed secrecy of his book. The king pities enemies who have since come to a bad end; Milton observes, 'to pity thus is to triumph' (p. 432). Of the king's apparently private prayers, Milton writes, 'He should have shut the dore, and pray'd in secret not heer in the High Street. Private praiers in publick, ask something of whom they ask not, and that shall be thir reward' (p. 456).

Milton was of course right in detecting an active purpose in the work which belied its tone of resignation. It was this internal contradiction which, from the beginning, raised doubts about its authorship. My own view on this point substantially agrees with that of the bibliographer F. F. Madan: John Gauden *was* responsible for heavy rewriting and editing of some papers of the king's, possibly with assistance from one or two fellow-clergymen. The best argument for Gauden's hand in the book is the external evidence. His claim was specific, and it was never denied by those in a position to know its truth. Gauden's role immediately before the Restoration had been that of a conciliator, working behind the scenes for the royal cause. For this, he was rewarded with a bishopric, that of Exeter, but when he became aware of the poverty of his new see he began agitating for something better, pointing out the need to keep up the dignity of his position: 'Nor have I been unaccustomed to generous methods of living wch to be sure are the only arts for us Bpps to get & preserve publiqe [*sic*] love and Honor to our persons and profession' (Wordsworth 1825, p. 31). He then explained the great service he had done the royalist cause, while stressing how fully he understood the need of keeping it secret. It is clear from his correspondence both with the Earl of Clarendon and with George Digby (now Earl of Bristol) that they both knew his claim to be true, and he eventually got the more lucrative post which he wanted. The mixture of carping and cringing in Gauden's letters is decidedly unattractive, but his eagerness for promotion can be understood if, as his wife later wrote, he already felt himself to be mortally ill and wanted to be sure of leaving his family well provided for. He died in September 1662, only four months after his election to the bishopric of Worcester.

The internal evidence for Gauden's authorship is also strong. The *Eikon* is quite consistent with his policy up to 1649. He was willing to accept moderate reform in the interest of preserving a state church with a properly paid ministry, something which he felt only monarchy could guarantee. To this end, he had preached before the House of Commons, taken the Covenant, and sat (at least for a time) on the Westminster Assembly. He thus represents the king as willing to acknowledge many errors, particularly with regard to church government in the 1630s, and eager for reconciliation with the Presbyterians. The king is made to declare, 'I believe many that love me and the church well may have taken the Covenant' (*Eikon* 1966, p. 79) and his supposed letter to the Prince of Wales emphasises the importance of forgiveness. Gauden thus prepares people's minds for the succession in case the worst should happen. Both Gauden and his wife later wrote that the king had known and approved of the book, though if Mrs Gauden's account can be believed, he would have preferred it to go out under someone else's name (Wordsworth 1825, p. 43).

The fervour with which royalists defended the king's authorship (and the fact that Gauden's silence was apparently considered worth buying) may seem strange in view of the widespread practice of 'literary borrowing' and the general recognition that royal writings were often ghosted. The editors of other works attributed to the king adopted a flexible attitude, including official resolutions and declarations as part of his writings, though well aware, as the editor of *Bibliotheca Regia* (1659) said, that 'many of them, and some of his messages too might be worded in the style of his *Secretaries*' ('To the Reader', sig. *6). Moreover, the device of putting fictitious words into the mouths of real persons is a common one in rhetoric and has a respectable precedent in king David himself, who, as one of Laud's sermons pointed out, 'sometimes speakes in his owne person, and sometimes in Gods' (Laud 1651, p. 145). The appropriation of ritualistic or biblical language was different from the impersonation of Charles's own manner. Like the composite royalist style already discussed, it enabled a number of writers to assume the same role.

The *Eikon* is only one of a number of works attributed to the king to be published by the royalist propaganda network. Since there was nothing to prevent either party from putting out supposedly royal poems, letters, or declarations, the authenticity of all these documents has to be regarded with suspicion. What is interesting is the consistency of their approach. *His Majesties Messages for Peace* (1648) appeared, almost certainly under the auspices of Richard Royston, in response to the decision of the two Houses to receive no more addresses from him. Its various declarations and messages were mostly authentic, but it includes a Declaration, dated 18 January, in which the King appeals directly and pathetically to his people. The provenance of this work is nearly as debatable as that of the *Eikon*, and was doubted almost at once. According to the introduction, it was written 'by His Majesties own hand', and came to light providentially, in some unspecified way. The introduction to this book is one of the earliest attempts to establish Charles's resemblance to Christ: the editor (Edward Symmons) laments that 'as our *Saviour* was, so hath our *Soveraign* been, shaddowed much from vulgar Eyes, by the black cloud of sclander and reproaches' (sig. A3–A3ᵛ). Later the editor quotes Pilate's question, 'Will you Crucifie your King?' (p. 121).

Charles's own language certainly shows that he was not averse to seeing himself as a martyr. In a letter to the Duke of Hamilton, dated December 1642, he had said, 'I will either be a glorious king or a patient martyr', though he added that he saw himself as 'not being the first, nor at the present apprehending the other' (quoted in Ollard 1979, p. 46). 'Glorious king' is something of a catch-phrase at this period. Apparently the term was used in a message from the House of Commons delivered to the king by Sir Henry Vane in May 1641: Parliament promised to make him 'as great, as glorious and as potent a prince as any of his ancestors ever were' (quoted Fletcher 1981, p. 34). Few parliamentary statements were repeated more frequently, and more bitterly, than this one. Throughout the war, the king was constantly asking his opponents whether their latest act of defiance was their way of carrying out their promise. The phrase is quoted in the *Eikon* itself ('But this is the strange method these men will needs take to resolve their riddle of making me a glorious king by taking away my kingly power' (p. 47)). A number of the poems on his death point out that, ironically, Parliament has finally kept its promise by sending him to a crown of glory.

Eagerness to turn the king into a Christ-figure and martyr is also apparent in the two published poems said to have been written by him in prison. *His Majesty's Complaint Occasioned by his late sufferings* (1647) is a loose imitation of Herbert's *The Sacrifice*, itself a monologue put into the mouth of Christ. *A Copy of Verses said to be composed by His Majestie, upon His first Imprisonment in the Isle of Wight* (1648) concludes, 'I'll die a martyr or I'll live a king'. Pathos and readiness for martyrdom were clearly the qualities which the royalist publicists wished most to emphasise in the king at this critical juncture. Gauden, under his own name, engaged in a similar though acknowledged impersonation in January 1649, when he addressed a letter to Lord Fairfax and the Council of War, urging them against putting the king on trial. 'Methinks I hear his Majesty in his Agony, Solitude, and expectation of an enforced death, calling on me, and all other his Subjects,' and he goes on to quote his Majesty. No doubt, he felt by this time that he had mastered the royal style (Gauden 1649, sig. A2^v). What Charles himself would have thought of this kind of thing may be gauged from his reaction in 1646 when the Presbyterian minister Alexander Henderson presumed to suggest what the Ghost of James I would say to him if it could speak. 'I must tell you,' Charles wrote, 'that I had the happiness to know him much better than you; wherefore I desire you, not to be too confident, in the knowledge of his Opinions' (*Reliquiae*, p. 200).

Besides making up the king's words, the press also made up his actions. It was the warning that he was in danger of assassination that made Charles flee from Hampton Court to Carisbrooke. In 1648 particularly, the royalist press played on the sense of the king's personal danger for propaganda purposes. *Mercurius Aulicus* (25 Jan.–3 Feb. 1648) says that the king 'is well, but sad, imploying yet him self in more diviner things, then earthly Crownes'. *Mercurius Dogmaticus* (27 Jan.–3 Feb. 1648) opens, in verse, 'Haste, haste, unto the Ile of Wight / And Rescue Charles from Death'. *Mercurius Bellicus* (14–20 Feb. 1648) claims that people have spat in his face – a story which would be repeated at the time of his trial. *Mercurius Melancholicus* (20 March 1648) reports him 'many times (as he walkes alone in his solitary Prison) suddenly making a stand, and casting up his eyes to heaven, and then prostrating himself upon his knees to prayers with lifted up hands to the King of Kings, imploring mercy for his Rebellious and stiffe-necked People'. Like the *Eikon Basilike* frontispiece, this is a vivid evocation of something which, by its nature, would have had no witnesses. The newsbooks sympathetic to Parliament countered with reports that the king was perfectly content and entertaining himself with light reading and exercise. There was even more scope for fantasy in the journalistic treatment of a minor incident early in 1648, when Colonel Hammond, the governor of Carisbrooke Castle, was trying to prevent the king from destroying secret correspondence. In royalist accounts, this developed into a sensational episode. *Mercurius Aulicus* (2–30 March 1648) gives one of the most highly-coloured versions: 'My Lord the King affronted, batter'd & bruis'd by cursed Caitiffs! – I cannot write for weeping'. The intention behind this pathos soon becomes clear, as the writer adds, 'The bells and bonfires on the Kings Coronation day, makes me think that there are in London thousands, that would revenge his Majestie on this cursed hell-hound.' Charles even appears as one of the speakers in the ballad verses which preface some of these journals. Thanks to the sensation-seeking press, in fact, he was becoming a much more vivid personality than he had ever been while still at freedom. The chief purpose of this constant insistence on the king's sufferings and readiness for martyrdom must have been to win popular sympathy and active support for his cause: several royalist uprisings did break out in the spring of 1648. At the same time, it sometimes seems as if his own party was unconsciously *willing* the king to die. Writers had created a fictitious saintly Charles I, and then fallen in love with their own creation.

The *Eikon Basilike* differs from the works just described in two respects. One was that it was supposed to be the work of a man who had just died, and thus had something of the authority of a deathbed utterance. The other was its supposedly unpremeditated nature. Both these qualities have to be seen in the context of the sensation already caused by the publication in 1645 of the private letters captured at Naseby, which had given such an embarrassing glimpse of the king's inmost thoughts. To counteract the damage done by the contents of the king's cabinet, it was essential to believe that the piety and forgiveness expressed in the posthumous book came from the still more secret cabinet of the king's heart. Abraham Wright wrote a poem on an *Eikon* which had been turned into a holy relic by being bound 'in a Cover coloured with His Blood'. The poem compares the book itself to treasure but then insists that 'The chiefest Jewel is the Cabinet' – that is, the cover which recalls the king's martyrdom (Wright 1927, p 54). It was as if the book, like his blood, had come straight from his heart. 'J.H.' (James Howell), whose brief 'Epitaph' was one of the earliest tributes to be printed with the *Eikon*, is one of many writers to declare that the king himself is his own best mourner:

> Thy heavenly virtues angels should rehearse;
> It is a theme too high for human verse.
> He that would know thee right, then, let him look
> Upon thy rare incomparable book
> And read it o'er and o'er; which if he do,
> He'll find thee king and priest and prophet too.

This is the constant emphasis of the tributes to the book: the secret, unknowable heart of the king had at last been revealed. The *Eikon* was a far more satisfactory image of the king than had been offered in any of his numerous writings; thanks to the execution, it was one which could be trusted never to change, never to disappoint its admirers. Not what it said, but what it symbolised, made it essential to believe in it as the king's own work.

Eikon *against* Eikon

The controversy over the authenticity of the *Eikon* began almost immediately. To some extent, it is even anticipated in the book itself. At several points, Charles is made to refer to his enemies' unwillingness to believe that his words and actions are his own. At one point he tells God, 'The less wisdom they are willing to impute to me, the more they shall be convinced of Thy wisdom directing me' (p. 61). Later, as if foreseeing an objection that was often to be made, he admits that in defending episcopacy 'I write rather like a divine than a prince' (p. 104). In the chapter on the capture and publishing of his private correspondence he notes that now men will at least believe that he is capable of acting and writing on his own initiative; he wishes that 'my subjects had yet a clearer sight into my most retired thoughts' (p. 130).

Reinforcing this 'evidence', a number of works published by royalists after the execution represent the king as anxious to be given credit for his own writing. *The Princely Pellican*, a royalist apologia published in early June 1649, describes him crying out, 'O that My Subjects knew but the integrity of mine Heart toward them!' In a rather unlikely tone of humility, and with a reference to his speech impediment, he tells his gentlemen,

the pretended losse of a State, has gain'd me a tongue. Passion, which usually made my tongue inarticulate, is become a stranger to me ... I am now become my owne Amanuensis. My Abilities, though meane, may now appear.
(*The Princely Pellican* 1649, pp. 2, 26)

Insofar as it was possible, Gauden and the others involved in writing the

Eikon Basilike attempted to make it seem like a work that had written itself. With its prayers based on the psalms and its very generalised and symbolic treatment of historical events, it belongs to the tradition of 'set and prescribed forms' which Charles had been asserting all along. Indeed, its chapter on the Prayer Book contains a defence of these:

Sure we may as well beforehand know what we pray as to whom we pray, and in what words as to what sense. When we desire the same things, what hinders we may not use the same words? ... I ever thought that the proud ostentation of men's abilities for invention and the vain affectations of variety for expressions in public prayer or any sacred administrations merits a greater brand of sin than that which they call coldness and barrenness ... Nor is God more a God of variety than of constancy; nor are constant forms of prayer more likely to flat and hinder the spirit of prayer and devotion than unpremeditated and confused variety to distract and lose it.   (pp. 96–7)

Philip Knachel, in his edition of the *Eikon Basilike* (1966), notes its detached and relatively impersonal tone, the fact that it rarely mentions anyone by name or otherwise descends to personalities (p. xiii). In this respect it is quite unlike, say, the unquestionably authentic Henderson correspondence. In addressing Henderson, the king is clearly writing with a definite correspondent in mind; he alternates between courtesy and sharpness, refers to 'the king my father' as an authority, and, while largely writing of himself in the role of king, occasionally states a personal view: 'For indeed, My humour is such, that I am still partial for that side, which I imagine suffers for the weakness of those that maintain it' (*Reliquiae*, p. 185). The *Eikon* shows none of the fluctuation of mood that one might expect in a work supposedly written over a long period of time and in many different circumstances. It is as uniform as possible – appropriate to its unhistorical mode and to the image of the king's constancy which it is determined to promote. He is indeed 'fixt', as the colours on the canvas of his portraits.

To some extent this impersonal tone was modified in later editions. New material was added after March 15, including an account of the king's last conversation with his children and four prayers which he was supposed to have used in prison and handed to Bishop Juxon on the scaffold. This is the first time that the source of a document is given – itself a sign that the book is taking account of its own historical context. The author of *The Princely Pellican* felt that the report of the king's family conversation ought to have been omitted, 'being onely familiar Expresses of Fatherly affection to his Children: and those so digested, as if he meant not they should be divulged' (p. 24). There seems to be more in this objection than a defence of the king's

Spectatum admissi risum teneatis .

The Curtain's drawne; All may perceiue the plot,
And Him who truely the blacke Babe begot :
Whose sable mantle makes me bold to say
A Phaeton Sol's charriot rulde that day .
Presumptuous Preist to skip into the throne ,
And make his King his Bastard Issue owne .
  The Authour therefore hath conceiu'd it meet ,
  The Doctor should doe pennance in this sheet .

8   Anon., frontispiece to *Eikon Alethine* (1649)

right to privacy with his own family. It reflects a royalist strategy which I
think was intuitive rather than explicit. The more removed the king was
from anything complex, personal and private, the easier it was to defend
him. He could be admired for what he was, not defended or attacked for
what he had done. Readers could, as Milton put it in a slightly different
sense, make 'the Book thir own rather then the Kings' (*Eikonoklastes*,
p. 328).

The book's imagery too is conventional: 'flames of discontent' (p. 12),
'my enforced darkness and eclipse' (p. 49), 'this Red Sea of our own blood'
(p. 68). Tumults of the people are compared with those at sea; the king is a
shepherd, a pilot, the sun, the oak, both father of his people and husband of
his kingdom. He is sometimes implicitly compared to king David or to
Christ, most obviously in the passage which probably inspired the frontispiece: 'I will rather choose to wear a crown of thorns with my Saviour than
to exchange that of gold, which is due to me, for one of lead, whose
embased flexibleness shall be forced to bend and comply to the various
and oft contrary dictates of any factions' (p. 28). The sheer amount of
this kind of language is one reason why both admirers and detractors called
the book poetic. One French translator had to admit that he had been to
some extent defeated by the fact that 'ce souuerain Autheur est extrème-
ment riche en Métaphores' (Cailloué 1649a, sig. c6). Thomas Corns's
analysis of the book's style by comparison with Milton's reveals that it is
indeed unusually dense with metaphorical language (Corns 1982,
pp. 69–73).

Parliamentary writers do not argue that metaphor and argument by
analogy are irrelevant to political issues; instead they attempt to appropriate the same language, or to invert it. Chapter 4 has indicated to what extent
the struggle between royalist and parliamentary writers was a struggle for
possession of certain powerful images. This struggle is continued in the
argument about the *Eikon*. Attacks on the book focus on its literary quality
as much as on its contents. Its authenticity is challenged on two counts:
either because it is not really by its supposed author, or because its author,
whoever he is, is not sincere. On the one hand, the attackers want to
discredit it as a literary work; on the other, they want to use its very
literariness against it. The first printed attack on the book – *Eikon Alethine*
(the Truthful Image) in 1649 – is like Milton's *Eikonoklastes* in that it treats
the book's author as a royal actor in the most derogatory sense of the term.
Eikon Alethine is based on the assumption that the book was really written
by a 'Divine' impersonating the king, and from the beginning it depicts the
discovery of the true author in dramatic terms. The frontispiece (plate 8)

The Curtain's drawne, all may perceive the plot :
And eas'ly see what yow my freind/have got.
Presumptuous coxcombe th'art, that thus would'st faine,
Murder the issue of the Kings owne braine.
If in the essence and the name of King,
Their is Divinity: know then, yow bring.
That which conduceth to the Kings owne praise,
As much as Crown's of Gold or wreath's of bayes.
Though as a King in's actions he did shine,
Yet in his writings he may be Divine.
  Do not then say one skips into his throne ;
  The Docter and the King may both be one.

9 Anon., frontispiece to *Eikon E Piste* (1649)

shows an unseen hand lifting a curtain to reveal a Doctor of Divinity. The verses make the point:

> The Curtain's drawne; All may perceive the plot,
> And Him who truely the blacke Babe begot:
> Whose sable mantle makes me bold to say
> A Phaeton Sol's charriot rulde that day.
> Presumptuous Priest to skip into the throne,
> And make his King his Bastard Issue owne.
>   The Authour therefore hath conceiu'd it meet
>   The Doctor should doe pennance in this sheet.

For the 'truthful' author, clearly, the book is simply a performance by a bad actor impersonating a king, who ought to be hissed off the stage like the ghost on the famous first night of Jonson's *Catiline*. This anti-theatrical critique springs from what seems to be a thorough acquaintance with the theatre: the author refers to Dr Faustus (p. 11), and to the king's attempt to act 'the second part of King Richard the second' (p. 100). When the *Eikon* rises to a high style, he treats it as a change of costume: 'here he layes by the Hood, and assumes the Purple Roab, and again venters to stalk on the stage with the affected long stride of Royalty' (p. 81). He is bewildered by the success of 'the King's book'. Why, he asks in his epistle 'To the Seduced People of England', should they be any more taken in by it than by the king's proclamations or actions in his lifetime? It is the same problem that troubled Sidney's Astrophil when he found that Stella was moved less by his 'real' woes than by stories of sad lovers. This problem was something for which no parliamentary supporter had an answer. In any case, the 'Truthful' Image was no truer than the one it attempted to replace, because its author was unable to give a real name or face to the Divine he was attacking. His book was quickly confronted by the 'Faithful' (royalist) Image, *Eikon E Piste*. In its frontispiece (plate 9), the attempt to replace the king by a doctor is foiled by someone in cavalier costume who, in revenge, puts a fool's cap on the head of the author of the anti-royalist *Eikon*. The picture is the best part of this hastily written book, although, like the verses beneath it, it depends largely on the ideas of its predecessor. Drawing a curtain might reveal a picture, an actor (like Catiline, so often referred to), or both at once (as in *The Winter's Tale*). The figure behind the curtain might or might not intend to be revealed. In both these frontispieces, we are left unsure of the identity of the hand drawing the curtain. In the *Eikon Alethine*, it might be either God's or that of the anonymous author. In the *Eikon E Piste*, presumably, it is God's, since the author is represented as a typical cavalier. This series of Chinese boxes includes both a 'revelation' (of the king as the genuine source of the meditations) and a 'discovery' (of the impertinent author's attempt to take this status away from him). The double meaning of discovery was anticipated in one of Charles's first appearances as a fictitious character, in Middleton's *Game at Chess*, where the white forces defeat the black by the move known as 'checkmate by discovery' (v.iii.160–1): moving a lesser piece to reveal a more powerful one – the king – which is in a position to deliver the final blow. The *Eikon* can be seen as the superlative example of this 'noblest mate of all', in which an apparently passive piece suddenly takes on an active role by its mere appearance, much as the ruler does in a masque.

Milton's *Eikonoklastes*, like the *Eikon Alethine*, tries to take Charles out of mythology and into history, where his words can be compared with his actions and where he can be tried and judged. Though he does not attempt to suggest that someone else is playing the part of the king, his discussion of the *Eikon*'s literary qualities is directed, throughout, to emphasising the extent to which Charles himself is playing a part. He frequently suggests that the book ought to be treated as a purely literary work, as if it were not worth arguing with it seriously: it might as well be called a 'peece of Poetrie': all it needs is rhyme (p. 406); Charles writes of his wife 'in straines that come/almost to sonnetting' (pp. 420–1). Milton ridicules a couple of unfamiliar coinages – 'demagogue' and 'effronterie' – as affected; ironically, as Corns (1982) points out (pp. 69–73), both these words have since been accepted into the language.

Another way in which Milton attacked the king's image was through analysis of the king's imagery. The *Eikon Alethine* had already made a point about the reversibility of metaphors, arguing that the images of Marshall's frontispiece might as easily be applied to Parliament (p. 2) and that Charles's view of himself as the sun and Parliament as the moon had inverted the correct view of their relationship (p. 59). Milton systematically takes apart Charles's traditional comparisons. With regard to one particularly striking passage – 'my reputation shall, like the sun (after owls and bats have had their freedom in the night and darker times), rise and recover itself to such a degree of splendor as those feral birds shall be grieved to behold and unable to bear' (p. 92) – he comments, no doubt reminded of *Richard II*, 'Poets indeed use to vapor much after this manner' (p. 502). His most original, and effectively offensive, device is his way of dealing with the *Eikon*'s comparison of king to husband and kingdom to wife. First, he implies that Parliament ought to play the male role in this relationship, then, pretending to accept the king on his own terms, he suggests that the proper relationship of a king to his country is that of son to mother. But, in that case, the king's claim that Parliament cannot bring forth any Acts without him also represents a desire for unnatural incest (p. 467). This rather far-fetched witticism is part of a larger attempt to invert the sexual imagery of kingship in order to replace the husband–father figure with an effeminate one, a king who was 'govern'd by a Woman' (p. 538). The most vicious of his inversions comes in the final chapter, where Milton declares that both Charles's book and his behaviour in his last days reflect the spirit inherited from his grandmother, Mary Queen of Scots. From her he has learned, 'as it were by heart, or els by kind, that which is thought by his admirers to be the most vertuous, most manly, most Christian and most Martyr-like both of his words and speeches heer, and of his answers and behaviour at his Tryall' (p. 51). Not only does the phrase deny Charles's status as Protestant martyr by associating him with the Roman Catholic queen; it simultaneously associates him with an actor who has learned his courage, like his prayers, by heart, and it denies his 'manliness' in the most literal sense of the word. Far from being an imitation of Christ, the king's performance becomes an imitation of the Whore of Babylon.

It is for this reason that Milton makes so much of his discovery that one of the king's supposed prayers (added to the *Eikon* only in later editions) was in fact extracted from the prison episode of Sidney's *Arcadia*. In the first edition he concentrates on the effeminacy and irreverence implied in the king's use of a prayer originally spoken by a woman in a romance set in pagan Greece. In the second edition, he enlarges on the subject of plagiarism, relating Charles's theft of Sidney's words to his theft of his subjects' property. Joseph Jane, answering Milton in his *Eikon Aklastos* (1651), missed the point when he contended that the prayer was Sidney's rather than Pamela's, 'neither made by a heathen woman, nor to a heathen God', but 'by the Author a Christian without reference to any heathen Deitie' (p. 82). The significance of the prayer, whoever was responsible for its insertion, is that it reflected the belief of the king's party in the timeless value of phrases from the past. Milton's reinserting of the prayer into its original context was designed to reinforce an argument not only against the *Eikon* but against the Book of Common Prayer. His comment on the presence of biblical language throughout the book is characteristic: 'It is not hard for any man, who hath a bible in his hands, to borrow good words in abundance, but to make them his own is a work of grace onely from above' (p. 553). In using Shakespeare's Richard III as an example of someone who parroted Scripture phrases for an evil purpose, Milton was linking the king's much-praised literary style with hypocrisy and his religious practice with play-acting. Thus, Milton's main attack on Charles, via his book, was that he was an actor in three senses; a hypocrite, whose actions contradicted his pious words; a mere formal mouthpiece of rituals and words which he had not made truly his own; and an effeminate puppet, not only controlled by women but modelling his language and behaviour on theirs. There is no evidence that any reader's view of the *Eikon Basilike* was changed either by the *Eikon Alethine* or by Milton. But the issues which they raised did nevertheless affect the royalist literary response to the execution.

Royalist elegies: problem and solutions

The first edition of the *Eikon* contained no commemorative poems; an edition of mid-March 1649 included, for the first time, a dedicatory poem by 'F.N.G.' (still unidentified), an epitaph by 'J.H.' (probably James Howell), and the first of several verse explanations of the frontispiece (by the printer, William Dugard). On 11 March Thomason received copies of an elegy by Bishop Henry King (also published as 'A Deep Groan') and a book called *Vaticinium Votivum*, which contained elegies on the king and other royalists. A collection of poems dedicated to Charles, *Monumentum Regale*, appeared three months later (Thomason's copy is dated 14 June). Many writers seem to have preferred to keep their works to themselves for the time being. A number of elegies which proclaim themselves to have been 'Written in 1649' were not in fact published until much later, and there is no way of knowing whether they were altered with hindsight. Whatever the reason for the delay, it made a rather unimpressive show by comparison with the usual rapid poetic response to the deaths of public figures. The passionately royalist *Man in the Moon* complained in its first number (16 April 1649):

The *Lyons* in the *Tower*, (since the King was murderd) have mourned extreamly, Roar'd out his *obsequies*, and are now (all but the Princes) dead: shall man, endued with *reason*, be more unnaturall then bruit beasts? must the best of Kings, goe to his silent *grave* with nothing but [the inscription on his coffin] KING CHARLS 1648?

The newsbook's indignation is perhaps rather specious, since it goes on to mention one work just out, which it claimed 'would distill tears from a Heart of Adamant'. This was *Regale Lectum Miseriae* (Thomason obtained his copy on 18 April), probably published by the same underground network that was responsible for *The Man in the Moon*. Its author was John Quarles, the son of the more famous Francis. He is the only published writer to attempt a historical narrative based on printed accounts of the trial and execution as well as his reading of the *Eikon* itself. This fact gives his work a certain interest despite its thudding metre and bathetic rhymes. Sometimes Quarles follows the courtroom dialogue quite closely, as in his description of the king's reaction on hearing the charge against him:

> He made a pause; but by, and by, he broke
> His silent lipps, and moderately spoke
> To this effect, May I desire to know
> From whence this great Authority doth flow
> That you pretend to act by? If it be
> Derivative, I shall desire to see,
> And know from whom; till then I shall deny
> To give my tongue a license to Reply.
> You are our Pris'ner Sir [says Bradshaw], you ought not to
> Demand what your apointed Iudges doe,
> For our Authority 'tis known at large
> Unto our selves; pray answer to your charge. (pp. 65–7)[1]

This 'Elegy' was printed with a 'Dream', consisting of Quarles's romantic fantasies about the king's last hours. He imagines that he hears Charles lamenting, and then (a vision within a vision) allows Charles to 'see' his queen. In their dream world they can say farewell to each other and even pray together, which, given their differences in religion, would probably have been impossible in real life. Adding to the printed account of Charles's last conversation with his children, Quarles makes him comfort them by reminding them of the mysteriousness of God's justice:

> Th'effect can never absolutely show
> The justnesse of a Cause, for oftentimes
> Just Heav'n is pleas'd to punish private Crimes
> With publique means; God knows my cause was just;
> And yet he lay'd my Armies in the dust. (p. 30)

Quarles, then, alternates between the romance model and an attempt to write a genuinely historical account of the event. One of the most personal touches is the reference in his 'Elegy' to the King's surprising fluency on the scaffold:

> Feare had no habitation in his breast,
> And what he spoke was readily exprest;
> Heav'ns sacred orator divinely typp'd
> His tongue with golden languages, and dipp'd
> His soul in Loves sweet fountaine. (pp. 81–3)

This is hardly an accurate description of Charles's nearly inaudible speech, but it refers indirectly to the fact that, as several witnesses attest, the king's notorious difficulty in speaking seemed to have been almost completely overcome during the period of his trial and execution (Wedgwood, p. 131). Interestingly, the speech impediment is mentioned by a number of elegists, giving perhaps the only touch of realism to their hagiographies. 'F.N.G.'s poem contrasts his awkward speech with his written eloquence:

> Great *Tully* had been silenc'd amongst men,
> Had but Thy *Tongue* been equal to Thy *Pen*:
> But this *Defect* doth prove Thy skil more choice,
> That makes the *Eccho* sweeter then the *voice*. . .

Few of the other elegies published during the first year show much conern with the historical, as opposed to the archetypal, Charles. Taking their tone from the *Eikon*, writers make him a representative of all the abstractions which hold society together, as in Henry King's early elegy, 'A Deepe Groane':

> Traytor and Soveraigne now inverted meet;
> The wealthy Olive's dragg'd to th'Brambles feet.
> The Throne is metamorphiz'd to the Barre,
> And despicable Batts the Eagle dare.   (King 1965, p. 115)

Images of inversion, witchcraft, uncreation, many of them biblical in origin like this example (Judges 9: 8–15), are piled on to express horror. In his second and better 'Elegy', published later, Henry King apologises for using the familiar comparison between Charles and Josiah:

> O pardon me that but from Holy Writ
> Our loss allowes no Parallel to it:
> Nor call it bold presumption that I dare
> Charls with the best of Judah's Kings compare.   (King 1965, p. 118)

The fear of such presumption did not trouble everyone. Some writers simply use the abbreviation 'Ch—' for both Christ and Charles, leaving the reader to choose between them. One sermon draws an explicit parallel, noting both the obvious similarities (their silence during the trial, for instance) and some which are frankly bathetic:

When our Saviour suffered, there were terrible signs and wonders, and darknesse over all the Land: so during the time of our Soveraigns Martyrdom, there were strange signs seen in the sky, in divers places of the Kingdom; and it was thought very prodigious, the Ducks forsook their Pond at Saint *Jameses*, and came as far as *Whitehall*, fluttering about the Scaffold.[2]

These examples indicate the difficulties involved in attempting an adequate literary response to the occasion. All elegies, of course, face the same problems: how to prove one's sincerity in a formal genre, how to control the expression of supposedly uncontrollable grief. But when the subject of the elegy is the embodiment of all traditional values on the one hand, and an unprecedented and shocking event on the other, the problem of steering between cliché and hysteria becomes particularly acute. However much they might disagree over improvisation versus 'set forms' in prayer, writers were basically agreed about the importance of a spontaneous effect in literary language. The author of *Eikon Alethine* had already contrasted the formality of the king's *Eikon* with his own definition of a genuinely moving style:

Not composures therefore adorned with Rhetoricall flourishes, nor smooth running sentences flowing from a *Ciceronian* tongue; but ejaculations abruptly broken with sobs, and prayers ending in unartificial sighes fetched from a heart truly contrite, are the most prevalent Oratory, with the Almighty. (p. 8)

Though he attacked his predecessor on every other point, the author of the *Eikon E Piste* (1649) obviously shared this particular view, to which he appealed when offering a much-needed justification for his own lapses of style:

if (therefore) you find any *abrupt breakings off, discoherences, or want of transition in my writing*, which my antagonist allowes, as the best oblations of a troubled spirit, I hope you will do no less for me. (dedication)

But the attempt to depict spontaneous grief ran into another danger, that of seeming weak and effeminate. The elegiac mode is not normally incompatible with a manly persona, and Vaughan's 'Elegy on R. Hall', published in *Olor Iscanus* (1651), seems comfortable with the idea that 'fair manhood hath a female eye' (lines 13–14). But accusations like those in *Eikonoklastes* had been levelled against royalists often enough to make some of them seem uncomfortable about expressing grief unless they could combine it with some proof of courage. The 'Elegy on Lord Francis Villiers' (Marvell 1972), published in 1648, begins by justifying heroic grief –

The purer fountains from the rocks more steep
Distill and stony valour best doth weep. (lines 21–2)

– and ends with the author's declaration that he and his friends will follow Villiers' example in leaving 'a whole Pyramid / Of Vulgar bodies' to his memory. In the same spirit, the verses on the king's death attributed to the Marquis of Montrose were said to have been written 'with the point of his sword', thereby enacting the writer's final assertion that he would 'write thy epitaph with blood and wounds' (*Reliquiae Sacrae Carolinae* 1650, p. 355). Few other authors of royal elegies were in a position to make such a claim, and their authors' uncertainty about themselves affects their uncertainty as to how to write about the king. 'How,' asks the author of 'Caroli', 'can I, / Who want *myself*, write him an Elegie?' (*Monumentum Regalie* 1649, p. 21). He seizes on the Longinian notion of the sublime to justify a sense of inadequacy to the subject:

> where the theme confounds us, 'tis a sort
> Of glorious Merit, proudly to fall short.

Another draws on the language of rhetoric only to reject it; 'Meiosis', a figure of understatement, will be the inevitable result of whatever he writes:

> Dread sir! What shall we say? Hyperbole
> Is not a Figure, when it speak's of Thee
> Thy Book is our best Language; what to this
> Shall e're be added, is Thy Meiosis:
> Thy Name's a Text too hard for us; no men
> Can write of it, without Thy Parts and Pen.
>   ([Francis Gregory], 'An Elegie' (['Com, com, let's mourne'],
>   in *Vaticinium Votivum* 1649, p. 69)

The use of emblematic techniques – black pages, as in *Regale Lectum Miseriae*, or red ink, as in *The Bloody Court* – is another way of trying to express the inexpressible. Behind the constant complaints about the difficulty of finding adequate language for an elegy lurks a fear of surrendering to the kind of emotion which seems appropriate to the scale of the subject.

Thus, despite their determination to make Charles a Christ figure, the way in which poets celebrate heroic suffering brings to a head all the contradictions inherent in the concept. The discomfort emerges particularly in their evident anxiety to avoid the 'feminine', or to displace it on to a female character. The best-known painting of the king's execution, by Weesop, resembles many paintings of the crucifixion in that the full effect of unrestrained public grief is depicted through the symbolic figure of a weeping or fainting woman. The anonymous author of *The Bloody Court, or the Fatal Tribunal* (1649) insists, 'My intention … is not to catch Womens Affections but to inform mens Judgements' (p. 5). He seems to be echoing Gauden's insistence, in his *Religious and Loyal Protestation* (January 1649), that the power of the Army leaders should be 'sweetened with Pitty, not foolish and *feminine*, which I would have below you, but *masculine*, Heroick, truly Christian and Divine' (sig. B3). Yet even while rejecting the hypothetical weeping woman, the writers use her to say what they cannot say in their own voices. In one biblical-sounding description of the execution, it is she who provides the key phrase:

The Sun shined that morning very clear without intermission, until the King came to the Fatal Block, and lay down, and then at that moment a Dark thick Cloud covered the face of the Sun, which for a time so continued, in so much, that a Gentlewoman standing by me to behold this Dreadful Tragedy, cryed out, Look, look, Sir, the Sun is ashamed and hideth his Face.   (*The Bloody Court*, p. 18)

Sometimes the author deals with emotion by displacing it on to the other side, where it becomes fanaticism. During the trial, Charles had constantly insisted on Reason and, more specifically, on the 'Reasons' which Bradshaw refused to let him give the court but which were finally published after the execution. Charles's 'Reasons', as Milton insisted in *Eikonoklastes*, were not the same as Reason. Nevertheless, the court's refusal to hear 'reason' and the obvious rhyme of 'reason' and 'treason' were easy targets for royalist satirists; a pamphlet published in July 1649 is called *Reason against Treason, or a Bone for Bradshaw to Picke*. One elegist reverses the usual accusation that royalists are living in a fantasy world, depicting the court instead as a nightmare of irrationality, 'a pageant Court ... Where Fairie Traytors murder aery Kings':

> No fond *Romance*, no fam'd *Arcadia* treats,
> Of such Eutopian, frantick Judgement Seats.
> ('An Elegie' ['Most Cruell men'] in *Monumentum Regale*, pp. 5–6)

Setting themselves in opposition to a hypothetical hysterical woman or raving fanatic is one way for writers to keep to the high ground of reason.

This royalist problem of sincerity – their own and the king's – may help to explain the prevalence of the actor image at this period. The notion of the execution as spectacle made its emotional effect more comprehensible. It also made sense of the Christ analogy by treating Charles as an imitator rather than someone presuming to see himself as Christ:

> This Scene was like the Passion-Tragedie,
> His Saviour's Person none could Act, but Hee.
> ('Com, com, let's mourne', *Vaticinium Votivum*, p. 69)

Another writer also refers to him as 'convoy'd ... to his last Theatre', where 'he acts his Passions part' (*Loyalties Tears Flowing* 1649). 'Passion', of course, means suffering; to act a passion would be hypocrisy, but to act a Passion is to accept a role in which one has been cast by Providence.

How far did the royal actor himself become a role on the stage as well as in print? Not at all, it seems, until after the Restoration. Anne Barton (1977) has noted that the author of *The Famous Tragedy* could not bring himself to introduce the king as a character; his execution is merely reported in the last act (p. 93), though it is clumsily dramatised later, in *Cromwell's Conspiracy*, a version of this play rewritten at the time of the Restoration (Potter 1981, pp. 292–3). Charles, of course, had one obvious disqualification for the tragic stage: his well-known stammer would have made it difficult to portray him without caricature.

One curious exception, however, deserves a brief notice. *The Kingdomes Faithful and Impartiall Scout* (31 Aug.–7 Sept. 1649) carries an account of an episode in Hampshire:

a Company of young Sparks had consulted to act a Tragedy of the Tryall of the late King of *England*, and putting the same into execution, Commissioners were appointed, a high Court of Justice called, and the severall Officers thereunto nominated; and having made choice of a Soldier to represent the Kings person, he was accordingly brought to the Bar, where he was impeached of high Treason, &c. and Sentence denounced, to have his head separated from his body.

The play continued up to the moment of the execution, whereupon the actor playing the Executioner astonished everyone by beheading the un-royal actor in earnest:

the rest of the Actors and Spectators were exceedingly astonish'd, and demanding the reason, why he did so, He replyed, *That it was his office, And he acted but his part, as they did theirs*; and after some further examination, the poor Executioner was ordered to be carryed away, and committed to safe custody: the rest of the Tragidicians [*sic*] departed in peace, and resorted every man, to their severall places of sanctuary.

This story appears to be pure fiction, like so much of what appears in the newsbooks. It would, however, be interesting to know whether it had any purpose apart from sensationalism. It seems to combine two familiar types of theatrical or anti-theatrical story which go back at least to ancient Rome: those which warn against acting, because jest may become earnest, and those which attribute an actor's biggest success to the fact that he was weeping over a real corpse or killing himself with real poison. But the newsbook-writer seems to hover on the edge of a recognition that all parties in the trial and execution had been acting the roles allotted them by fate. Just as the tragicomic model, which threw the responsibility for a happy ending on to Providence, absolved royalists from the need to do anything to help their cause, so did the notion of Charles as a tragic actor, perhaps the victim of a hereditary curse on the house of Stuart. One of the oldest meanings of the world-as-stage image is associated with the stoic philosophers: it is the idea that we have no choice as to the part we play, but must simply try to play it as well as possible. Playing down Charles's individual and personal responsibility for events made it easier for both sides to reconcile themselves to those events, and thus to each other.

J. W. Draper (1929), the author of the fullest study of the broadside elegies of this period, suggests that the cavaliers finally abandoned the form and resorted to satire because they had 'failed to win over for the royal martyr the sympathy of the broadside-reading public' (p. 123). This account is over-simplified. The decrease in the number of royalist publications in the course of 1649 must be linked to the Printing Act, which came into effect in September of that year. Other elegies continued to be produced (on the three royalist lords executed in April 1649, on the various victims of Worcester in 1651, and on those executed for other royalist plots). The most striking is Robert Wild's elegy on fellow-Presbyterian Christopher Love, which he calls a tragedy and writes in five sections, with a prologue and epilogue. It out-Clevelands Cleveland in its unlikely choice of topics to be witty about, particularly when he opens his account of the execution by borrowing the subtitle of *Philaster* for a truly appalling pun, 'Love lies a-bleeding' (Wild 1671, p. 27). The tendency for elegies to become witty and satiric already existed (it can be seen, for instance, in such poems as Cleveland's elegy on the execution of Laud). Even in the elegies for the king, writers sometimes leap with surprising readiness, even relief, from the expression of deepest grief to cheap jibes about the parliamentarians. For instance, John Quarles presents *Regale Lectum Miseriae* as the product of deep depression, says that he is about to go abroad, and that he writes 'out of a disturbed minde'. He apologises for the printing errors, because 'it is generally known that errours in griefe, are incident to all'. Yet the opening expression of the author's grief turns abruptly into an irrelevant account of a Puritan seducing his 'sister'. Similarly, Bishop Henry King writes his most effective lines when he turns from praising Charles to satirising his enemies' notorious promise to make him a 'great and glorious king':

> Yet have You kept your word against Your will,
> Your King is Great indeed and Glorious still,
> And You have made Him so. We must impute
> That Lustre which His Sufferings contribute

To your preposterous Wisdoms, who have done
All your good Deeds by Contradiction:
For as to work His Peace you rais'd this Strife
And often Shot at Him to Save His Life;
As you took from Him to Encrease His wealth,
And kept Him Pris'ner to secure His Health;
So in revenge of your dissembled Spight,
In this last Wrong you did Him greatest Right,
And (cross to all You meant) by Plucking down
Lifted Him up to His Eternal Crown.

(King 1965, 'Elegy', lines 463–76)

It sometimes seems that writers find it easier to deal with the execution indirectly, or in an aside linked to some other subject. One of the most obvious cases is *Lachrymae Musarum* (1649), the collection of elegies on the young Lord Hastings, where most of the authors are really using the occasion to lament the general state of the world from which the young man has mercifully escaped, and to suggest that his death is a punishment for the sins of others. Dryden, for instance, compares Hastings's smallpox-pimples to subjects rebelling against their lord, then calls them 'Gems sent to adorn his Skin, / The Cab'net of a richer Soul within' (lines 63–4). The notion of the body as a cabinet for the jewel of the soul is traditional in elegy; in 1649, however, no reference to cabinets could fail to have reverberations. Like many of the other poets in this collection, Dryden also digresses into social satire (on the dull, elderly men who have had the bad taste to continue living now that young Hastings is dead) and then explains that 'Grief makes me rail.'

It is not, then, that poets have failed to win sympathy for Charles, but that they preferred to present themselves in the aggressive stance of his avengers rather than in the passive one of his mourners. In poems written after 1649 the tension between grief and anger seems, curiously, to resolve itself by dividing itself between the objects of these emotions, Charles I and Cromwell. One reason for the fascination which Marvell's 'Horatian Ode' has always exercised is that its attention to, and sympathy for, both figures creates a Hegelian sense of tragic conflict. But in later poems, including even Marvell's, the contrast between the two men ceases to be a conflict. Writers direct purely elegiac sentiments toward Charles, while focusing the energetic, celebratory, 'manly' tone on his successor. Charles's Christ-like passivity is increasingly stressed. After the execution, one writer claimed that the king's personal device had been the pelican (Arnway 1649, p. 89). This seems not to have been true, but the symbolism of the pelican being devoured by her own children was too appropriate not to use. Sir

William Denny's *Pelecenicidium* (1653), supposedly a religious treatise against suicide, has as its frontispiece a pelican. Though deliberately obscure in detail, it seems to me a typical example of the obvious yet covert royalist work, offering visions or parables which it then explains, or explains away. For instance, one episode depicts a stag hunt:

> Behold, pursu'd by many furious Hounds,
>   From ore the hills a deadly Chase!
>   In that spoyl'd Grove's his heavy Case.
> The Stagge doth fall, and weepeth to his wounds,
>   While th' Huntsmen winde the death of this their prize,
>   A live Hart from dead Stagge doth rise,
> Starts up; they all pursue for Prey. Past reach he flies.   (pp. 229–30)

The 'Perspective' on this poem, supposedly supplied for the benefit of female readers 'of a weaker Apprehension', explains that the stag stands for the condition of man before and after conversion; he is changed into a hart by faith (pp. 244–5). The Moral is that we cannot serve God and Mammon, and 'there is but one Phoenix' (p. 246). While all these images might be religious – the Phoenix is a common symbol for Christ's resurrection – the fact that *Cooper's Hill* had already made the stag hunt a political allegory leaves little doubt that in this case the stag is Charles I and the hart Charles II (with special reference to his escape after Worcester). In the biblical lament for Jerusalem: 'her princes are become like harts that find no pasture, and they are gone without strength before the pursuer' (Lamentations 1:6).

Marvell's 'Nymph Complaining for the Death of Her Fawn' has, not surprisingly, been suspected of some association with this imagery of a king hunted to death. It is characteristic of Marvell that he should feminise the subject, making the victim a pet fawn rather than a stag, its death an almost accidental killing, and the lament that of a young and obviously naive girl. The source of the story may be Ovidian, but it may also (Marvell certainly knew Fanshawe's translations) recall the episode in *Il Pastor Fido* where the scornful Silvio accidentally wounds Clorinda, who has long loved him in vain, and, through his remorse, learns to love her. In Marvell's poem, 'inconstant' Silvio has betrayed the nymph, and the fawn which he gave her on parting has been killed by 'wanton troopers'. The language of violence is transformed into that of romance and casual infidelity. The poem need not be directly about the king at all, but it appeals to the same emotions that were being allowed to cluster around him: pathetic, feminine, safely inactive, a logical development of the contrast already implicit in the Horatian Ode.

10   After William Faithorne, 'Cromwell between the Pillars', emblem dating from
the early 1650s

Charles and Cromwell: Shakespeare as political unconscious

Cromwellian iconography, inevitably, grew out of royal iconography, just as Cromwell's court, in many respects, was a royal court (see Sherwood 1977). The effectiveness of the emblematic pictures of Charles is borne out by the fact that William Faithorne in 1653 produced one of Cromwell (plate 10), with an elaborate mixture of traditional emblems (the soldier's helmet becoming a hive for bees) and allegory (Cromwell as St Michael conquering the Whore of Babylon or a pilot steering the biblical ark between the classical Scylla and Charybdis). But the emphasis is so markedly different as to suggest a deliberate contrast with the *Eikon* frontispiece. Though he holds a Bible, Cromwell's pose is an active one; he is in armour, and his military success is indicated by the army behind him and by the figure of Fame. The three crowns of the *Eikon* reappear, but now they encircle his sword and are being offered to him by personifications of England, Scotland, and Ireland. At the bottom of the picture are depicted various figures engaged in peaceful and profitable occupations. A dove with an olive branch alludes to the sign of God's mercy on England after its stormy past, and, incidentally, to Cromwell's name. His initials form a sun and a moon, adorning one of the pillars whose significance in royal iconography goes back to the Emperor Charles V (see Yates 1975, p. 23). The ark on Ararat in the sunshine may be meant to balance the stormy landscape in the *Eikon* frontispiece. Abraham's near-sacrifice of Isaac, depicted below it, is left tantalisingly unexplained. There may be a carefully veiled allusion to the interpretation suggested in *Mercurius Britanicus* (22–9 May 1649), where the story is an allegory of the execution: 'God was about to sacrifice the Kingdom, and destroy it, but he in compassion spared it ... and in regard that better one man dye than a people perish, *Gregory* [the executioner] one of the servants of Old Father *Time*, turned about and saw a Ram and sacrificed it'.

A similar contrast is developed in Marvell's two other Cromwell poems, where traditional images of royalty are used to undermine the institution of kingship in the abstract. In the 'First Anniversary', kings are oaks – slow-growing trees, too slow for a time which needs the speed of the lightning or the hawk-like qualities of the divinely inspired leader. While Charles's role as Davidic musician had been compared (by Quarles, for example, in *Divine Fancies*, 1644) to the careful harmonising of different strings, Cromwell's music, like Amphion's, makes cities rise (lines 49–74). Cromwell controls time; a king is only the wooden head on his viol or one of the images which 'with vain Scepter, strike the hourly bell' (lines 41–2).

Marvell may be remembering Richard II's description of himself as Boling-broke's 'Jack o' the clock'.

Samuel Sheppard's almanac for 1654 gives a list of kings followed by the verse:

> When Kings are lost, and Subjects do decay,
> Though hearts may speak, tongues must not dare to say.

If, as I think, this last line echoes the words of the groom to the imprisoned Richard II, 'What my tongue dares not, that my heart shall say' (v.v.97), it is one of the very few references to a play which could be described as the repressed subtext for the whole period. Repressed, perhaps, because it was too open to conflicting interpretations. When Cotgrave selected two quotations for his *English Treasury*, it is significant that he passed up the now-famous passages of patriotism and lament. He also ignored the prison scene, which differs from those of the poems discussed in chapter 4 in showing that the hero's thoughts, far from enabling him to escape, only reinforce his sense of imprisonment. Cotgrave chose instead Mowbray's words, which he placed in a section headed 'Of Credit, Reputation':

> The purest treasure mortal times afford
> Is spotless reputation; that away,
> Men are but gilded loam, or painted clay.   (p. 61)

His other extract, the Duchess of Gloucester's rebuke to John of Gaunt, appears under the heading 'Of Patience':

> What we in mean men, oft call patience
> Is pale cold Cowardice in noble breasts.   (p. 214)

While it may be misleading to rely too much on Cotgrave's own prefer-ences, his choice of these passages corresponds sufficiently to other writing of the 1650s to suggest that what the period responded to most in the play was not its depiction of the king as martyr but the criticism of his assump-tion of that role, which rarely inspires anything but irritation in his followers. His pious reactions to crisis ('Must he lose / The name of King? A God's name, let it go'; 'Our holy lives must win a new world's crown') are described by others as 'frantic' or unkingly. The possibility that Chris-tian resignation had no place in a ruler was one of those things which, in the aftermath of the king's execution, might be felt but never said.

The ethic of justification by success did, of course, have to come to terms with the fact of Cromwell's death. To some extent, the event has the effect, for Marvell, of assimilating the Lord Protector to the tradition of other mortal rulers and thus to their imagery: in the 'Poem upon the Death of His Late Highness the Lord Protector', he becomes the oak whose slow growth had been used earlier as a reproach to kings (lines 261–70), and lightning, which he had once embodied, is now able to strike him too. By attributing Cromwell's death to grief for the loss of his daughter, Marvell even introduces the tones of erotic tenderness hitherto associated in his poetry with the deaths of royalist heroes. As if thinking of poems like Denny's *Pelecenicidium*, he asks, rhetorically,

> Who now shall tell us more of mournful swans,
> Of halcyons kind, or bleeding pelicans?   (lines 79–80)

However, the poem also draws a deliberate contrast with the king's death and with the whole idea of the royal actor. Something which royalists were later to use against Cromwell, perhaps had already used against him, was his lack of any literary or theatrical quality. 'I think', Cowley wrote after Cromwell's death, in his *Discourse by Way of Vision, Concerning the Government of Oliver Cromwell*, 'you can hardly pick out the name of a man who ever was called Great, besides him we are now speaking of, who never left the memory behinde him of one wise or witty Apothegm even amongst his Domestique Servants or greatest Flatterers' (Cowley 1906, p. 363). Marvell's elegy makes a virtue of this fact. The poem's opening lines deny both the vulgar desire for drama and the need for a stage at all:

> The People, which what most they fear esteem,
> Death when more horrid so more noble deem;
> And blame the last *Act*, like *Spectators* vain,
> Unless the *Prince* whom they applaud be slain.   (lines 7–10)

Dryden's significantly titled 'heroic stanzas' on Cromwell also contain an implicit contrast with Charles. It was suggested long ago (Parsons 1904, pp. 47–9) that stanza 15 of the poem is intended to set Cromwell's un-impeded success against the images in the *Eikon* frontispiece:

> His *Palmes* though under weights they did not stand,
> Still thriv'd; no *Winter* could his *Laurells* fade;
> Heav'n in his Portraict shew'd a Workman's hand
> And drew it perfect yet without a shade.

Sun rather than shade, competence in ruling rather than patience in suffering: these qualities must have looked particularly attractive when, after Cromwell's death, it looked as if chaos might be about to come again.

Those attempting to prepare the way for a restoration of Charles II

11a   Anon., first frontispiece to *Bibliotheca Regia* (1659)

THE
EXPLICATION
OF THE
FIRST FIGURE.

WE *here prefent King* CHARLS *upon his* Throne,
  Ruling three Kingdoms, and all three as one ;
Not clad in folitude *and fhades of night,*
Spending his penfive thoughts in Meditations,
But Acting powerfully *in all mens fight* ;
Such actings *beft become the Kings of mighty Nations.*

A Crown begirts his Sacred Head, to fhew
That GOD *above made him a* GOD *below,*
Heavens great Vice-gerent ; *by his Supreme word,*
Not awing more the Paifant *than the* Lord.
Difpenfing Graces , *paffing* Laws ; *and when*
Religion *was concern'd, directing by his* Pen.

The blefsings of his Scepter *thofe* ; *But more*
His Trident *speaks him for the Oceans King,*
To whom the VVater-Nymphs *their prefents bring* :
Reigning from fea to fea, from fhore to fhore,
Brideling the waves with his Imperial *Fleet,*
And holding Sea *and* Land *under his* Royal *Feet.*

11b   Verse caption to first frontispiece

12a   Anon., second frontispiece to *Bibliotheca Regia* (1659)

· THE
EXPLICATION
OF THE
SECOND FIGURE.

A S *a tall* Ship *difputes the power of* F A T E,
   Though the winds roar upon the tottering Main :
So CHARLS *makes good the* Ship *of* Church *and* State
Embroil'd *at home, ingag'd with* France *and* Spain :
The Helm *he governs with a conftant hand,*
His Trident aws *the* Sea, *the* Seas *fecure the Land.*

   Fill'd *with a* Leading gale *he cuts the waves,*
   Or *by a* fide-wind *gains the* Port *defir'd;*
   Sometimes *he* bears *againft the ftorm, and braves*
   The raging flood, *with it's own fury tir'd,*
   And *fometimes wifely lets the* Veffel *drive,*
Complying *with the* ftream, *when 'tis in vain to ftrive.*

   A Tempeft *from the* North, Crofs-winds *at home*
   Create *foul weather to difturb his way ;*
   But *ftill he rides upon the angry foam,*
   Teaching *the* VVinds *and* Tempeft *to obey.*
   Till *from the* helm *remov'd by envious fate,*
The Tempeft *finks the* Church, *the* Winds *fubvert the* Su

12b   Verse caption to second frontispiece

responded to the new spirit. In 1659, Henry Seile, an associate of Royston, published a volume of previously uncollected writings by Charles I, *Bibliotheca Regia*. These are mainly papers from the years before the war, so it is not surprising that the two illustrations commissioned for the volume should depict a young, active and successful ruler on his throne or at the helm of the ship of state. But the verses accompanying them show that the editor is eager to offset the pathetic image of the *Eikon* frontispiece. The first figure (plate 11a) makes an explicit contrast with it, showing the king

> Not clad in *solitude* and shades of night,
> Spending his pensive thoughts in *Meditations*,
> But *Acting powerfully* in all mens sight;
> Such actings best become the Kings of mighty Nations.

The king holds not only a sceptre but a trident, because, the writer notes, he is also 'the Oceans King ... Brideling the waves with his *Imperial* Fleet'. The growth in importance of the British navy, usually thought of as a specifically Cromwellian achievement, is here backdated and credited to Charles. Verses explaining the second illustration (see plates 12a and b) emphasise his skilful steering of the ship of state rather than the fact that he is eventually 'from the *helm* remov'd by envious fate'. Casting the responsibility for his defeat and death onto Fate, rather than Parliament or the Army, is an obvious way of healing old discords within a comforting myth of the civil war which all sides could accept.

Patrick Cruttwell (1954) has observed that Charles I and Cromwell 'made realities' out of a contrast which had already been prepared in the drama of the previous age and 'set the patterns of thought and emotion' for those who lived through these events in real life (p. 188). His prototype for Cromwell is Tamburlaine, also a self-made man and 'fortune's son'; Charles I is in the tradition of Richard II and the saintly Duncan in *Macbeth*. He goes on to argue that, once the civil war had forced people to 'take sides', the complexity of the drama was coarsened by the needs of propaganda.

Imagine a *Macbeth* written after the execution of King Charles. It would then have been quite impossible to preserve, as Shakespeare does, both the mystical reverence for legitimate kingship, the sense that its destruction involves a violation of the divine and the natural orders, and the sympathetic dramatic presentation of the murderous usurper.   (p. 198)

Cruttwell's interpretation of the play is debatable (is Shakespeare ambivalently apolitical? is Macbeth sympathetically presented?), but the existence of two later versions of the story makes it possible to examine the validity of the hypothetical contrast which he sketches here. Milton's short sketch of a proposed tragedy of *Macbeth* was probably written before Charles I's execution (the most likely date for it is the early 1640s), but it obviously dates from a period when the nature of his kingship was a matter of debate. An extensive revision of Shakespeare's play, usually attributed to Davenant, was first produced (probably) in 1663–4 (Davenant 1965, p. 14) and influenced the performance text well into the nineteenth century. It is of course difficult to say much about Milton's project from the evidence of a few sentences: he says that it will begin with the meeting of Malcolm and Macduff; observing the unities, it will deal with Duncan's murder through a narration by his ghost. The only thing obvious from this account is that the play will have to consist mainly of debate about what to do to combat Macbeth's tyranny. David Norbrook (1987) has suggested that the debate might have focused on the conflict in Scotland between hereditary and elective succession, and hence about the justice of Macbeth's claim to the throne. I myself should guess that Milton's decision to begin the play at the English court shows his determination to make the plot as relevant as possible to the situation in the early 1640s, when English and Scottish forces united to overthrow a tyrant. The play's shape would then have been similar to that of *Samson Agonistes*, beginning at the lowest point of despair and ending with the recovery of resolution.

The question whether rebellion against a tyrant can ever be justified was also the aspect of the play which most interested Davenant, though from a different point of view. As a play about darkness, witchcraft, regicide, and a monstrous birth – and a play whose one comic scene is a display of drunkenness – *Macbeth* embodies the dominant images of royalist writing. Perhaps this is why it never seems to be quoted in the literature of 1640–60. It is as if its imagery had detached itself from its own story, like a virus from a laboratory, to multiply in the society outside. Davenant clearly recognised, and did his best to underline, the topicality of the plot. We are told of Macbeth that 'there is a Civil War / Within his Bosom' (v.ii.17–18), and when Malcolm pronounces the fate of the dead tyrant, he seems to recall what happened to the regicides at the Restoration:

> Drag his Body hence, and let it Hang upon
> A Pinnacle in *Dunsinane*, to shew
> To future Ages what to those is due,
> Who others Right, by Lawless Power pursue.
>
> (Davenant 1965, v.ix.31–4)

The last lines of the play are, however, given to Macduff, whose role at this point becomes obviously reminiscent of General Monk's. It is he, and not Malcolm or the saintly Duncan, who provides the play's chief contrast to Macbeth. His wife's role is equally developed. At Lady Macbeth's first appearance, she is accompanied by Lady Macduff, who is staying with her in the castle while their husbands are away at war:

> *La. Macb.* Madam, I have observed since you came hither,
> You have been still disconsolate. Pray tell me,
> Are you in perfect health?
> *La. Macd.*   Alas! how can I?
> My Lord, when Honour call'd him to the War,
> Took with him half of my divided soul,
> Which lodging in his bosom, lik'd so well
> The place, that 'tis not yet return'd.
> *La. Macb.*   Methinks
> That should not disorder you: for, no doubt,
> The brave *Macduff* left half his soul behind him,
> To make up the defect of yours.   (I.v.1–10)

The contrast between the two women's language reflects their contrasting moral values. Lady Macbeth shares the parliamentarian contempt for romantic figurativeness, pretending to take literally her companion's clichéd image of the divided soul. The contrast sharpens as she learns that her companion is still under the influence of past fears even though she has learnt that Macduff is safe, and that the thought of 'the bright glories which / He gain'd in battle' (I.v.20–1) gives her no pleasure. Like Gondibert, Lady Macduff expresses the scepticism common among defeated royalists about military glory (especially that which wins 'popular applause'):

> *La. Macd.* The world mistakes the glories gain'd in war,
> Thinking their Lustre true; alas, they are
> But Comets, Vapours! By some men exhal'd
> From others bloud, and kindled in the Region
> Of popular applause, in which they live
> A-while; then vanish; and the very breath
> Which first inflam'd them, blows them out agen.   (I.v.22–8)

Having finally got rid of Lady Macduff, Lady Macbeth is able to read her husband's letter and embark on the soliloquy which follows it. Though her words correspond largely to Shakespeare's, they have been transformed by their context. 'What thou highly covet'st / Thou covet'st holily!' (I.v.55–6) suggests the hypocrisy of a Puritan general, while her determination to 'chastise with the valour of my tongue' his 'too effeminate desires'

(I.v.62–5) makes her part of the world of preaching women to which Lady Macduff's properly female royalism is contrasted. The contrast is further emphasised when Lady Macbeth deliberately 'unsexes' herself so as to be fit for the task of regicide.

The witches' appearance to Macduff and his wife in II.v provides the opportunity for extra spectacle, but this is not its only purpose. Davenant not only enlarges the two roles with which his spectators were most likely to identify themselves, but emphasises the difficulties in their attempt to maintain their integrity in an evil world. As often in this play, Lady Macduff is seen as her husband's good angel, not only balancing the role of Lady Macbeth but also, perhaps, vindicating the royalist respect for women and the controversial role of Henrietta Maria. The witches, who are warmongers, prophesy that Macbeth will 'spill much more bloud: / And become worse, to make his Title good' (II.v.37–8); meanwhile they 'shou'd rejoyce when good Kings bleed' (II.v.40). The successes of the parliamentary armies, often claimed to be proof of supernatural assistance, here become what their opponents often called them: the work of witchcraft. In the final scene Macduff declares that if Macbeth surrenders he will be

> Led
> About the World and Gazed on as a Monster,
> More Deform'd than ever Ambition Fram'd,
> Or Tyrannie could shape. (v.viii.27–30)

Macbeth is compared to a monster in Shakespeare as well, but Macduff's use of the term sets it in the context of the language of the 1640s and 1650s, where Reformation is Deformation. It is not surprising that Davenant's part of the Dryden–Davenant *Tempest* (1667) should have elaborated the relationship of the monster Caliban and the rebellious sailors with a new character, the monster's equally unattractive sister Sycorax, equally ready to pair off with either of the rival rulers of the island.

Yet it is not easy to read Davenant's *Macbeth* as pure divine right royalism. Its very language works against such a reading. Davenant's alterations undoubtedly make the play more explicitly political, but they also remove from regicide much of the imagery of sacrilege and damnation. Although in his most famous soliloquy the Restoration Macbeth recognises the bars against killing Duncan in terms of his relationship of kinsman, subject and host, he is worried only about the effect of the murder on his own peace of mind; Davenant cuts the extraordinary apocalyptic poetry in which Pity is personified first as a naked newborn babe and then as heaven's cherubim. The night of the murder is unruly, even if the porter is not allowed to be drunk, but when Macbeth departs to kill Duncan, he hears the bell not as one 'that summons thee to heaven or to hell' but one 'That rings my Coronation, and thy Knell' (II.i.49–50). Davenant may have wanted to avoid the drunkenness so strongly associated with the cavaliers as well as the excesses of biblical language so strongly associated with the Good Old Cause. But he was in any case, as *Gondibert* had notoriously shown, a writer committed to offering a rational account of events rather than relying on supernatural machinery. In the early part of the play, Lady Macbeth seems to share this view, and her sarcastic comment on Lady Macduff's romantic language is witty enough to suggest that the writer may have had some sympathy with her at this stage.

At the same time, the play's treatment of the Macduffs emphasises rather than taking for granted the moral choices forced on them by their situation. The scene which must have been most agonisingly relevant to many members of its Restoration audience was the new one (III.ii), entirely in heroic couplets, where Macduff and his wife debate what he should do about Macbeth's usurpation. Lady Macduff, who takes a Providential view of history, argues against Macduff's eagerness to take an active role in helping destiny:

> *Macd.* From *Duncan's* Grave, methinks, I hear a groan
> That call's a loud for justice.
> *La. Macd.*   If the Throne
> Was by *Macbeth* ill gain'd, Heavens Justice may,
> Without your Sword, sufficient vengeance pay.
> Usurpers lives have but a short extent,
> Nothing lives long in a strange Element.   (III.ii.9–15)

Lady Macduff fears that her husband may be guilty himself of ambition without realising it – and his insistence that 'My aim is not to Govern, but Protect' (III.ii.40), shows, in that now loaded verb, the ambiguity of his position. For that majority of Davenant's audience who had been quiescent under Cromwell, this argument externalises an inner conflict which badly needed ventilating. In this respect, his *Macbeth* is a forerunner of those heroic plays which, as Susan Staves (1979) puts it, seem primarily intended 'to assuage the guilt of the postwar generation over its abandonment of the legitimate monarch' (p. 110). A later scene between the Macduffs makes the sense of abandonment explicit: Lady Macduff at first begs her husband not to leave her unprotected, then, on hearing of Banquo's murder, urges him to escape at once. He has already tried to reassure her that

> You will your safety to your weakness owe
> As Grass escapes the syth by being low.   (III.vi.13–14)

Could Davenant have seen Marvell's 'Upon Appleton House', where the poet laments the accidental killing of the rail?

> Unhappy birds! what does it boot
> To build below the grass's root;
> When lowness is unsafe as height,
> And chance o'ertakes, what 'scapeth spite?   (lines 409–12)

That Lady Macbeth's disinterested and virtuous advice is the cause of her own death is a source of a tragic irony like that which pursues Macbeth himself. In Macbeth's final encounter with Macduff, prophecy meets prophecy, for the witches have already hailed Macduff too, promising that 'He'll bleed by thee, by whom thou first hast bled' (II.v.81). The play, ultimately, justifies both those who act and those who merely wait for the prophecies to be fulfilled. What it does *not* justify is Divine Right; Macbeth, as the final words make clear, is not a fiend from hell, but a man who has pursued 'others Right, by Lawless Power'.

It is not surprising that Davenant should give Lady Macduff such strong arguments for letting fate take its course, since he himself, as his enemies never tired of pointing out, had been willing to compromise with the *de facto* government and to act as a theatre impresario under Cromwell. If Cruttwell can praise Shakespeare for the complexity with which he balances 'the mystical reverence for legitimate kingship' with 'the sympathetic dramatic presentation of the murderous usurper', one might argue that Davenant's play, balancing a largely secular sense of kingship against the unsympathetic portrayal of a usurper, is equally complex. What weakens it is that it dramatises most effectively, not the consciousness of the central character, but the external debate between different responses of other characters to the evil political world which he has created.

Conclusion

This book has been dealing with a number of paradoxes: a dominant culture in a politically repressed position; a desire for self-expression which could be satisfied only through anonymous publication; the concealment of meaning by devices which drew attention to themselves as codes; the depiction of apparently fantastic situations which were essentially true; and exuberant self-display which, on inspection, turns out to have borrowed someone else's words and voice. The most important royalist book of the period is also the one which pretends to be most secret, the *Eikon Basilike*. Supposedly a totally private and unmediated expression of the king's thoughts, it was really written with publication in view. Its real secret, unknown to its first readers, was that it was only partly (if at all) a work by Charles I; the image of consistent, single-minded royalty was a fictitious construct. At this point it seems appropriate to ask whether the study of these paradoxes serves any larger purpose. It seems to me that three conclusions have emerged from it.

1. One purpose behind the writing of this book was the attempt to distinguish not only between royalist and puritan writers but between royalist and puritan styles. I think the difficulty of this task has become apparent. Both sides see themselves as part of the same biblical and classical literary world. Both also refer to romances and to the theatre, though from different perspectives, and both accept the Providential model on which the formal structure of these works is based. This means that both sides also accept, as the basis of all explanations of human events, the doctrine of secret purposes. In my first three chapters I looked at the notions of meaning emerging from obscurity, the sun shining through the clouds, the ruler's true nobility being perceived despite his disguise or misfortunes. This is the language of transcendence; it assumes the existence of an inherent and unchanging reality. But also an inscrutable reality. The various codes have one thing in common: although everything means something else, at the end of the sequence of interpretation one invariably finds 'secret purposes', which, like 'final causes', throw all ultimate responsi-

bility on the will of the king and, beyond that – '*O altitudo!*' – on the will of God.

Stanley Fish has suggested that the real division between seventeenth-century minds is not that between the rival political and religious positions summed up by Joan Webber (1968) in the terms 'conservative Anglican' and 'radical Puritan'. Rather, he argues, the distinction is epistemological:

On the one hand there is the assumption that the mind, either in its present state or in some future state of repair, is adequate to the task of comprehending and communicating the nature and shape of reality; and on the other, the assumption that the mind is a prisoner of its inherent limitations, and that the apprehension, in rational or discursive terms, of ultimate truth, is beyond it. (Fish 1972, p. 377)

This distinction would correspond roughly to the emotional polarities I have been setting up between the distrust of mystery and the fascination with it. I would argue, however, that such an opposition is historically conditioned rather than innate. Mystery is an advantage for any party in power, and, since knowledge is power, any party out of power will naturally demand further access to it. At the same time, any party which is denied access to the open expression of its views will express them covertly if it can. Royalist style, as it formed itself under pressure, was marked by a taste for obscurity, mystery, and playfulness. This was because, first, these were qualities which could be seen as distinguished from those of the vulgar; second, because they facilitated deception at a time when it was a necessary survival tactic; and, third, because they justified that deception by invoking a language in which context was everything and literal meaning nothing. There may be tactical reasons for wishing to think that truth is ultimately unknowable, and one of them is the fact that one has just been caught telling a lie. Thus, I would argue, it is largely the circumstances in which writers were working, rather than an immutable set of assumptions, which create the distinction between royalist and parliamentarian writing.

2. My second conclusion has implications for another subject on which there has been much emphasis in recent years: the extent to which seventeenth-century writers were affected by censorship. Because of this threat, it is argued, their works must be interpreted on the assumption that they all mean something more subversive than they dare to say. This kind of interpretation is not difficult. Almost any work can be read subversively if we accept the principle that both analogy and contrast may be used as means of attack on authority. But the approach is inherently contradictory. If a literary work is meant to be genuinely unintelligible to such contemporaries as do not already share the author's opinions, it is hard to see how it

can be subversive, though it might be supportive. I would not wish to deny
the importance of the political element in the interpretation of civil war
literature. Every political authority of the period certainly disliked and, as
far as possible, prevented really damaging attacks on itself in print, while
virtually no one defended the right to publish anything contradictory to
the Christian religion. Awareness of the possibility of punishment must
have coloured the act of writing, even though the authorities were ca-
pricious in their choice of writers of whom to make examples. Whatever
their original intentions, the works of victimised writers were bound to
become subversive as a result of their punishment.

But how secret is a code which can be cracked by anyone with some
knowledge of the history of the period and some training in this way of
reading? The only code that is really impenetrable to an unsympathetic
reader is the aesthetic one; there is a natural tendency to assume that
literature expressing views which one dislikes is over-simplistic while that
with which one agrees is complex – too complex for its opponents to
understand, and hence by definition invulnerable to their criticism. I
remain convinced that what writers fear most is not the censor but censure,
and that they emphasise their danger from the former as a way of protecting themselves from the latter.

3. These two conclusions go together: the instability of the conditions in
which writers were working, and their own uneasiness about the value of
what they wrote, explain their need to find a principle of constancy behind
their work. My final conclusion has to do with their devotion to that
symbol of constancy, Charles I. By 1645, the events of the civil war had
reached a point where Charles needed either to be condemned as a devious
schemer or condoned on the dubious grounds that he had not really known
what was going on. To refuse to accept either proposition – to attribute to
the king a degree of wisdom which was totally independent of his observed
actions – required such an effort of double-think that it is worth trying to
unpick its tangled motives.

A cult of personality is capable of surviving even the most damning
discoveries: the believer abstracts the 'real' hero from the confused mass of
words and actions which are his historical being. The process requires an
act of faith like the one which Wordsworth says one has to make towards
the poet:

> And you must love him e'er to you
> He will seem worthy of your love.

In this respect, there is little difference between political and aesthetic commitment. The language of much contemporary literary criticism, with words like 'project', 'conspiracy', and so on, tends to imply that all ideologies are imposed from above as part of a plan of repression. But of course those *not* in power are equally a part of the conspiracy. The image of the ruler as the sun behind the cloud may most obviously seem to serve the interests of the ruler himself, as when Richard II and Prince Hal attempt to make the darkening of their image something for which they have given temporary permission but which they can end at any time. But it also offers the ruler's subjects a poetic reconciliation of two contradictory views: on the one hand, disasters are not the ruler's fault; on the other hand, he *is* in control, and there is a purpose to events. Shakespeare's sonnets, where the beloved is equated with the sun, show how the lover's interests are also served by this myth, which allows him to feel his betrayal without having to see the beloved as a betrayer. A more thorough study of this subject might look still further at the eroticism which figures so strangely in the literary treatment of Charles I, the fact that the king is often seen as a husband or lover rather than as the father of his kingdom, and the nervousness about femaleness which is the other side of the royalist taste for romance. This confusion of sexual roles is part of a general confusion between active and passive roles which, I have already argued, allows both parties to escape full responsibility for their feelings and actions.

Edmund Wilson's *Patriotic Gore* (1962), a study of the literature of the American Civil War, notes the extent to which Union writers, the descendants of the New England parliamentarians, were influenced by memories of their predecessors. He suggests that one of the influences on Julia Ward Howe's famous 'Battle Hymn of the Republic' was Macaulay's 'The Battle of Naseby', which, like the 'Battle Hymn', draws on the imagery of Isaiah 63:1–6. Wilson's analysis of one stanza of the Hymn is particularly interesting:

> In the beauty of the lilies Christ was born across the sea,
> With a glory in his bosom that transfigures you and me:
> As he died to make men holy, let us die to make men free,
>   While God is marching on.

Wilson cannot guess where the lilies in this stanza come from, and can suggest as sources only Easter lilies and the lilies of the parable that neither toil nor spin; I suspect that Mrs Howe is being influenced by the lyrical eroticism of the Song of Songs which so often occurs in Marvell's verse. But notice what Wilson goes on to say about the effect of this reference to the lilies and the Hymn's location of Christ 'across the sea':

they serve to place Him in a setting that is effeminate as well as remote. The gentle and no doubt very estimable Jesus is trampling no grapes of wrath. And now come on, New England boys, get in step with the marching God! (Wilson 1966, p. 96)

This is what lies just below the surface in *Richard II* and the royalist elegies: the aspect of Christianity which stresses passive suffering and martyrdom is essentially an embarrassment. For a victorious army, religious and military values need not be perceived as conflicting, but a defeated army naturally seeks to explain events in terms of secret purposes which require a response of passive acceptance. The embodying of these qualities in the figure of Charles the Martyr eventually made it possible to distance them, to relegate them, like the 'gentle and no doubt very estimable Jesus', to the world of romance and female suffering. Admiration for the deeply religious Cromwell is, paradoxically, a secular admiration: the Protector is admired for his achievements rather than for his (genuinely mysterious) character. When Marvell, in his Elegy, wishes to suggest a softer side to this hero, he can do so only through the romantic aura which he creates around Cromwell's relationship with his daughter. The displacement of uncomfortable emotional responses on to a female figure continues into Restoration literature, where the need to believe in something mysterious finds its last refuge in the myth of the incomprehensible woman. In Congreve's *Love for Love*, a rueful couplet about the mysterious behaviour of Angellica (whose name belongs both to romance and to religion) expresses both the desire to believe in her magic and the scepticism about it:

> For Women are like Tricks by Sleight of Hand,
> Which to Admire, we need not Understand.

What this suggests is a possible explanation for the codes, the disguises, the elaborate mystifications, which I have been describing. The people for whom they were most necessary were the writers themselves, and the creation of so many mysteries was designed to conceal the terrifying possibility that, behind all these, there might be no mystery at all.

NOTES

1 'Secrecie's now publish'd': royalists and the press, 1641–1660

1 I am grateful to Katherine F. Pantzer for identifying Royston as the 'Reston' who is listed in D. F. McKenzie, *Stationers' Company Apprentices 1605–1640*. He was the son of a tailor in Oxford, apprenticed first to the stationer Josias Harrison and then, for some reason, rebound to the typefounder John Grismond. He later used a printer named John Grismond, presumably some relation of his former master, for some of his more clandestine publications. It would be interesting to know whether he deliberately changed the spelling of his name for the sake of the pun on 'roi'.

2 This leaf is also bound in with the British Museum's copy of *The British Bell-Man* for 13 May 1648 (E442.2). Possibly it was distributed separately; possibly the Crouches and their confederates enclosed it in other pamphlets and newsbooks which were being sold at this time.

2 'Our cabbalistical adversaries': secret languages

1 Howell, *Parables Reflecting upon the times* (1644), published anonymously. It was later published and acknowledged in his *Twelve Treatises* (1661). See Patterson 1984, p. 209.

2 Some editions contain illustrations of these devices, though they appear to have been made in the next century. Sloane MS 5427, in the British Library, is a collection of Parliamentary devices, most of them in colour. Among the Clarke papers at Worcester College, Oxford, are two contemporary drawings illustrating the colours of Horse Regiments. These drawings were used in the early eighteenth century as the basis for a large plate, originally intended to be bound in with Clarendon's *History*, which is most easily accessible in Ollard (1976). See also Wilkinson (1927), pp. 279–80 and n.

3 Genre as code: romance and tragicomedy

1 The importance of Rowe's pamphlet for the history of the theatre was first pointed out by Thornton S. Graves in 'Notes on Puritanism and the Stage', *Studies in Philology*, XVIII (1921), 141–69, and Hyder S. Rollins, 'Contribution to the History of the English Commonwealth Drama', *Studies in Philology*, XVIII (1921), 267–333.

4 Intertextuality and identity: literary codes

1 Sheppard is identified as its author in *The Perfect Weekly Account*, no. 11, May 1648, pp. 17–24, where his arrest is reported.
2 Ironically, this page of explanatory verse is missing in the British Museum copy of the book, so the illustrated title page is only partly intelligible.
3 Modernised from the commonplace-book of Christopher Wase (Bodleian MS Rawlinson Poet. 117), p. 127.

5 The royal image: Charles I as text

1 The reason for the odd numbering is that the reverse of each page of the 'Elegy' is black, which means that the poem is printed only on alternate pages.
2 *The Life and Death of King Charles the martyr, Parallel'd with our Saviour in all his Sufferings* (1649). This is an extract, printed in London, from a sermon by Henry Leslie, the Bishop of Down, *The Martyrdome of King Charles, or his conformity with Christ in his Sufferings*, preached at The Hague before Charles II in June 1649 and apparently printed there.

REFERENCES

The place of publication is London unless otherwise stated.

An Act Against Unlicensed and Scandalous Books and Pamphlets, and for Better Regulating of Printing 20 Sept. 1649.

An Act Declaring What Offences Shall be Adjudged Treason 17 July 1649.

An Act for Setting apart a Day of Solemn Fasting and Humiliation, and Repealing the former Monthly Fast 23 April 1649.

Act of Common Council 9 Oct. 1649.

The Anti-Panegyrike, Answering the Panegyrike n.d. [1653?].

Arnway, John 1649. *The Tablet, or Moderation of Charles the I, Martyr, with an Alarm to the Subjects of England* (2nd ed.).

'Assheton's Memoranda' [c. 1642]. Yale Beinecke Library Osborn MS (208220) b 101, pp. 126–7.

Bacon, Francis 1905. *The Philosophical Works of Francis Bacon.* Ed. John M. Robertson (based on texts and translations of Ellis and Spedding). London: George Routledge & Sons Ltd.; New York: E. P. Dutton & Co.

Barber, C. L. 1959. *Shakespeare's Festive Comedy, a Study of Dramatic Form and its Relation to Social Custom.* Princeton: Princeton University Press.

Barclay, John 1625. *Argenis.* Trans. Kingsmill Long (prose) and Thomas May (verse).

1628. *Argenis.* Trans. Robert Le Grys (prose) and Thomas May (verse).

Barish, Jonas 1981. *The Anti-Theatrical Prejudice.* Berkeley, Los Angeles, London: University of California Press.

A Bartholomew Fairing 1649.

Barton, Anne 1975. The King Disguised: Shakespeare's Henry V and the Comical History. In Joseph Price (ed.), *The Triple Bond.* University Park, Penn., and London: Pennsylvania State University Press.

1977. He that Plays the King: Ford's *Perkin Warbeck* and the Stuart history play. In Marie Axton and Raymond Williams (eds.), *English Drama, Forms and Development.* Cambridge: Cambridge University Press.

Barwick, Peter 1724. *The Life of the Reverend Dr. John Barwick, DD.* Trans. John Bedford.

Bentley, Gerald Eades 1943. John Cotgrave's *English Treasury of Wit and Language* and the Elizabethan Drama. *Studies in Philology*, XI, 186–203.

1945. *Shakespeare and Jonson, their Reputations in the Seventeenth Century Compared.* Chicago: University of Chicago Press.

216 *References*

Berkeley, Sir William 1987. *The Lost Lady*. Ed. D. Rowan, Oxford: Malone Society Reprints.

Bibliotheca Regia, or The Royal Library 1659.

The Black Book Opened 1660.

Blagden, Cyprian 1958. The Stationers' Company in the Civil War Period. *The Library*, 5th series, XIII, 1–17.

1960. *The Stationers' Company, a history, 1403–1959*. London: Allen & Unwin.

The Bloody Court, or the Fatal Tribunall . . . published by a Rural Pen, for general satisfaction 1649.

Blount, Thomas 1648. *The Art of Making Devices* [a translation of Henri Estienne's *L'Art de Faire les Devises*]. 2nd ed.

1654. *The Anatomy of Eloquence, Containing a Compleat English Rhetorique, Exemplified, With Common-Places, and Formes, digested into an easie and methodical way to speak and write fluently, according to the mode of the present times.*

Bosher, Robert S. 1951. *The Making of the Restoration Settlement. The Influence of the Laudians 1649–1662*. Westminster: Dacre Press.

Boyce, Benjamin 1955. *The Polemic Character 1640–1661, A Chapter in English Literary History*. Lincoln, Nebraska: University of Nebraska Press.

Braithwait, Richard 1641. *Mercurius Britannicus, or the English Intelligencer. A Tragi-Comedy. At Paris. Acted with Great Applause*. Wing B4270.

Brett-James, Norman G. 1935. *The Growth of Stuart London*. London & Middlesex Archaeological Society. George Allen & Unwin Ltd.

A Brief Relation of the Death and Sufferings of the Most Reverend and Renowned Prelate the L. Archbishop of Canterbury 1645. Oxford.

Britanicus Vapulans n.d.

The British Bell-Man 13 May 1648.

Browne, Richard 1644. *The Lord Digbies Designe To Betray Abingdon*.

Browne, Thomas 1964. *Religio Medici and Other Works*. Ed. L. C. Martin. Oxford: Clarendon Press.

Bulwer, John 1648. *Philocophus: or the Deafe and dumbe Mans Friend*.

1653. *Anthropometamorphosis: Man Transformed, or, the Artificiall Changeling*.

1974. *Chirologia: or the Natural Language of the Hand, and Chironomia: or the Art of Manual Rhetoric*. Ed. James W. Cleary. Carbondale and Edwardsville, Ill.: Southern Illinois University Press; London and Amsterdam: Feffer & Simons, Inc.

Bunyan, John 1966. *Grace Abounding to the Chief of Sinners and The Pilgrim's Progress from this World to that which is to come*. Ed. Roger Sharrock. London, New York, Toronto: Oxford University Press.

Burnet, Gilbert 1897. *History of My Own Time*, 2 vols. Ed. Osmund Airy. Oxford: Clarendon Press.

Burroughs, Jeremiah 1641. *Sion's Joy*. Reprinted in Robin Jeffs (ed.), *Fast Sermons to Parliament*, vol 1. Cornmarket Press.

Burton, Robert 1955. *The Anatomy of Melancholy*. Ed. Floyd Dell and Paul Jordan-Smith. New York: Tudor Publishing Company.

Bush, Douglas 1945. *English Literature in the Earlier Seventeenth Century 1600–1660*. Oxford: Clarendon Press.

Butler, Martin 1984. A Case Study in Caroline Political Theatre: Braithwaite's *Mercurius Britannicus* (1641). *The Historical Journal*, XXVII, 947–53.

'C.J.' 1654 *The Idol of the Clownes*.

C.R. in a Cloud 1647.

[Cailloué, D. (trans.)] 1649a. *Eikon Basilike, Le Pourtraict du roy de la Grand-bretagne, Fait de sa propre main, durant sa Solitude & ses Souffrances*. Paris. 1649b. *La Métamorphose des Isles Fortunées*.

Calendar of State Papers Domestic [*CSPD*] [Charles I], vols. XXII (1648–9), XXIII (1649–50, and Addenda, 1625–49)), XLIII (1644–5).

Canterbury's Change of Diet 1641.

Carlton, Charles 1983. *Charles I, the Personal Monarch*. London: Routledge & Kegan Paul.

Cartwright, William 1651. *Comedies, Tragi-comedies, with other poems*.
　1951. *The Poems and Plays of William Cartwright*. Ed. G. Blakemore Evans. Madison, Wisc.: University of Wisconsin Press.

Cavendish, Margaret 1662. *Plays written by the Thrice Noble, Illustrious and Excellent Princess, the Lady Marchioness of Newcastle*.
　1664. *CCXI Sociable Letters Written by the Thrice Noble, Illustrious, and Excellent Princess, the Lady Marchioness of Newcastle*.
　1668. *Plays, Never Before Printed*.

Cavendish, William 1956. *The Phanseys of William Cavendish, Marquis of Newcastle, addressed to Margaret Lucas and her letters in reply*. Ed. Douglas Grant. Nonesuch Press.

Chernaik, Warren 1968. *The Poetry of Limitation: A Study of Edmund Waller*. New Haven and London: Yale University Press.

Cleveland, John 1967. *The Poems of John Cleveland*. Ed. Brian Morris and Eleanor Withington. Oxford: The Clarendon Press.

Clyde, William M. 1934. *The Struggle for the Freedom of the Press from Caxton to Cromwell*. London: Oxford University Press.

Coates, Willson H., Anne Steele Young, and Vernon Snow (eds.) 1982. *The Private Journals of the Long Parliament, 3 January to 5 March 1642*. New Haven and London: Yale University Press.

Compton, James, Earl of Northampton. Untitled play ['Leontius']. British Library, Additional MS 60279.

Considerations touching the late treaty for a Peace held at Uxbridge 1645. Oxford.

A Copy of Verses said to be composed by His Majestie, upon His first Imprisonment in the Isle of Wight 1648.

Corbet, John 1647. *True and Impartiall History of the Military Government of the Citie of Gloucester*.

Corbett, Margery, and R. W. Lightbown 1979. *The Comely Frontispiece, the emblematic Title-page in England 1550–1660*. London, Henley and Boston: Routledge and Kegan Paul.

Corbett, Margery, and Michael Norton 1964. *Engraving in England in the Sixteenth and Seventeenth Centuries, Part III, The Reign of Charles I*. Cambridge: Cambridge University Press.

Corns, Thomas N. 1982. *The Development of Milton's Prose Style*. Oxford: Clarendon Press.

Corns, Thomas N. 1986. Publication and Politics, 1640–1661: An SPSS-based Account of the Thomason Collection of Civil War Tracts. *Literary and Linguistic Computing*, 1, 74–84.

Cotgrave, John 1655a. *The English Treasury of Wit and Language, Collected out of the most, and best of our English Drammatick Poems; Methodically digested into Common Places for Generall Use.*

  1655b. *Wit's Interpreter, or The English Parnassus, or, a Sure Guide to those Admirable Accomplishments that Compleat our English Gentry, in the Most Acceptable Qualifications of Discourse, or Writing.*

Cotton, Anthony 1971. London Newsbooks in the Civil War: Their Political Attitudes and Sources of Information. Unpublished D.Phil. thesis, University of Oxford.

Cotton, Charles 1923. *Poems of Charles Cotton, 1630–1687.* Ed. John Beresford. Richard Cobden-Sanderson, 17 Thavies Inn.

Cowley, Abraham 1905. *Poems; Miscellanies; The Mistress; Pindarique Odes; Davideis; Verses Written on Several Occasions.* Ed. A. R. Waller. Cambridge: Cambridge University Press.

  1906. *Essays, Plays and Sundry Verses.* Ed. A. R. Waller. Cambridge: Cambridge University Press.

Craftie Cromwell, pt 1, and *The Second Part of Crafty Crumwell* 1648 (*see also under* Howlett, T. R. (ed.) 1978).

Cressy, David 1980. *Literacy and the Social Order: Reading and Writing in Tudor and Stuart England.* Cambridge: Cambridge University Press.

Cromwell's Conspiracy. A Tragi-comedy. Relating to Our Latter Times . . . Written by a Person of Quality 1660.

Cruttwell, Patrick 1954. *The Shakespearean Moment.* Chatto and Windus.

CSPD. See Calendar of State Papers Domestic.

Davenant, William 1965. *Macbeth.* In Christopher Spencer (ed.), *Five Restoration Adaptations of Shakespeare.* Champaign, Ill.: University of Illinois Press.

  1971. *Sir William Davenant's 'Gondibert'.* Ed. David F. Gladish. Oxford: Clarendon Press.

Davies, Neville 1967. The History of a Cipher, 1602–1772. *Music and Letters*, XLVII (1967), 325–9.

Davys, John 1737. *An Essay on the Art of Decyphering. In Which is inserted a Discourse of Dr Wallis. Now first publish'd from his Original Manuscript in the Publick Library at Oxford.*

de Marsys (trans.) 1649. *Les Memoires du Feu Roy de la Grand'Bretagne Charles Premier, Escrits de sa Propre Main dans sa prison.* Paris.

Denham, John 1928. *The Poetical Works of Sir John Denham.* Ed. T. H. Banks, Jr. New Haven: Yale University Press; London: Humphrey Milford; Oxford: Oxford University Press.

Denny, Sir William 1653. *Pelecenicidium, or the Christian Adviser Against Self-Murder.*

Digby, George 1642. *The Lord George Digbie's Apologie for Himself.*

Donaldson, Ian (ed.) 1985. *Ben Jonson.* Oxford and New York: Oxford University Press.

Donno, Elizabeth Story (ed.) 1978. *Andrew Marvell: the Critical Heritage.* London, Henley and Boston: Routledge and Kegan Paul.

Draper, John W. 1929. *The Funeral Elegy and the Rise of English Romanticism.* New York: New York University Press.

Dryden, John 1972. *The Poems and Fables of John Dryden.* Ed. James Kinsley. London, New York, Toronto: Oxford University Press.

Duke Hamilton's Ghost, or the Underminer Countermined 1659.

Dury, John 1649. *The Reformed School.*

Dyve, Sir Lewis 1958. *The Tower of London Letter-Book of Sir Lewis Dyve, 1646–47.* Ed. H. G. Tibbutt. Bedfordshire Historical Record Society, vol. XXXVIII.

Eikon Alethine, The Pourtraicture of Truths most sacred Majesty truly suffering, though not solely, wherein the false colours are washed off, wherewith the Painter-Steiner had bedaubed Truth, the late King and the Parliament, in his counterfeit Piece entitled EIKON BASILIKE 1649.

Eikon Basilike, The Portraiture of His Sacred Majesty in His Solitudes and Sufferings 1966. Ed. Philip A. Knachel. Ithaca, N.Y.: Cornell University Press (for the Folger Shakespeare Library).

Eikon E Piste, or, the faithfull Portraicture of a Loyall Subject, in Vindication of Eikon Basilike 1649.

Eisenstein, Elizabeth 1979. *The Printing Press as an Agent of Change,* 2 vols. Cambridge: Cambridge University Press.

Epulae Thyestiae, or, The Thanksgiving Dinner 1648.

Evelyn, John 1955. *The Diary of John Evelyn,* 6 vols. Ed. E. S. de Beer. Oxford: Clarendon Press.

Everett, Barbara 1979. The Shooting of the Bears: Poetry and Politics in Andrew Marvell. In R. L. Brett (ed.), *Andrew Marvell, Essays on the tercentenary of his death,* pp. 62–103. Oxford: Oxford University Press (for the University of Hull).

The Famous Tragedy of Charles I 1649.

Fane, Mildmay 1938. *'Raguaillo d'Oceano' and 'Candy Restored'.* Ed. Clifford Leech. Materials for the Study of the Old English Drama, xv. Louvain: Librairie Universitaire (repr. 1963).

Fanshawe, Richard 1964a. *A Critical Edition of Sir Richard Fanshawe's 1647 Translation of Giovanni Battista Guarini's Il Pastor Fido.* Ed. Walter F. Staton, Jr. and William E. Simeone. Oxford: Clarendon Press.

1964b. *Shorter Poems and Translations.* Ed. N. W. Bawcutt. Liverpool: Liverpool University Press.

Farrar, James Anson 1892. *Books Condemned to be Burnt.* London: Elliot Stock, 62 Paternoster Row.

[Featley, Daniel] 1644. *The Sea-Gull, or the New Apparition in the Starchamber at Westminster.*

Ferne, Henry 1649. *A Sermon Preached before his majesty at Newport in the Isle of Wight.*

Fish, Stanley 1972. *Self-Consuming Artifacts.* Berkeley, Los Angeles, London: University of California Press.

Fletcher, Anthony 1981. *The Outbreak of the English Civil War*. London: Edward Arnold.

Forker, Charles R. 1965. Robert Baron's Use of Webster, Shakespeare, and Other Elizabethans. *Anglia*, LXXXIII, 176–98.

1986. *Skull Beneath the Skin, the Achievement of John Webster*. Carbondale and Edwardsville, Ill.: Southern Illinois University Press.

A Form of Prayer to be Used for Both the Days of Publique Thanksgiving For The Seasonable and happy reducing of the LEVELLERS, being Thursday June 7. And all England over on Thursday June 28.

Fortescue, G. K. 1908. *Catalogue of the Pamphlets, Books, Newspapers and Manuscripts relating to the Civil War, the Commonwealth, and Restoration, collected by George Thomason, 1640–1661*, 2 vols.

Frank, Joseph 1961. *The Beginnings of the English Newspaper*. Cambridge, Mass.: Harvard University Press.

1980. *Cromwell's Press Agent: a Critical Biography of Marchamont Nedham, 1620–1678*. Lanham, Md.: University Press of America.

Free-Parliament Quaeries, propposed to tender consciences. ('by Alazonomastix Philalethes') 1660.

The Frontispiece of the King's Book Opened, With a Poem annex'd: The Insecurity of Princes. Considered in an occasionall Meditation upon the King's late Sufferings and Death, 1649.

Fuller, Thomas 1845. *The Church History of Britain*, vol. VI. Ed. J. S. Brewer. Oxford: Oxford University Press.

Gardiner, S. R. 1897–8. *History of the Great Civil War*, 4 vols. Longmans, Green & Co.

Gauden, John 1649. *The Religious and Loyal Protestation, of John Gauden, Dr in Divinity*.

Gayton, Edmund 1654. *Pleasant Notes upon Don Quixote*.

Gethner, Perry 1987. Affairs of State and French Tragicomedy in the Seventeenth Century. In Nancy Klein Maguire (ed.), *Renaissance Tragicomedy, Explorations in Genre and Politics*, pp. 177–95. New York: AMS Press.

Gibson, John. Commonplace Book. British Library Additional MS 37719.

Gilbert, Allan H. 1939–40. The Monarch's Crown of Thorns: The Wreath of Thorns in *Paradise Regained*. *Journal of the Warburg and Courtauld Institutes*, III, 156–60.

Gilman, Ernest B. 1986. *Iconoclasm and Poetry in the English Reformation, Down Went Dagon*. Chicago and London: University of Chicago Press.

Gimmelfarb-Brack, Marie 1979. *Liberté, Egalité, Fraternité, Justice! La vie et l'Oeuvre de Richard Overton, Niveleur*. Frankfurt, Berne, Las Vegas: Peter Lang.

Goldsmith, M. M. 1981. Picturing Hobbes's Politics? The Illustrations to *Philosophical Rudiments*. *Journal of the Warburg and Courtauld Institutes*, XLIV, 232–7.

Grand-Mesnil, Marie-Noële 1967. *Mazarin, La Fronde, et la Presse, 1647–1649*. Paris: Armand Colin.

Graves, Thornton S. 1921. Notes on Puritanism and the Stage. *Studies in Philology*, XVIII (1921), 141–69.

Gray, Arthur B. 1935. The Portrait of King Charles I in St. Michael's Church, Cambridge. *The Cambridge Public Library Record*, VII (1935), 101–7.

Green, Mary Anne Everett (ed.) 1857. *The Letters of Queen Henrietta Maria, including her private correspondence with Charles the First.*

Greg, W. W. 1939–59. *A Bibliography of the English Printed Drama to the Restoration*, 4 vols. London: Oxford University Press.

Guarini, Giambattista 1914. *Il Pastor Fido e Il Compendio della Poesia Tragicomica.* Ed. Gioachino Brognoligo, Scrittori d'Italia. Bari: Gius. Laterza & Figli.

Hamilton, James 1649. *The Several Speeches of Duke Hamilton Earl of Cambridge, Henry Earl of Holland, and Arthur Lord Capel, Upon the Scaffold.*

Harbage, Alfred 1936. *Cavalier Drama.* New York: Modern Language Association; repr. New York: Russell & Russell, 1964.

Hardacre, Paul H. 1956. *The Royalists during the Puritan Revolution.* The Hague: Martinus Nijhoff.

[Hausted, Peter] 1644. *Ad Populum, or, a Lecture to the People.* Oxford.

HCJ. See *House of Commons Journals.*

Heinemann, Margot 1978. Popular Drama and Leveller Style – Richard Overton and John Harris. In Maurice Cornforth (ed.), *Rebels and Their Causes, Essays in Honour of A. L. Morton.* London: Lawrence & Wishart.

Hermans, Theo 1985. Images of Translation, Metaphor and Imagery in the Renaissance Discourse on Translation. In Theo Hermans (ed.), *The Manipulation of Literature, Studies in Literary Translation.* London and Sydney: Croom Helm.

Herrick, Robert 1965. *The Poems of Robert Herrick.* Ed. L. C. Martin. London, New York, Toronto: Oxford University Press.

Hetet, John 1985. The Wardens' Accounts of the Stationers' Company, 1663–79. In Robin Myers and Michael Harris (eds.), *Economics of the British Booktrade 1605–1939*, pp. 32–59. Cambridge and Alexandria, Va.: Chadwick–Healey.

His Majesty's Complaint Occasioned by his late sufferings 1647.

The History of Arcadia, or an Addition to and a Continuance of Sir Phillip Sydney's ARCADIA: Usually Styled The Countesse of Pembrokes ARCADIA [c. 1650]. Yale Beinecke Library Osborn MS. b.107.

HLJ. See *House of Lords Journal.*

Hobbes, Thomas 1651. *Philosophical Rudiments.*

1968. *Leviathan.* Ed. C. B. Macpherson. Harmondsworth: Penguin.

Hotson, Leslie 1928. *The Commonwealth and Restoration Stage.* Cambridge, Mass.: Harvard University Press.

House of Commons Journals, III (1642–4), V (1647–8).

House of Lords Journals, X, 1647–8.

Howell, James 1642. *The Vote, or a Poeme Royall, Presented to His Majestie for a New Yeares Gift.*

1647. *A New Volume of Letters.*

[Howell, James] 1644. *Parables Reflecting upon the times.*

Howlett, T. R. (ed.) 1978. *Crafty Cromwell, part one. AEB (Analytical and Enumerative Bibliography)*, II.

Hutton, Ronald 1982. *The Royalist War Effort 1642–1646.* London and New York: Longman.

Hutton, Ronald 1985. *The Restoration, a political and religious history of England and Wales 1658–1667.* Oxford: Clarendon Press.

Hyde, Edward 1857. *The Life of Edward Earl of Clarendon . . . in which is included a Continuation of his History of the Grand Rebellion,* 2 vols. Oxford University Press.

   1888. *History of the Rebellion and Civil Wars in England,* 6 vols. Ed. W. Dunn Macray. Oxford: Clarendon Press.

[Jane, Joseph] 1651. *Eikon Aklastos, The Image Unbroken. A Perspective of the Impudence, Falshood, Vanitie, and Prophanenes, Published in a Libell entitled EIKONOKLASTES against EIKON BASILIKE.*

Jansson, Maija, and William B. Bidwell (eds.), 1987. *Proceedings in Parliament 1625.* New Haven and London: Yale University Press.

Joseph, B. L. 1951. *Elizabethan Acting.* London: Oxford University Press.

K. [Kirkham], R. *Alfred, or Right Reinthron'd, being a Tragicomedy* [a translation of William Drury, *Alfredus, sive Aluredus*]. Bodleian Library MS Rawlinson Poet. 80.

Kahn, David 1967. *The Codebreakers, the story of secret writing.* New York: Macmillan.

Kettering, Alison 1983. *The Dutch Arcadia, Pastoral art and its audience in the golden age.* Totowa and Montclair, N.J.: Allanheld & Schram; Woodbridge, Suffolk: The Boydell Press.

A Key to the King's Cabinet 1645. Oxford.

King, Henry 1965. *The Poems of Henry King.* Ed. Margaret Crum. Oxford: the Clarendon Press.

King Charles His Speech Made upon the Scaffold 1649.

The Kingdomes Faithfull and Impartiall Scout (31 Aug.–7 Sept. 1649).

The Kingdomes Weekly Intelligencer.

The King's Cabinet Opened, or, Certain Packets of Secret Letters & Papers, written with the King's own hand, and taken in his Cabinet at Naseby Field June 18 1645 1645. See *Reliquiae Sacrae Carolinae.*

The King's Most Gracious Messages for Peace and a Personal Treaty 1648.

Knowlson, James 1975. *Universal Language Schemes in England and France, 1600–1800.* Toronto and Buffalo: University of Toronto Press.

Kogan, Stephen 1986. *The Hieroglyphick King, Wisdom and Idolatry in the Seventeenth-Century Masque.* Cranbury, N.J.: Associated University Presses.

La Bruyère, Jean de 1962. *Les Caractères de Théophraste traduits du grec avec Les Caractères ou les Moeurs de ce Siècle.* Ed. Robert Garapon. Paris: Garnier Frères.

Lachrymae Musarum: the tears of the muses, Exprest in Elegies: written by divers persons of Nobility and Worth, upon the death of the most hopefull, Henry Lord Hastings 1649. Ed. Richard Brome.

Lambert, Sheila 1987. The Printers and the Government, 1604–1640. In Robin Myers and Michael Harris (eds.), *Aspects of Printing From 1600,* pp. 1–29. Oxford: Oxford Polytechnic Press.

Langbaine, Gerard 1691. *An Account of the English Dramatic Poets.* Aldershot, Hants.: Scolar Press, 1971.

The Last Will and Testament of Tom Fairfax and the Army under his Command 1648.

Laud, William 1651. *Seven Sermons Preached Upon severall occasions by the Right Reverend and Learned Father in God, William Laud, Late Archbishop of Canterbury.*

Leo, William 1645. *A Sermon Preached at Lambeth April 21 1645. At the Funerall of that Learned and Polemicall Divine, Daniel Featley, Doctor in Divinity, Late Preacher there, with a Short Relation of his Life and Death.*

Leslie, Henry, Bishop of Down 1649. *The Martyrdome of King Charles. Or his Conformity with Christ in his Sufferings.* The Hague.

L'Estrange, Sir Roger 1663. *Considerations and Proposals in Order to the Regulation of the Press.* Reprinted, 1974, in *Freedom of the Press: Sir Roger l'Estrange's Tracts and others, 1660–1681,* ed. Stephen Parks, London: Garland Publishing.

A Letter in Which the Arguments of the Annotator and three other speeches upon their Majesties Letters published at London, are Examined and Answered 1645. Oxford.

The Liar: or, a Contradiction to Those Who in the titles of their Bookes affirmed them to be true, when they were false; although mine are all true, yet I terme them Lyes 1641.

The Life and Reign of King Charles, or, the Pseudo-Martyr Discovered 1651.

The Life and Death of King Richard the Second, who was deposed of his Crown, by reason of His not regarding the councell of the sage and wise of His Kingdom, but followed the advice of wicked and lewd councell 1642.

The Life and Death of Mrs. Rump 1660.

Lilburne, John 1649. *A Discourse betwixt Lieutenant Colonel John Lilburne Close prisoner in the Tower of London, and Mr Hugh Peter: upon May 25, 1649. Published by a friend, for the Publick benefit.*

Lily, William 1715. *Mr William Lilly's History of His Life and Times.*

Loftis, John (ed.) 1979. *The Memoirs of Anne, Lady Halket, and Ann, Lady Fanshawe.* Oxford: Oxford University Press.

Lovelace, Richard 1930. *The Poems of Richard Lovelace.* Ed. C. H. Wilkinson. Oxford: Clarendon Press.

Loyalties Tears Flowing After the Blood of the Royal Sufferer, Charles the I 1649.

'M., J.' 1642. *News from Hell, Rome, and the Innes of Court.*

McCormack, John R. 1973. *Revolutionary Politics in the Long Parliament.* Cambridge, Mass.: Harvard University Press.

McKenzie, D. F. 1961. *Stationers' Company Apprentices 1605–1640.* Charlottesville, Va.: Bibliographical Society of the University of Virginia; and Oxford: Bodleian Library.

Madan, Falconer 1912. *Oxford Books, a Bibliography of Printed Works Relating to the University and City of Oxford or Printed or Published There,* vol. II (Oxford Literature 1641–50).

Madan, Francis F. 1923. Milton, Salmasius, and Dugard. *The Library,* 4th series, IV, no. 2, 119–45.

1949. *A New Bibliography of the Eikon Basilike,* Oxford. Oxford Bibliographical Society Publications, N.S., III.

Malcolm, Joyce 1983. *Caesar's Due: Loyalty and King Charles 1642–1646*. Royal
  Historical Society; Atlantic Highlands, N.J.: Humanities Press Inc.
The Man in the Moon 1649–50.
Manuche, Cosmo. *The Banished Shepherdess*. British Library Additional MS
  760273.
  Love in Travel. British Library Additional MS 60275.
  1652. *The Loyal Lovers*.
Marcus, Leah S. 1986. *The Politics of Mirth: Jonson, Herrick, Milton, Marvell, and
  the Defense of Old Holiday Pastimes*. Chicago and London: University of
  Chicago Press.
Martz, Louis B. 1965. The Rising Poet. In Joseph H. Summers (ed.), *The Lyric and
  Dramatic Milton: Selected Papers from the English Institute*. New York and
  London: Columbia University Press.
Marvell, Andrew 1971. *'The Rehearsal Transpros'd' and 'The Rehearsal Tran-
  spros'd the Second Part'*. Ed. D. I. B. Smith. Oxford: The Clarendon Press.
  1972. *The Complete Poems*, Ed. Elizabeth Story Donno. Harmondsworth:
  Penguin. Repr. 1976.
Mason, Wilmer G. 1974. The Annual Output of Wing-Listed Titles 1649–1684.
  The Library, 5th series, XXIX, 219–20.
May, Thomas 1854. *The History of the Parliament of England* [1647]. Oxford:
  Oxford University Press.
Mayhew, Thomas 1660. *Upon the Joyful and Welcome Return*.
Mazzeo, Joseph Anthony 1964. *Renaissance and Seventeenth-Century Studies*.
  New York: Columbia University Press; London: Routledge and Kegan Paul.
Mercurius Anti-Pragmaticus 1647.
Mercurius Aulicus (1) 1643–5.
Mercurius Aulicus (2) 1648.
Mercurius Brittanicus (1) 1643–6.
Mercurius Brittanicus (2) 1648.
Mercurius Censorius 1648.
Mercurius Civicus 1644.
Mercurius Dogmaticus 1648.
Mercurius Elencticus 1647–9.
Mercurius Insanus Insanissimus 1648.
Mercurius Melancholicus 1647–9.
Mercurius Mercuriorum, Stultissimus 1647.
Mercurius Morbicus, or Newes from Westminster, and Other Parts (1, 2, and 3)
  1647.
Mercurius Phanaticus 1660.
Mercurius Pragmaticus 1647–9.
'Mercurius Pragmaticus', *The Levellers Levelled* 1647.
Miles, Josephine 1948. *The Primary Language of Poetry in the 1640s*. Berkeley and
  Los Angeles: University of California Press.
Milton, John [1642] 1953. *An Apology Against a Pamphlet call'd A Modest Confu-
  tation of the Animadversions upon the Remonstrant against Smectymnuus*. In
  Don M. Wolfe (ed.), *Complete Prose Works*, vol. 1. New Haven: Yale Uni-
  versity Press; London: Oxford University Press.

Milton, John [1644] 1959. *Areopagitica, a Speech of Mr. John Milton For the Liberty of Unlicenc'd Printing, to the Parlament of England*. In Ernest Sirluck (ed.), *Complete Prose Works*, vol. II. New Haven: Yale University Press; London: Oxford University Press.

Milton, John [1650] 1962. *Eikonoklastes, in answer to a Book Intitl'd Eikon Basilike, the Portraiture of his sacred Majesty in his Solitudes and Sufferings*. In Merritt Y. Hughes (ed.), *Complete Prose Works*, vol. III. New Haven and London: Yale University Press.

Miner, Earl 1971. *The Cavalier Mode from Jonson to Cotton*. Princeton: Princeton University Press.

1974. *The Restoration Mode from Milton to Dryden*. Princeton: Princeton University Press.

(ed.) 1977. *Literary Uses of Typology*. Princeton: Princeton University Press.

Mistress Parliament Brought to Bed of a Monstrous Child Reformation 1648. See Potter 1987.

Mistress Parliament Her Invitation to Mrs. London 1648. See Potter 1987.

Modell of the Fire-Workes to be presented in Lincolnes Inn Fields on the 5th of Novemb. 1647. (BL TT669.f.11.92).

The Moderate 1649.

The Moderate Intelligencer 1649.

Montague, Walter 1659 [misprinted as 1629]. *The Shepherds Paradise*.

Monumentum Regale: or a Tombe Erected For that Incomparable and Glorious Monarch, Charles the First ... in select Elegies, Epitaphs, and Poems 1649.

Morrill, John 1982. The Church in England, 1642–9. In John Morill (ed.), *Reactions to the English Civil War, 1642–1649*. London & Basingstoke: Macmillan.

Muddiman, J. B. 1908. *A History of English Journalism to the Foundation of the Gazette*. London: Longmans.

Nelson, C. and M. Seccombe, 1986. *Periodical Publications 1641–1700*. Occasional Papers of the Bibliographical Society, no. 2.

Newmarket Fair 1649.

Nicéron, Jean-François 1638. *La Perspective Curieuse, ou Magie Artificielle des Effets Merveilleux*. Paris.

Nicholas, Donald 1955. *Mr. Secretary Nicholas (1593–1669). His Life and Letters*. London: Bodley Head.

Norbrook, David 1987. *Macbeth* and the Politics of Historiography. In Kevin Sharpe and Steven N. Zwicker (eds), *Politics of Discourse. The Literature and History of Seventeenth-Century England*. Berkeley, Los Angeles, New York: University of California Press.

O Hehir, Brendan 1969. *Expans'd Hieroglyphics, a Critical Edition of Sir John Denham's 'Coopers Hill'*. Berkeley and Los Angeles: University of California Press.

Old Sayings and Predictions verified and fulfilled touching the Young King of Scotland 14 July 1651.

Ollard, Richard 1976. *This War without an Enemy, a History of the English Civil Wars*. London: Hodder & Stoughton.

1979. *The Image of the King, Charles I and Charles II*. London: Hodder & Stoughton.

Ong, Walter J. 1971. *Rhetoric, Romance and Technology, studies in the interaction of expression and culture.* Ithaca and London: Cornell University Press.

Ormonde's Curtain drawn: in a short discourse concerning Ireland 1646.

Osborne, Dorothy 1928. *The Letters of Dorothy Osborne to William Temple.* Ed. G. C. Moore Smith. Oxford (repr. 1947).

Osborne, Francis 1658. *Historical Memoires on the Reigns of Queen Elizabeth and King James.* Oxford.

   1983. *The True Tragicomedy Formerly Acted at Court.* Ed. Lois Potter. New York and London: Garland Publishing (the Renaissance Imagination).

Overton, Richard [?] 1646. *A Defiance against all Arbitrary Usurpations or Encroachments.*

Parker, Martin 1641. *The Poet's Blind Mans Bough, or Have among you my blind harpers.*

The Parliaments Post 1645.

Parry, Graham 1981. *The Golden Age Restor'd. The culture of the Stuart Court, 1603–42.* Manchester: Manchester University Press.

Parsons, E. S. 1904. Note in *MLN* xix, 47–9.

Patterson, Annabel 1978. *Marvell and the Civic Crown.* Princeton: Princeton University Press.

   1984. *Censorship and Interpretation. The Conditions of Writing and Reading in Early Modern England.* Madison, Wisc.: University of Wisconsin Press.

Peacham, Henry. *Heroica Emblemata.* Bodleian Library MS Rawl. Poet. 146.

Perfect Occurrences of Every Day's Journall in Parliament 1647–8.

The Perfect Weekly Account 1648.

Plant, Marjorie 1939. *The English Book Trade, An Economic History of the Making and Sale of Books.* London: Allen & Unwin. 3rd ed., 1974.

Plomer, H. E. 1904. Secret Printing during the Civil War. *The Library*, N.S. v, 374–403.

   1907. *A Dictionary of the Booksellers and Printers Who Were at Work in England, Scotland, and Ireland from 1641 to 1667.* London: Bibliographical Society.

Potter, Lois 1981. The Plays and the Playwrights, 1642–1660. In Lois Potter (ed.), *The Revels History of Drama in English*, vol iv. Methuen.

   (ed.) 1987. The *Mrs Parliament* Political Dialogues. *AEB (Journal of Analytical & Enumerative Bibliography)*, N.S. 1, 101–70.

   1988. Marlowe in the Civil War and Commonwealth: Some Allusions and Parodies. In K. Friedenreich, R. Gill, and Constance B. Kuriyama (eds.), 'A Poet and a filthy Play-maker', New Essays on Christopher Marlowe. AMS Press, New York, pp. 73–82.

The Presbyterians Letany to be used for the more speedy suppressing of the growth of Independency, now in a very thriving way 1648.

The Princely Pellican, royall resolves presented in sundry choice Observations. Extracted from His Majesties Divine Meditations: with satisfactory reasons to the whole kingdome, that his Sacred person was the Onely author of them 1649.

Proquiratio Parainetike, or, a Petition to the People [dated September 1642].

Prynne, William 1657. *King Richard the Third Revived.*

Quarles, John 1648. *Fons Lacrymarum, or a Fountain of Tears; from whence doth flow Englands Complaint.*

1649. *Regale Lectum Miseriae, or, a Kingly Bed of Miserie, In which is contained A Dreame: with an Elegie upon the Martyrdome of Charls, late King of England.*

Rainbowe, Edward 1649. *A Sermon Preached at Walden in Essex, May 29. At the Interring of the Corps of the Right Honorable Susanna, Countesse of Suffolke.*

Randall, Dale 1965. *Jonson's Gypsies Unmasked, background and theme of The Gypsies Metamorphosed.* Durham, N.C.: Duke University Press.

Raymond, John 1648. *Il Mercurio Italico, An Itinerary Concerning a Voyage Made through Italy, in the yeare 1646, and 1647.*

Reed, John Curtis 1930. Humphrey Moseley, Publisher. *Oxford Bibliographical Society Proceedings and Papers*, vol. II, 57–142.

Reliquiae Sacrae Carolinae 1650.

Ristine, Frank Humphrey 1910. *English Tragicomedy, its origin and history.* New York: Columbia University Press. Repr. Russell & Russell, 1963.

Rivers, John [as 'John Abbott'] 1647. *Devout Rhapsodies.*

Rollins, Hyder E. 1919. Martin Parker, Ballad-Monger. *Modern Philology*, XVI, 449–74.

1921. A Contribution to the History of the English Commonwealth Drama. *Studies in Philology*, XVIII, 267–333.

1923. *Cavalier and Puritan, Ballads and Broadsides Illustrating the Period of the Great Rebellion 1640–1660.* New York: New York University Press.

1927. Samuel Sheppard and His Praise of Poets. *Studies in Philology*, XXIV, 509–55.

Rowe, John 1653. *Tragi-Comoedia. Being a Brief Relation of the Strange, and Wonderfull hand of God discovered at WITNY, in the Comedy Acted there February the third.* Oxford.

The Royal Legacies of Charles the First of that Name 1649.

Rump, or an Exact Collection of the Choycest Poems and Songs Relating to the Late Times by the Most Eminent Wits, from Anno 1639 to Anno 1661 1662. 2 vols.

Runciman, Steven 1975. *Byzantine Style and Civilisation.* Harmondsworth: Penguin.

'S., J.' 1651. *The Prince of Prig's Revels.*

'S., S.' [Samuel Sheppard?] 1653. *Paradoxes, or Encomiums.*

'S., W.' *Commonplace Book.* Yale Beinecke Library Osborn MS b.230.

Saltonstall, Wye 1946. *Picturae Loquentes.* Repr. with introduction by C. H. Wilkinson. Oxford: The Luttrell Society, Basil Blackwell.

Salzman, Paul 1985. *English Prose Fiction 1558–1700.* Oxford: Clarendon Press.

Sams, Eric 1985. Cryptanalysis and Historical Research. *Archivaria*, XXI, 87–97.

A Satyr Occasioned by the Author's Survey of a Scandalous Pamphlet Intituled The King's Cabinet Opened 1645. Oxford.

The Scottish Politick Presbyter Slain by an English Independent 1647.

A Second Discovery of the Northern Scout of the Chiefe Actions and attempts of the Malignant Party of Prelates and Papists, Proctors and Doctors, and Cavaliers, that are now resident in the county of York 1642.

Selden, John 1934. *Table Talk* [1686], in *Table Talk by Various Writers from Ben Jonson to Leigh Hunt*. London and Toronto: J. M. Dent & Sons, Ltd.

Sharpe, J. A. 1985. 'Last Dying Speeches': Religion, Ideology and Public Execution in Seventeenth-Century England. *Past and Present*, CVII, 144–67.

Shelton, Thomas 1642 and 1647. *A Tutor to Tachygraphy, or, Short-Writing* (1642), and *Tachygraphy* (1647). Augustan Reprint Society, with an Introduction by William Matthews, UCLA, 1970.

Shepherd, Simon 1986. *Marlowe and the Politics of Elizabethan Theatre*. Brighton: The Harvester Press.

Sheppard, Samuel 1646. *The False Alarm*.

   1647. *The Committee-man Curried, a Comedy presented to the view of all men*.

   1649. *The Loves of Amandus and Sophronia*.

   1651. *Epigrams Theological, Philosophical, and Romantick*.

   1984. *The Fairie King*. Ed. P. J. Klemp. Salzburg Studies in English Literature.

   [as 'S.S.'] 1652. *The Weepers, or the Bed of Snakes is Broken*.

   [as 'Raphael Desmus'] 1653 and 1654. *Mercurius Anonymus. An Almanack, and no Almanack. A Kalendar, and no Kalendar*.

[Sheppard, Samuel] 1648. *Ecce The New Testament of our Lords and Saviours, the House of Commons at Westminster*.

Sherwood, Roy E. 1977. *The Court of Oliver Cromwell*. London and Totowa, N.J.: Croom Helm.

A Short View of the Life and Reign of King Charles, (the Second Monarch of Great Britain) From his Birth to his Burial 1658.

Shrapnel, Susan 1971. The Poetry of Andrew Marvell in Relation to his contemporaries and contemporary history. Unpublished Ph.D. thesis. University of Nottingham, 1971.

Sidney, Philip 1655. *The Countess of Pembroke's Arcadia*. 10th edition.

Siefert, Fredrick 1952. *Freedom of the Press in England, 1476–1776, the rise and decline of government controls*. Champaign, Ill.: University of Illinois Press.

Simmons, Edward 1647. *A Vindication of King Charles: or, a Loyal Subjects Duty*.

Sloane MS 5247, British Library [a collection of illustrations, some in colour, of Parliamentary devices].

Smith, David Eugene 1917. John Wallis as a Cryptographer. *Bulletin of the American Mathematical Society*, XXIV, 82–96.

Snow, Vernon F. and Anne Steele Young (eds) 1969. *Private Journals of the Long Parliament, 7 March to 1 June 1642*. New Haven and London: Yale University Press.

Spencer, Lois 1958. The Professional and Literary Connexions of George Thomason. *The Library*, XIII.

   1959. The Politics of George Thomason. *The Library*, XIV.

Spufford, Margaret 1981. *Small Books and Pleasant Histories: Popular Fiction and its Readership in Seventeenth-Century England*. London: Methuen.

Staunton, Edmund 1644. *Phinehas's Zeal in Execution*.

Staves, Susan 1979. *Players' Scepters, Fictions of Authority in the Restoration*. Lincoln, Nebraska, and London: University of Nebraska Press.

Strange Newes from Scotland, or a strange relation of a terrible and prodigious monster 1647.

Strong, Roy 1972. *Van Dyck: Charles I on Horseback*. Art in Context Series. London: Allen Lane, the Penguin Press.

Suckling, John 1971. *The Works of Sir John Suckling (Non-Dramatic)*. Ed. Thomas Clayton. Oxford: Clarendon Press.

The Sussex Picture, or, an Answer to the Sea-Gull. 1644.

Tate, Nahum 1681. *The Sicilian Usurper.*

Taylor, John 1640. *Differing Worships, Or the Oddes, between some Knights Service and God's. Or Tom Nash his Ghost (the old Martin queller).*

1643. *Mercurius Aquaticus, or the Water-Poets Answer to all that has or shall be Writ by Mercurius Britanicus*. Oxford.

1645a. *Aqua-Muse: or Cacafogo, Cacadaemon, Captain George Wither Wroung in the Withers*. Oxford.

1645b. *Crop-Eare Curried, or, Tom Nash His Ghost*. Oxford.

The Terrible, horrible, Monster of the West 1650.

A Testimony to the Truth of Jesus Christ, and to Our Solemn League and Covenant, as also against the Errours, Heresies and Blasphemies of these times, and the toleration of them. 1648.

Thomas, Keith 1978. *Religion and the Decline of Magic*. Harmondsworth, Peregrine Books. First published by Weidenfeld and Nicolson, 1971.

Thomas, P. W. 1969. *Sir John Berkenhead, 1617–1679, a Royalist Career in Politics and Polemics*. Oxford: Clarendon Press.

Thomason, George 1647. 'For the renowned Apprentices of this famous Citie', a copy in Thomason's hand of a royalist sheet. Thomason Tracts: E.392.7.

Townshend, Dorothea 1924. *George Digby, Second Earl of Bristol.*

Treadwell, Michael 1987. Lists of Master Printers: the Size of the London Printing Trade, 1637–1723. In Robin Myers and Michael Harris (eds) *Aspects of Printing From 1600*, pp. 141–70. Oxford: Oxford Polytechnic Press.

Trevor-Roper, H. E. 1964. The Fast Sermons of the Long Parliament. In H. R. Trevor-Roper (ed.), *Essays in British History Presented to Sir Keith Feiling*. London and New York, pp. 85–138.

A True Diurnall, with some perfect occurrences, weekly and moderate intelligence 31 May 1647.

Underdown, David 1960. *Royalist Conspiracy in England, 1649–1660*. New Haven: Yale University Press.

1971. *Pride's Purge, Politics in the Puritan Revolution*. Oxford: Oxford University Press.

1987. *Revel, Riot, and Rebellion, Popular Politics and Culture in England 1603–1660*. Oxford and New York: Oxford University Press.

Vaticinium Votivum, or Palaemon's Prophetic Prayer 1649.

Vaughan, Henry 1976. *Complete Poems*. Ed. Alan Rudrum. Harmondsworth: Penguin (rev. 1983).

Vines, Richard 1644. *Magnalia Dei ab Aquilone; set forth in a sermon.*

Wallace, John M. 1968. *Destiny His Choice, The Loyalism of Andrew Marvell*. Cambridge: Cambridge University Press.

Waller, Edmund 1901. *The Poems of Edmund Waller*. Ed. G. Thorn Drury. London: A. H. Bullen; New York: Charles Scribner's Sons.

Wallerstein, Ruth 1965. *Studies in Seventeenth-Century Poetic*. Madison and Milwaukee, Wisc.: University of Wisconsin Press.

Wallis, John. Letters 1. to Dr John Fell, 8 April 1685, transcribed by Thomas Smith, 6 August 1698; 2. to Thomas Smith, 29 Jan. 1696–7. Bodleian Library MS Smith 31.

Walpole, Horace 1862. *Anecdotes of Painting in England: with Some Account of the Principal Artists and Incidental Notes on other Arts. Also a Catalogue of Engravers who have been born or resided in England. Collected by the late George Vertue*. 3 vols. London: Henry G. Bohn.

Wase, Christopher. Commonplace Book. Bodleian Library MS Rawlinson Poet. 117.

  1649. *The Electra of Sophocles, presented to her highness the Lady Elizabeth, with an Epilogue Shewing the Parallel in two poems, 'The Return' and 'The Restauration'*. The Hague [i.e., London].

[Weaver, Thomas] 1654. *Songs and Poems of Love and Drollery*.

Webber, Joan 1968. *The Eloquent 'I': Style and Self in Seventeenth-Century Prose*. Madison, Milwaukee, London: University of Wisconsin Press.

Webster, John 1959. *The White Devil*. Ed. J. R. Brown. London: Revels Plays, Methuen & Co., Ltd.

  1964. *The Duchess of Malfi*. Ed. J. R. Brown. London: Revels Plays, Methuen & Co., Ltd.

Wedgwood, C. V. 1960. *Poetry and Politics under the Stuarts*. Cambridge: Cambridge University Press.

  1964. *The Trial of Charles I*. London: Collins.

The Weekly Intelligencer 1651.

Wells, Stanley, and Gary Taylor, 1987. *William Shakespeare: a Textual Companion*. Oxford: Oxford University Press.

Werstine, Paul (ed.) 1982. *1 Newmarket Fair. AEB (Analytical and Enumerative Bibliography)*, 6.

Whitelock, Bulstrode 1853. *Memorials of the English Affairs from the Beginning of the Reign of Charles the First to the Happy Restoration of King Charles the Second*. 4 vols. Oxford: Oxford University Press.

Wilcox, Helen 1990. Exploring the Language of Devotion in the English Revolution. In Thomas Healy and Jonathan Sawday (eds), *Literature and the English Civil War*. Cambridge: Cambridge University Press.

Wild, Robert 1671. *Iter Boreale. With other Select Poems*.

  1963. 'Iter Boreale'. In *Poems on Affairs of State, vol. I. 1660–1678*. Ed. George deF. Lord. New Haven: Yale University Press.

Wilding, Michael 1986. Milton's *Areopagitica*: Liberty for the Sects. In Thomas N. Corns (ed.), *The Literature of Controversy, Polemical Strategy from Milton to Junius. Prose Studies*, vol. IX, pp. 7–38.

  1987. *Dragon's Teeth, Literature in the English Revolution*. Oxford: Clarendon Press.

Wilkins, John 1641. *Mercury, or the Secret and Swift Messenger: Shewing, How a Man may with Privacy and Speed communicate his Thoughts to a Friend at any Distance*.

Wilkinson, C. H. 1927. The Library of Worcester College. *Oxford Bibliographical Society*, I, 263–320.

Williams, William P. 1973. The First Edition of *Holy Living*: An Episode in the Seventeenth-Century Book Trade. *The Library*, 5th ser. XXVIII.

Wilson, Edmund 1966. *Patriotic Gore, Studies in the Literature of the American Civil War*. New York: Galaxy.

Wilson, John F. 1969. *Pulpit in Parliament*. Princeton: Princeton University Press.

Wither, George 1649. *Carmen Eucharisticon: a private thank-oblation exhibited to the glory of the Lord of Hosts.*

Wolfe, Don M. 1947–8. Unsigned Pamphlets of Richard Overton: 1641–1649. *Huntington Library Quarterly*, XXI, 167–201.

Wood, Anthony a 1813. *Athenae Oxonienses ... To Which are added The Fasti, or Annals of the Said University.* 4 vols. Ed. Philip Bliss.

Wordsworth, Christopher 1825. *Documentary Supplement to 'Who Wrote EIKON BASILIKE?', including Recently Discovered Letters and Papers of Lord Chancellor Hyde, and of the Gauden Family.* John Murray.

(ed.) 1892. *The Manner of the Coronation of King Charles the First of England at Westminster, 2 Feb. 1626.* Henry Bradshaw Society, vol II.

Wormald, B. H. G. 1951. *Clarendon, Politics, History & Religion 1640–1660.* Cambridge: Cambridge University Press.

Wortley, Sir Francis 1647. *The Loyal Song of the Royal Feast.*

1648. *Mad Tom a Bedlam's Desires of Peace.*

Wright, Abraham 1927. *Parnassus Biceps* (1656). Ed. G. Thorn-Drury. Frederick Etchells & Hugh Macdonald.

Wright, Louis B. 1934. The Reading of Plays During the Puritan Revolution. *Huntington Library Bulletin*, VI, 73–108.

Yates, Frances A. 1975. *Astraea, The Imperial Theme in the Sixteenth Century.* London: Routledge and Kegan Paul; Harmondsworth: Peregrine Books (1977).

Zwicker, Steven N. 1977. Politics and Panegyric: the Figural Mode from Marvell to Pope. In Earl Miner (ed.), *Literary Uses of Typology*, pp. 115–46. Princeton: Princeton University Press.

INDEX